Lofty Aims & Lowly Duties

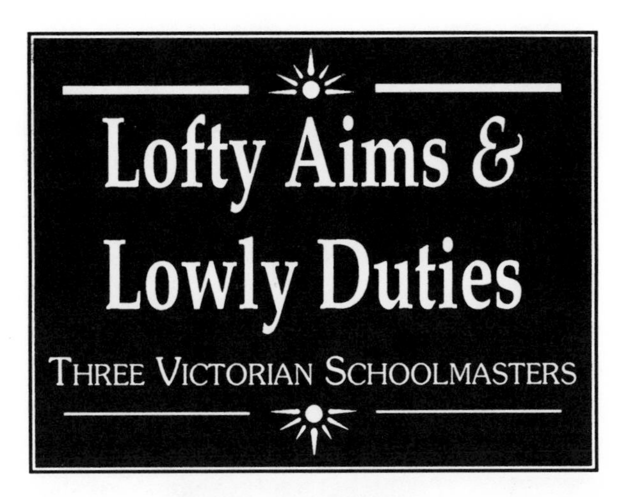

Ruth Jennings

Sheffield Academic Press Ltd
343 Fulwood Road
Sheffield S10 3BP
England

Printed on acid-free paper in Great Britain
by The Charlesworth Group
Huddersfield

British Library Cataloguing in Publication Data

Jennings, Ruth
Lofty Aims and Lowly Duties:
Three Victorian Schoolmasters
I. Title
371.10092

ISBN 1-85075-495-0
ISBN 1-85075-453-5 pa

Whatever may be the sources whence the income of the schools may be derived—how abundant soever that income may be—under whatever management each school may be placed—by whatever local or central administration the inspection and regulation of schools may be conducted—and whatever may be the course of instruction intended to be given—all must fail to exert a civilising influence on the people, unless the teachers are in numbers, skill and knowledge equal to the duty they have to discharge.

Sir James Kay-Shuttleworth
Memorandum on Popular Education
(London: Ridgeway, 1868), p. 6;
(London: Woburn Press, facsimile, 1969).

CONTENTS

Part III
SCHOOLMASTERS AND FAMILY MEN

Part IV
THE SCHOOL BOARD PERIOD

ACKNOWLEDGMENTS

Among the pleasures of writing this book were the new localities to explore, the hours of work in well-run libraries and record offices and, not least, acquaintance with the many people who gave so much willing help, officially or unofficially, at every stage of the research. Foremost among these was Richard Barnes, great-grandson of William Barnes, one of the schoolmasters depicted here. Richard, easily traced as a descendant of this distinguished man, shared with me at once the fruits of his own family research and, in the last year, went on to make the set of stylish drawings which help us to visualize the original character of the various houses and schools. All of these buildings—except the Chatsworth school, cleaned and well-maintained by the Liverpool Education Committee (and now portrayed on the cover of this book) are demolished or sadly run-down.

Then there are those, too numerous to list completely, who responded by post to queries about their own ancestry while some, like Sheila Cassidy in London and Joan Leach in Knutsford, searched local records on my behalf. Others, like Revd Alan Munden and Trevor Earl, gave generously of their special expertise in long letters of advice.

For access to information from particular records I would like especially to thank Dr John Addy of the College of Ripon and York St John; Mr John Davies of Leeds Grammar School; Mr Edgar Newton MBE of Melling; Mr Charles Roome, guardian of the Farnley School log books; Mr George Bartle (British and Foreign School Society archive); Miss C. Sibbitt of the Alice Ottley School, Worcester; Miss L. Groves of the College of St Hild and St Bede, Durham; Mrs J. Read (Froebel Society archive); Miss A. Phillips of Newnham College, Cambridge and Dr Helen Jewell, author of a history of the Leeds Girls High School.

I acknowledge most gratefully the helpfulness of staff in Liverpool, at the Central Libraries and Record Office, the University Library, the Athenaeum Library and the library of St Katharine's College (now part of the Liverpool Institute of Higher Education); in Wakefield, at the District Library and Register of Deeds; in the Local History Library in Halifax and in the archive sections of the Chester, Cheshire and Diocesan Libraries in Chester. Useful material was also gleaned from local libraries and archives in Knutsford, Kendal, Carlisle and Sowerby Bridge. The main depositories in London also gave excellent service—the various branches of the Public Record Office, the British Library in Great Russell Street and Colindale and the archive centre of the National Society (then at Westminster).

On a more personal note I would like to thank Bill Marsden of the School of Education, Liverpool University (now Professor W.E. Marsden), who steered me through the work for a Masters degree in 1986, who read the script of the book, proffered some good advice and encouraged me to seek a publisher.

Finally, I would like to to acknowledge permission to make use of the following illustrations: figs 8, 9, 10, 12, 13, 16 and the cover sketch by Richard Barnes RIBA; fig. 2 Local History Library, Halifax; fig. 3 Wakefield Art Gallery; figs. 4, 7, 15, 17 West Yorkshire Archive Service; fig. 5 Library of the National Union of Teachers; fig. 6 National Society archive; fig. 8 photograph obtained from the Farnley and District Community Association; fig. 9 photograph lent by Joan Leach; fig. 10 photograph supplied by the Liverpool City Engineers Department; fig. 14 by courtesy of the University of Liverpool; fig. 16 photograph supplied by Leeds City Library.

List of Illustrations

Introduction

> The teacher in an elementary school of poor and perhaps neglected children can scarcely have a more animating watchword than 'lofty aims and lowly duties'.

When Miss Bailey, Inspectress to the Liverpool School Board, wrote these lines in her booklet on kindergarten method in 1876 teachers of the poor were a crowd large enough to be addressed collectively and publicly in books, speeches and sermons. Many, by then, were paid directly from public funds, others partly and indirectly; about half were employed by local School Boards, the rest by churches, chapels, manufacturers and charitable trusts. Go back only fifty years, though, and school teachers—at this level of society—were fewer by a factor of several thousand, scattered individuals without a national identity. What happened in between was the slow and laborious growth of a state machine for elementary education and with it the emergence of a new profession.

This book charts the progress of three boys who were born in the 1830s, ready for the first phase of teacher expansion in the late 1840s. It shows how the training, employment and direction of teachers became more public and more systematic decade by decade and how throughout this time—and despite their rising status—teachers were constantly exhorted by officials of church and state in exactly the terms used by Miss Bailey.

What was to become the state system of education in Britain made its tentative start in 1833 when tax payers' money was first used to support promote schools for the poor, but it was the Education Act of 1870 which brought a new all-embracing, public commitment. Through it, a net was cast nation-wide and within a couple of decades both the provision of places for the 'labouring classes' and attendance at school were made compulsory. But it was earlier in this period, in 1846, that the crucial step was taken to promote, and pay for, a new career plan for teachers, a plan that was to benefit a whole succession of young men and women from the humbler ranks of society who chose to follow this vocation.

This we clearly see as three young men, all the sons of skilled artisans, were drawn into the first government-sponsored pupil-teacher scheme after 1846 and moved on to be trained at a state-supported Church of England college in 1854 and 1855. After that, they followed out their different careers in the West Riding of Yorkshire, Liverpool, nearby Cheshire and Lancashire, experiencing between them a variety of schools: inner city, industrial town, country town and isolated village. In their later years all were involved in the work of major School Boards; one as a headmaster in Leeds, another as elected member in this town, the third as a local inspector in Liverpool.

But the growth of the secular machinery was one thing; its dependence on and tensions with the voluntary authorities was another. Dominant among these was the Church of England and all three men were born and bred close (if not then committed to) this institution. It will become evident how, in activities local and national the Established Church was both a great provider of education for the working classes and, at the same time, a source of opposition and conflict. No individual churchmen trained and working in the schools during this period could avoid its powerful embrace nor, as the role of the state increased, the inevitable strains upon his loyalty.

It was, of course, within the church sector (still with a confident presence today) that the old emphasis on 'lofty aims and lowly duties' remained strong. But schoolmasters throughout the nineteenth century and almost everywhere were charged with leading the children of the poor into dutiful, religious adulthood, endowing them with basic skills to be used for the common good. It was constantly said that the work of the schoolmaster would be arduous, the rewards slender: ambition and 'find gentleman airs' were discouraged. But teachers in due course won for themselves—together with professional confidence—higher living standards and a measure of public esteem. Indeed the lives depicted here show how this new social machinery was able to carry the sons of artisans into the lower middle class and some of their sons and daughters to a higher milieu still.

The whole picture has been compiled for three quite unknown and, at first, unimportant individuals, entirely from public sources. The wide extent of these from church and registration records, the census, school documents, inspectors' reports, local newspapers and so on, has made possible not only the portrayal of these men at home and at work but also the character of their schools, managers and employers. Setting these separate but connected biographies in the context of the broader social and political movement by which they were shaped yields a narrative which spans seventy years and takes in a plait of themes—all of them bearing on the fluctuating commitment of Victorian society to the betterment of its sprawling under-class.

Part I

Early Days

I

Origins

In the year 1837, as Queen Victoria came to the throne, the National Society for the Education of the Poor in the Principles of the Established Church[1] was hard at work in its London office dealing with requests for help and advice. Two of the clergy who wrote to them that year were men who by their labours helped to advance the careers of the schoolmasters who are the subject of this book.

Revd James Gratrix of St James church, Halifax, told the National Society in January how he wished to attach an infant school to his present Sunday school for the benefit of the 'large and dense population' served by his church.[2] A few months later, in October, Revd Fielding Ould of Christchurch, Hunter Street, Liverpool wrote to say he was about to build a school for the 'large and destitute population of the district'.[3] These clergy, like so many of their colleagues, were seeking National Society grants and, at the same time, a share in the annual sum voted by Parliament since 1833 for the building of schools. In distributing this money the Privy Council took recommendations from the National Society (for church schools) and from the British and Foreign School Society (for those which were undenominational). Hordes of children had already gained from this combination of voluntary effort and public largesse. Soon to join them were three boys resident in the 'populations' described above. These were William Barnes, born in Liverpool in 1837, his friend John Daniel Crosfield born in 1834 and Edwin Foster, also born that year, in Halifax.

By the time of these births there was a nation-wide preoccupation with the task of educating the poor; indeed the concern was far from new in the 1830s. But who were the 'poor'? Good

Christian men were only too aware that they were extremely numerous—however one tried to define the limits of this great under-class. Needing education, they were often referred to as the 'labouring classes' but many who were in the direst need could not find work and those who 'laboured' were anything but uniform in skill, income and life-style. They were an obvious, a problematic, but not a distinct class, far too many for even the most visionary of schemes to embrace completely.

So it is not surprising that in these early decades of the nineteenth century the children of the 'poor' in the state-assisted elementary schools were a variegated lot, the schools differing widely in their intake of pupils and the standards they tried to achieve. It follows that because we are concerned, in this book, with three boys who became teachers themselves—and did better than average in the profession—we need to ask exactly where their families stood within the 'poor' populations referred to above.

This first chapter locates a starting-point from which to develop an account of the progress and social advancement of each young man. From other than humble origins they would not have found themselves in the state-assisted elementary schools in the first place but where should we locate them in the stratified society of the urban Victorian poor in the particular towns where they lived? On what kinds of labour were these families supported and where exactly were their homes?

To establish the physical setting for each family let us take the second question first. For all these boys their earliest recollections would have been of dirty, crowded and busy streets but the towns into which they were born and in which they grew up were very different from each other. Liverpool in the early nineteenth century was flourishing as a seaport, focus for world trade and the nation's second city. Prosperous merchants were still building themselves houses in the town in the 1820s and 1830s, but in spite of the fresh on-shore breezes, Liverpool was on record as one of the unhealthiest towns in Britain and it was certainly the most over-crowded. While the Corporation estate, worth £3 million in 1837, was drawn on for both town improvements and charitable causes and the evidences of private wealth were everywhere to be seen, poverty and destitution, sickness and squalor in the small back-streets were the precarious base of this community's success. And all the town's social problems were increased with the influx of desperate Irish fleeing the potato famine in the late 1840s.[4]

In Halifax, the same contrasts could be seen but on a much smaller scale. Less than one-tenth the size of Liverpool, Halifax lay in the 'bleak and mountainous region' where Yorkshire borders on Lancashire, a town flourishing in its own way, a centre for the manufacture of worsteds and woollens. 'Picturesquely situated' on the slopes of the River Hebble,[5] most of its factories were using water power well into the nineteenth century. But with the advent of steam in the 1830s came the attendant problems of noise and dirt and this, with the migration of factory labour and the rise of population to around 20,000, meant that for much of the town conditions were far from healthy.[6]

Let us now focus more closely on the Barnes and Crosfield households in Liverpool. Each family moved several times between the 1830s and 1854 when the young men left home but they were always to be found within a mile or so radius of St George's Hall, to the north, east and west of the town centre. From this vantage point in the mid-nineteenth century one could view, to the west, in the dock hinterland some of the most squalid and overcrowded streets to be found in any town anywhere. To the right, eastwards, the ground was higher and further away on these slopes could be seen a range of handsome villas with gardens (Fig. 11). Christchurch, Hunter Street, and the school which Barnes and Crosfield attended lay within a quarter of a mile of St George's Hall, on a contour which roughly divided the poorer, lower sections of north Liverpool from the pleasanter suburbs on the slopes of Everton.

It is impossible, now, to be sure what any particular house was like to live in, even those which can be located for certain in particular streets, but the characteristics of neighbourhoods can easily be read from maps, census returns and contemporary accounts. On this basis we can say that the least salubrious of the identifiable addresses for these families were the Crosfields' homes in Manchester Street and Smithfield Street, the Barnes's home in Johnson Street, where William was born, and a much earlier home for this family in Midghall Lane (1810). All of these were in the lower, western side of the town within half a mile of the river. Here were numerous warehouses and small manufacturies; tanneries, soaperies, iron foundries and—just off Johnson Street itself—a substantial lime-works.

However, it is likely that these two families occupied some of the better houses in this part of town. In Manchester Street, for instance, in 1841 the Crosfields had for neighbours men and families in secure if humble occupations; a draper, a printer, a saddler, an auctioneer, a bookseller and a quill-dresser. There were no unskilled labourers in this row of houses and several had living-in servants. Behind such houses, though, and the shops, factories and public houses which also fronted these streets were rabbit-warrens of back alleys with tiny units of building or 'backhouses', later infill of what had been yards or even gardens. Here was demonstrated

> the cutting-up of ground by square inches in order to make money by packing human beings together as if they were cotton bales.[7]

Such 'courts' were entered by narrow, often covered, passageways from the street and within were dwellings for hundreds of families. Hardly better was the planned working class housing at this side of town. Minute 'cottages' were built in terraces, often back-to-back; such were the tiny houses in Midghall Street where William Barnes's father was born in 1810. Some years later this locality was given over to the labouring Irish.

In these first decades of the nineteenth century the whole of the inner city was in a state of flux with the older resident population moving out to make way for new commercial premises. It was therefore generally true that the move inland was to find some improvement in residential accommodation. Thus drawn, perhaps, the Barnes family moved, soon after William was born, to Rose Place, a side-street running east off Scotland Road. Here they were just above the area of greatest overcrowding (outside the notorious Vauxhall Ward) but the housing was a patchwork of old and new, large and small, in which some of the better properties were being vacated to make way for lower class residents. In Rose Place itself in the 1820s there were homes 'set back in gardens and embowered in umbrageous foliage' but the builders moved in and 'lawn and parterre gave way to alley and back street'.[8] The Barnes family lived for many years in Rose Gardens, a small terrace of four houses in a cul-de-sac off Rose Place, each still with its own patch of front garden. In 1824 the residents of this end of Rose Place included one 'gentleman', two 'gentlewomen' and one ladies' seminary. By 1841 it was a busy commercial street with numerous small craftsmen and traders.

In 1845 the Crosfields lived in Birkett Street not far away and this, like Rose Place, was the home of small tradesmen and artisans. As hinted above, it would tempting to read into the topography and the sequence of moves a progression, west to east, lower to higher, worse to better housing, but clearly the situation was more complicated than this. The Crosfields in fact moved 'down' to Smithfield Street from Birkett Street then 'up' again by the mid-1850s. Moreover, the Barnes family went from Rose Place, from what had once been quite a respectable little house, a few hundred yards away into a 'court'. Was this a move 'up' or 'down'? By the 1840s the older courts were undoubtedly cramped and unhygienic but local Housing Acts were forcing builders to spend more and give more space and among these newer courts was Conway Place, off Rose Hill, where the Barnes family lived in 1851.

This court was entered from Rose Hill by a passageway about six feet wide, open to the sky. Inside, there was a yard about twenty feet by forty-five separating two terraces of three houses each, the terraces back-to-back with those of the neighbouring courts. These houses were a little over fifteen feet square in ground plan, that is, one room deep, but this was the most generous lay-out to be found in such courts; some of the smaller units were less than ten feet by ten.

How was this space used? In 1851 there were altogether in the six dwellings in Conway Place fourteen adults, four teenagers at work and fourteen younger children. The Barnes household included the two parents, William, a daughter Sarah aged eleven, a grandfather and a nephew aged eighteen. Even with the maximum capacity in such a house—two main rooms plus attic plus cellar—it was hardly spacious especially if we remember that each room had also to accommodate a section of the stairway. If there were fixed toilet facilities they would have been in the yard and water had to be fetched from pumps outside in the street. Was this an improvement on Rose Gardens? It is difficult to say. Back there in 1851 the four houses were all severely crowded; the Barnes's old house now had family of five in it and six lodgers.

Both these Liverpool families made further moves after William and John had been away to college and returned. In 1855, John Crosfield's mother and her elder son were in new homes to the east of Christian Street and the Barnes family was by then a mile further out, up the slope above Shaw Street, all in small terraced houses, the latter, in Gregson Street, quite newly built. The nature and location of all these homes can be kept in mind to compare with the houses occupied by William Barnes after he was married and by Edwin Foster when he came to Liverpool later.

What then of Edwin Foster's home-base? He was born on 10 October 1834, just a few months after John Crosfield, but he was not baptized until Christmas Day 1836 when his parents were living in Foundry Street. This is the only address we have for the family while they were in Halifax, a street in the poorer north-east section of the town, running steeply downhill from Northgate to the river a couple of hundred yards below the North Bridge. There had been factories upstream of the bridge from the early 1830s and soon after this a new concentration of industry downstream as well. The Foundry Street area of working-class dwellings was therefore subjected to fumes and smoke from the factories, effluvia from the river and, because the town still had many open drains, downflow from the streets above.[9] However, this particular street was not one of the worst in this quarter of the town. Though the houses were small—of the same dimensions as the Barnes's house in Conway Place and similarly in a terrace and back-to-back—the terrace fronted on to the street and the Fosters and their immediate neighbours each had a separate dwelling. There were much more squalid conditions in nearby streets where, as in the poorer parts of Liverpool, cellars were occupied by whole families.

The Fosters were here until 1843 when Edwin was around nine years old. Sometime during that year, the whole family moved to Wakefield,

> an opulent and handsome market town pleasantly situated on the north side of the River Calder regarded in many civil matters as the capital of the West Riding.[10]

For something like twenty years the Foster family was based in Kirkgate, an important commercial street running from the centre of the town southwards towards the river. Some of its sidestreets and enclosed yards were as bad as anything in Halifax but upper Kirkgate was another matter. The Fosters had house-and-shop premises first at number 84 then even more centrally at number 51. When Wakefield became an incorporated borough in 1848 this ward was seen as the most important 'as regards the total number of its assessments, the wealth of its inhabitants and the possibility of its increase'.[11] Without doubt the Fosters had moved up in the world.

It is clear thus far that none of these families was desperately poor. We do not find them in lodging-houses, cellars or the smallest courts. We do find them with neighbours in skilled trade or petty commerce. So what exactly were their own sources of their own income? There is no way of telling how large these were but we do know that each father was a skilled artisan.

William Foster was a last-maker and it seems he worked with a relative, James Foster, in a business which produced not only lasts for boot and shoe-making but also clogs, pattens and boot-trees. James had premises more central in Halifax with a shop in Crown Street and their predecessors had been resident in the town, in various trades, since at least the end of the eighteenth century. Once in Wakefield William Foster was among the more solid and respectable citizens. His name appears among the Parliamentary electors for 1851; he would probably have qualified from about 1845. His neighbours in 51 Kirkgate were, on one side, a confectioner, a furniture broker and a gunsmith and, on the other, a firm of solicitors, a hairdresser and a cutler.

Like the Fosters, the Crosfields had something of a family tradition in business. For at least three generations they had been joiners and up to and including John's father, Thomas, there was a line of Freemen of Lancaster,[12] the title, with its trading privileges, passing from father to son. Unlike the Fosters, though, the Crosfields were more dispersed. From their origins in Lancaster in the eighteenth century it seems there were moves to both

Liverpool and London. Though Thomas had a number of younger siblings all born in Liverpool, he himself came to (or returned from) the town from London in the early 1830s with a wife and several children. In Liverpool he worked as a furniture dealer but his elder son Thomas took up the joinery trade which they pursued alongside. After Thomas (senior) died in 1850 his brother Richard, a coach-builder, joined the household and helped to support his widowed sister-in-law.

For William Barnes, by way of contrast, there is no evidence of a continuity of family business into which he might have been drawn. His father Richard was a watch-case maker born, and presumably apprenticed, in Liverpool but his grandfather, John Barnes, a mariner, came originally from Norwich. Nor did Richard Barnes run his own workshop; he was an employee or 'journeyman' contributing one of the numerous subsidiary crafts to the production of complete watches.

With all these trades we can assume the families enjoyed, if not a large, at least a steady income. There was always a market for household joinery and furniture. Handmade wooden lasts were essential to the shoe-making process and the small workshop had a role whenever the trade itself was small-scale and localized. Even when factory production became more general later in the nineteenth century there was still a demand for the skilled last-maker in bespoke shoe and boot-making for the gentry.[13] No doubt William Foster who died in 1861 found more work of this latter kind in Wakefield than he had in Halifax. As for watches, the trade in Liverpool flourished up to the time of the American Civil War when the important American market virtually collapsed. Looking back to the 1850s a writer in the *Liverpool Review* recollected that

> any mechanic in connection with the trade could easily earn several pounds a week—manufacturers and jewellers picked up money to any tune.[14]

Before these times were over Richard Barnes had died and his son had embarked on his own career.

So it is clear that though these breadwinners cannot have been immune to fluctuations in trade they were not characteristic of the huge mass of labouring poor. Indeed they were probably among the better-off citizens to be using the church elementary schools at this time and the boys would have found themselves, day by day, with a much rougher element in the schoolroom, both in dress and manners. So should we call them 'working class' like most of the schools' clientele or could any of these families be said to have reached 'lower-middle class' status?

It is ironic that while perceptions of social hierarchy would always have been sharp within small communities it was not easy, then, for outsiders to guess exactly how different households in a street or parish, say, would align themselves and almost impossible, now, after a lapse of time, without a mass of personal records. However, a short time after these young men left home the government became anxious about the flow of money into the elementary schools and some decisions had to be made as to what kinds of families should be allowed to benefit; it was just at this skilled artisan/shopkeeper level that the problems of classification arose. At first there was a simple rule that

> the object of the grant is to promote the education of children belonging to the classes that support themselves by manual labour.[15]

Soon after this, the definition was seen to be both too wide and too narrow and more detailed guidance followed. Thus, a manual worker would be above the line if he was a master employing journeymen or apprentices, a non-manual worker below it if, either he could not afford to pay 9d a week for each child (the maximum fee allowed in grant-earning schools) or if he 'associated with the workmen of the place' rather than the tradesmen.

It was suggested that 'simple policemen, dock and railway porters' be regarded as 'working men' but that careful enquiries should be made for men in such trades as 'masons, carpenters, tailors, blacksmiths etc.' and for such petty officials as excisemen and clerks. A little later managers of schools were told they could include shopkeepers 'who have only petty stocks and employ no-one but members of their own family'.[16]

Though set out with such care in the 1860s these rules were not, it seems, generally enforced but the formal wording based on what clergy and officials believed they saw as real social distinctions can be used here to separate the 'working' from the lower reaches of the 'middle' class. With this rule of thumb, none of these families quite qualifies as middle class—unless there were employees in the Foster or Crosfield workshops (a fact usually noted in the census)—or if these men regularly consorted with tradesmen who were themselves masters. Perhaps Foster did so—he had relatives at this level—but on the whole such facts are hard to come by for this early period.

All we can do within this narrative is to chart the indicators of change, making use of direct clues to social standing whenever these come to hand. For example, we shall see how, for all these men who were born in the 1830s, increased status came with the progression to non-manual work, to payment by salary instead of weekly wage, to larger incomes and better housing and to the keeping of servants. Undoubtedly all were middle class—on any measure—by the time each was in his last phase of employment in the 1870s and 1880s. By then, though, the character of each household was defined not only by its working head but by the activities and aspirations of the next generation. Chapter XII will look at the role of these factors in locating each man on the social map of his time

From that final vantage point we can see how far the careers of Barnes, Crosfield and Foster had brought them from their own origins and also—with a glance at each of their family trees set out in the Appendix—their separation in life-style from surviving relatives. Meanwhile there is a ladder of opportunity to be revealed, based at first on the most rudimentary schooling for aspiring teachers but expanding year by year under the controlling influences of church and state as the notion grew that even those in elementary schools might be considered 'professional'.

II

Locality, Church and School

The ordinary working-class child in the 1830s and 1840s was fortunate if he had parents willing to find him the rudiments of an education—and even more so if there were well-run schools within reach of his home—but prospects for children in the large towns were rather better than for those in the more isolated places. The painful and unignorable facts of urban poverty and overcrowding had called forth exceptional efforts and the result in any sizeable town was a patchwork of schools, Sunday or weekday, large or small, private or denominational, the latter exclusive or more open. Some were free; others, and not necessarily the best, charged fees. For William Barnes, John Crosfield and Edwin Foster in Liverpool, Halifax and, later, Wakefield, there was a range of elementary education on offer. How did they make use of it? From the course of their later careers it would be reasonable to assume that the three boys were schooled early and well. From 1848 we can attach them with certainty to two schools (one in Liverpool and one in Wakefield) and Foster, before this, less surely, to a couple in Halifax. To understand the origins of these schools and their significance in these towns we need to look first at the general pattern of elementary education by then established and then at more local problems and issues.

The period between 1834 when John Crosfield was born and 1848 when all three boys were settled as scholars, was one of energetic school building as clergy, ministers and laymen pressed forward to avail themselves of the Treasury grants first offered in 1833. This first step in government funding was not the result of one single, purposeful act of legislation; it followed a series of failed Education Bills and was not even intended as an annual event. When it became so, the level of individual grants was pegged down to match the amounts that could be raised locally and the money was handed out, then, only through the National Society (for church schools) and the British and Foreign Schools Society whose schools were undenominational.

In 1839–40 the grants system underwent a major consolidation; under the aegis of a new Committee of the Privy Council for Education a full-time Secretary was appointed and, shortly after, a first group of Her Majesty's Inspectors, (HMIs). But the funding of elementary education was never free of controversy and the contentions of these years—all provoked by religion—were not resolved by the series of practical decisions which were made, necessary though these were. The lives of aspiring schoolmasters and their pupils were at all times in the hands of the warring parties. The number and location of schools, the daily curriculum, teaching methods, the style of management all were affected by the shifting patterns of local and national opinion. The schoolmaster's own prospects were dependent on his standing with managers, clergy and Her Majesty's Inspectorate and thus indirectly on the habits and attitudes he had picked up during the course of his own education and training. So in setting the context for certain schools in particular towns we can reveal something of the important social and religious influences that William Barnes, John Crosfield and Edwin Foster experienced as they moved from boyhood into adolescence and towards their future as trainee schoolmasters.

Turning first to Liverpool, in 1835–36 a committee of the Manchester Statistical Society reviewed the 'State of Education' in the borough. They found that even then some 30,000 poor children, about half those aged between five and fifteen, were attending schools of one kind or another—Sunday schools, dame schools, charity schools and the so-called public schools. These last were run by clergy, managers or trustees and not for private profit. Many dating from this period were built with government funds and could offer at least minimal efficiency. The Manchester survey counted nearly fifty public schools in Liverpool and commented that this was a higher proportion than in most towns, catering for more than a third of all the children being educated.[1] In 1837 twenty-two of these schools in Liverpool were affiliated to the National Society[2] the other thirty or so were most of them nonconformist, a few were Roman Catholic. Perhaps half a dozen of the church schools were on the northern side of the town centre and accessible to the Barnes and Crosfield households by the late 1830s and early 1840s.

Though we have no strong evidence of Church of England affiliation in these two families at this early stage—only the records of church baptisms, marriages and burials—it is likely in view of the boys' later careers that they went to church schools. It is difficult to be more precise because the families moved around and the records do not always make clear when schools were opened. However, it would be fair to say that William and John were probably at the Christchurch National School in Christian Street by 1845 because twins in the Barnes family were baptized in the church in 1844. We know for certain they were both there in 1848.

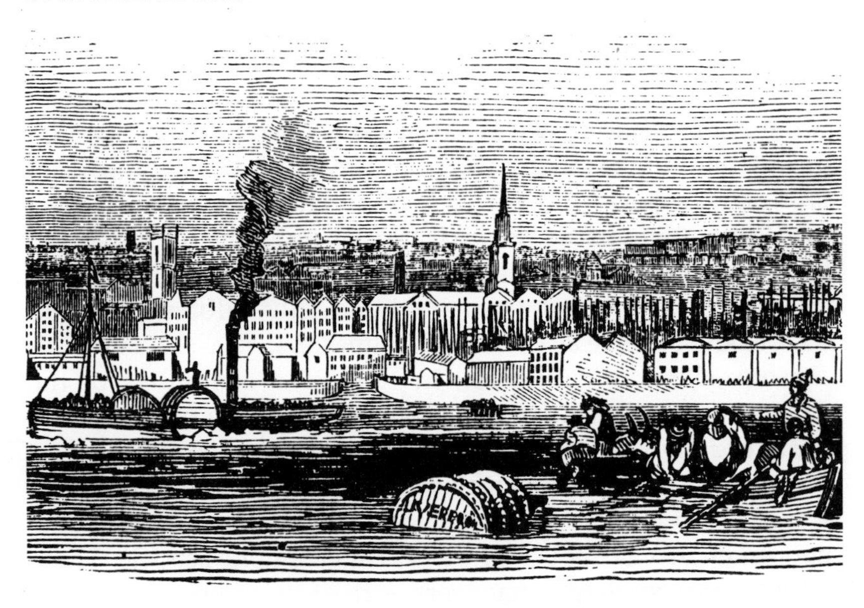

Figure 1. *Liverpool from the Mersey in 1849*
(From the Illustrated London News of 1 August)

Now it so happens that Liverpool in the late 1830s was conducting its own unique religious and political drama[3] and this led in due course to the founding of a new batch of Church of England schools, among them Christchurch, Christian Street. Let us return to the Revd Fielding Ould and his letter to the National Society on 29 June 1837. Ould wrote to explain that he wished to build a school for a population of about 15,000, in his own words composed of 'shopkeepers, mechanics and many labouring poor'.[4] The schools were to be open week days and Sundays for 725 pupils, boys, girls and infants and supported by annual subscriptions, charity sermons and small weekly payments by the children (1d or 2d). He reckoned they would need an income of about £250 a year for a master, mistress, books etc. This proved an underestimate as did the cost of the building which the trustees hoped would be around £2000 but later came to £3500. A formal application for a Treasury grant countersigned by the Bishop of Chester was sent to the National Society (for their initial approval) in 1837.

Over a year later, Revd Ould gratefully acknowledged the support of the National Society and their assurance that £337 had been promised by the Lords of Her Majesty's Treasury as soon as the buildings were completed, the bills paid and the accounts drawn up. But in October 1838, though building was under way the trustees were in difficulties, being forced to raise a loan to pay the contractors and with no prospect of further income. The National Society responded with a grant of £250 and backed the trustees in a further 'memorial' to their Lordships claiming that the excessive cost of the site justified an extra grant. But their Lordships were unmoved and it was not until May 1841 with a further £50 from the National Society that the trustees were free of debt. The schools had been opened, successfully, in May 1840 (when Crosfield was six and Barnes three years old). By 1841 the school had six managers, five local businessmen and one cleric in addition to the trustees. In April that year the school had been visited by Her Majesty's Inspector, Revd Baptist Noel, who had said it was 'the best to be seen in this place'.[5]

The investment of time and money in such a venture was considerable. What inspired Revd Ould to move when he did? And how did he raise the £1000 or so which came from local sources? Clues are to be found within the Trust Deed[6] for the school whose aims and purposes were declared to be

> for the instruction of poor children of both sexes resident in Liverpool and the neighbourhood thereof...on Sundays in reading in the Church Catechism and in the principles of the Christian religion according to the Articles and Liturgy of the Reformed and United Church of England and Ireland...and on working days in reading, writing and common arithmetic and other useful matter...

The trustees, a minimum of three, were all communicant members of the Church of England; the incumbent was chairman with a casting vote. Earlier, in October 1837, the school was affiliated to the National Society and the following rules were accepted:

> ...the National system of teaching will be adopted as far as practicable: the children will be instructed in the Liturgy and Catechism of the Established Church and constantly attend Divine Service at their Parish Church or other place of worship under the Establishment as far as the same is possible on the Lord's Day: no religious tracts will be used in the Schools but such as are contained in the Catalogue of the Society for Promoting Christian Knowledge.

The request to affiliate was signed by Revd Ould and his curate, Francis Power, secretary to the trustees. The clue to their particular state of mind lies in the phrase in the Trust Deed referring to the 'Reformed and United Churches of England and Ireland'.

In these years, men and women with a strong concern for the integrity of the church stood up to be counted on how they saw the Reformation and how they used the terms Protestant and Catholic. Even before 1800 the evangelicals had started to question the authority of the church and the quality of its spiritual and pastoral care. In 1833 a rather different campaign was mounted to revitalize the church from within and to fend off what were seen as current threats to its special place in the life of the nation. By the late 1830s and for the rest of the century and beyond there were two strong parties in the church. On the 'high' side were those who resisted any subjection to or dependence on the state, who extolled the example of the early Christian fathers and who declared the authority of the church through the Apostolic Succession and the efficacy of its sacraments. From its origins in 1833 this was sometimes known as the Oxford Movement and its followers, Tractarians, after the publication of a series of 'Tracts for the Times' which gave the group its identity. Later in the movement came a revival of ritual practices which scandalized its opponents while antagonizing some of its own supporters.

In the evangelical or 'low' church camp were those who looked back only to the Reformation, to the clearing of 'superstitious rubbish',[7] to a freeing of the individual's approach to his Maker and to Scripture rather than the priesthood as a source of authority. These people were not opposed in principle to church and state working together and they had some interests in common with the nonconformists—notably on the place of the Bible in elementary education—but evangelicals within the church were not always friendly to their fellow Protestants who had separated themselves earlier from the Establishment; Barnes, Crosfield and Foster were under such influence for most of their lives.

An emphasis on the church as 'Reformed' therefore puts Ould and Power in the low church party and they were, in fact, members of a militantly Protestant group in the town. Between 1835 and 1841 these men conducted a vigorous campaign against the Roman Catholic community and against the Liberal council elected after the reform of local government in 1835. The resulting clamour formed the background to the religious life of ordinary families, of whatever persuasion, for several years.

What happened was this. Soon after the reformed Council took office, two large elementary schools, built and maintained by the Corporation since 1827, were converted from their role as essentially church schools to undenominational ones, on the principle that all who contributed to their upkeep should have equal access, Protestants and Catholics alike. At the start of each day it was agreed that all should sing a hymn together and read from a set of Scripture lessons[8] and in the last hour of school, arrangements were made for separate religious instruction under the appropriate clergy who were invited in for the purpose.

This hour was carefully designated 'after school' to ward off charges of indoctrination but it provoked the response from Protestant activists that Protestant children were being deprived of the 'complete and unmutilated Scriptures' during school hours. A strident and bitter dispute was carried on for several years until a new Conservative council in 1841 changed the regime in the schools back to the Church of England pattern and all the Catholic children left.

The prime mover in all this campaigning was the minister of St Jude's church, Revd Hugh M'Neile, Irishman, orator and rabble-rouser. Among his numerous followers were both Revd Ould and Revd Power, his curate. James Murphy, in his account of the Corporation schools 'experiment' considered that Ould was second only to M'Neile in his distaste for the Corporation schools and all they stood for but since

> he apparently had little of M'Neile's intelligence and debating skill his hostility was much less effective.[9]

Nevertheless, he and Francis Power who in 1846 moved to the new church of St Alban's Bevington set, between them, a firmly Protestant tone for the churchgoers in this district of north Liverpool.

The liberal experiment in the schools was defeated within a few years but the Protestant movement in Liverpool had wider targets. In October 1835 a huge public meeting resolved

> that it is the duty of all men who value the rights and privileges of conscience—of true religious and civil liberty—to endeavour to oppose and counteract the encroachments of Papal darkness and Papal tyranny in the United Kingdom.[10]

Nine months later (July 1836) they reassembled to form a 'Church of England School Society' to collect money and lay plans for the building of church schools.[11] On the anniversary of the Protestant Association meeting of October 1835 yet more money was collected at the door and by 1837 it was reported that the Society was extending its influence within the borough and that funds stood at £11,000.[12] It was with some of this money that the Christchurch school was built; it followed two others, the North and South Church of England schools both opened in 1837. Justifying his use of these funds, Ould claimed in 1841 that his school was giving

> a thoroughly Scriptural and Church of England education to seven or eight hundred pupils from one of the most populous and poorest districts of Liverpool'.[13]

Not surprisingly, Ould chose the first trustees for the school from among his fellow activists. All four were wealthy merchants and they were among the large crowds of middle-class lay people who came to meetings and delved into their pockets to subscribe for the cause. But what was the mood of the working people for whom the new schools were designed? In the National Society's Annual Report of 1837 the senior Rector of Liverpool said:

> the working classes have shown great attachment to the Protestant Bible system of teaching adopted in our schools and I am happy to express my feeling that this feeling is increasing.[14]

As another observer put it, the cry against the Corporation schools raised by the clergy was 'loudly echoed by their agitated flocks'.[15]

Is it possible that the Barnes and Crosfield parents were caught up in this movement and took their children to the nearest Protestant school? Possibly, or they may simply have responded to the good reputation the Christchurch school soon acquired in its own right. We shall never know, but throughout the school careers of young Barnes and Crosfield Revd Ould maintained a strong presence in his church and in the town. In the 1850s (before the boys left home) he was a protagonist in a new Protestant campaign directed this time against a high church section of the National Society's administration—a national not a local squabble—and important for this narrative because the Church of England training schools were involved. These matters will be discussed later (Chapter IV).

We must now return to Halifax and Wakefield and the schools with which Edwin Foster was associated. These Yorkshire towns had two distinctive features which, in the context of early church schooling, made them very different from Liverpool. One was the much greater strength of nonconformity—and the virtual absence of Roman Catholics—the other, the widespread use of child labour. The nonconformists were particularly strong in the factory towns. They came in where the Church of England had failed to expand fast enough to keep up with the growth in the working population and succeeded with the strength of their evangelical zeal, their readiness to build schools and chapels and the appeal of a more participatory style of church-going.

Starting with Halifax, it seems that by the time of the religious census in 1851 the Established Church was ahead of the nonconformists there with rather more than fifty per cent of the Sunday attendance on the day of the census.[16] Back in 1843, however, according to Edward Baines[17] the town had a place in chapel for one of two of the population with the church offering only one place in five. (In Liverpool that year the church supplied about half the total Sunday seating for worship; the other half was shared about equally between the nonconformists and the Roman Catholics). In 1835, the year after Edwin Foster was born, Halifax had three churches and ten chapels. Whether or not all these figures are to be trusted—and there is a difference between seats provided and seats filled—nonconformity was strong enough in Halifax to pose a constant threat to the Anglican authorities who were already concerned that the people of England were slipping away from them. Nor were the nonconformists of Halifax all poor and working-class; they included some of the most wealthy and influential mill-owners.

The problem for the Established Church was not only that of expanding territory and capturing souls—the nonconformists, where they were numerous, could exert an unwelcome political influence in those areas of local government which directly affected the church. The setting for much of this warfare was the Vestry which, under common law, was responsible for the upkeep of the parish church. To maintain the fabric of the church the local community of rate-payers were obliged to elect churchwardens and to set and collect a church rate. Not unreasonably, those who did not use the church and who gave support to their own chapels and schools came to resent the imposition of the church rate and up to 1868, when the compulsory church rate was abolished, there were constant skirmishes and some more serious confrontations in Vestries nation-wide.

It was in January 1837 between two such heated meetings in Halifax that Revd James Gratrix made his first approach to the National Society and by April that year he had completed and returned an application for 'Aid towards the building of two schoolrooms'. These were to form the basis of the first of two schools that Gratrix was to build for his locality. In his letter he explained that the church of St James had been erected only five years earlier 'by the Commissioners for expending the Parliamentary Grant', money from the Exchequer whose distribution was authorized by the Church Building Act of 1818.[18] Halifax, like many other populous areas had gained by the addition of a new church but, as Gratrix went on to complain, this meant that there were no endowments and all the running expenses fell upon himself and his congregation. Gratrix was therefore obliged to raise a constant flow of cash to 'defray all the ordinary expenses' of his church and to support the existing Sunday school of 300 children. So, like Revd Ould, he was begging for money.[19]

At this stage Gratrix estimated that he would need £694 for a new building to house the present Sunday school plus an infant school; later this sum rose to £725 and £225 for the land. A plot was chosen on the north-west margin of the town and after the school was built Victoria Street was constructed on its southern boundary. The National Society made a grant of £300 but Gratrix was to spend several more years pestering the authorities for supplementary grants to keep the schools going.

Then there were other problems. In the hostile atmosphere of this largely nonconformist town Gratrix complained in 1839 that 'the Dissenters have at present 19 parts out of 24 of the rising generation of Halifax in their Sabbath schools'.[20] A later estimate (Baines, 1843) put the Anglican share of Sunday school pupils rather higher, about one-third,[21] but like many of his fellow clergy Gratrix felt obliged to battle on to maintain an effective presence for the Established Church in the locality.

It became part of his strategy to open the school to all sects; this way he hoped to draw in more of the factory children who, under current legislation[22] were obliged to spend two hours of each day in school. To this end he approached the National Society to ask for a relaxation of the rule on the use of the Catechism. Would they allow this element of church instruction to be waived 'where the Parents or Guardian of the child positively object to it?'[23]

Briefly, the answer to this question was at first 'Yes' and then 'No', the apparent change of mind due to a sharpening of divisions within the Society just then and a series of tactical difficulties with the government over new arrangements in 1839, both of which merit detailed description at this stage. It is significant that a few months earlier the Society had replied to a similar query pointing out that in the Rules

> it is not strictly laid down that under all circumstances every pupil is made to learn the church Catechism [but] with reference to the interpretation of the rule much responsibility must rest on the Diocesan Board...to secure the great principle of instruction in conformity with the doctrine and discipline of the Established Church.[24]

Gratrix was not sent this statement of policy. Instead, the matter was deferred to a special meeting planned for nearly six months ahead.

On 29 April 1840 'a very full Committee'[25] composed of the Archbishops of Canterbury and York, one Member of Parliament, nine bishops, four other clergy and several laymen, heard Gratrix's letter and granted his request. Two senior Factory Inspectors had written, too, and one of them, Leonard Horner, had spoken to the Bishop of London beforehand. Horner tells us that after the meeting Lord Ashley wrote to him saying the resolution had been carried unanimously. To Horner this was gratifying; 'a step gained towards a better feeling on the subject'.[26] But his satisfaction was short-lived. The General Committee of the Society on 6 May declined to confirm the resolution. Meeting again on 23 May 1840 with letters from Horner, a colleague, Saunders, and 24 clergy they resolved that 'no sufficient reason has been given for departing from the Terms of Union'.[27]

Possibly for James Gratrix this was the end of the matter for there is nothing to suggest that he rebelled against the decision either in the conduct of this school or of his next school which was expressly built for factory children. The Trust Deed for this first St James's school was drawn up in December 1839, after Revd Gratrix had made his request to the National Society and some months before he received an answer. It is therefore interesting that in the Deed the purposes of the school are described thus:

> to be used and occupied as and for a schoolhouse and place wherein the education and instruction of poor children may be carried on...according to the system of the National Society...with such variation and changes in the said system as shall from time to time be adopted and approved by the same Society.[28]

Gratrix appears to have been quite ready to obey whatever rules the Society chose to set—or did he calculate this was a reasonable price to pay for financial aid?

But how could the National Society have set aside the wishes of the high-powered committee which they themselves had called together to adjudicate? This was no outside advisory committee—all the Bishops were members of the Society's executive, ex-officio. It is important to find an answer to this question because after this time relationships were never to be easy again, either within the various sections of the church, or between the church and the government, where the management of schools was concerned.

It so happened that the National Society just then was effectively powered by a new ancillary committee led by a group of high churchmen and under them it had made some useful progress towards setting up Diocesan Boards of Education across the country. But this 'Committee of Enquiry and Correspondence' also had plans for a Church of England Normal (or Training) School and this at a time when the government was fighting to preserve a new set of proposals for a National Training School which would cater for all denominations. With all this in the background the Catechism problem for pupils in factory schools was a relatively minor one but the limited concession which the upper hierarchy was willing to make in April 1840 did not please the General Committee who were, by then, thoroughly on the defensive where the autonomy of the Society and its rules were concerned. From that time the high church section within the National Society were influential, with serious consequences for the credibility of the Society and its standing in the community. This episode thus forms part of the background for the in-fighting which was to affect some of the existing training colleges later (see Chapter IV).

The government meanwhile withdrew its proposal for a Normal School but early in 1839 it had embarked on the consolidation of its education plans mentioned previously and the new Committee of Council on Education was proposing to appoint a team of Inspectors. Not surprisingly, the prospect of the invasion of church schools and colleges by state officials, no doubt imposing new conditions for the award of grants, stirred up the bitterest feelings yet between the National Society and leading politicians. It took until the summer of 1840 for a concordat to be worked out;[29] under this the church would have control over the choice of Inspectors and would also direct their functions in relation to religious education. Her Majesty's Inspectors very soon became the Committee of Council's front men in the community and the schools for Christchurch, Liverpool and St James, Halifax were among thousands to come under regular inspection from 1840 onwards.

We can now return to Halifax and the question of Edwin Foster's schooling. He was, perhaps, sent to Revd Gratrix's new school in Victoria Street opened, with an infant department, when the boy was about five years old. The other, Parish, church school was long-established but on the far side of town from Foundry Street where the family lived. But we have seen how Gratrix's main problem was the sectarian divide; can we be sure that the Fosters were allied to the church at this time? It is true that Edwin was baptized in the Parish church and another child of the family at St James in 1835 but a later decision of William Foster's must raise some doubts.

What happened was this. A second son was born in early 1841 and William registered him as 'John Feargus'. Now this uncommon second name carried strong political connotations just then with Feargus O'Connor, the Chartist leader and many of his colleagues in prison for subversive activities. What is more, O'Connor's *Northern Star*, published in Leeds and circulated widely in Halifax, carried a weekly column in which followers

Figure 2. *Chartist rioters at the North Bridge, Halifax, 1842*
(From the Illustrated London News of 15 August)

declared their loyalty by sending in notice of 'Young Patriots', boys—and girls—to be named after the martyrs in prison. They would tell of remonstrations, resistance or even refusal on the part of clergy to baptize children with the names of those who were 'exciting the people to insurrection and rebellion'.[30] So it seems unlikely that William Foster would have risked being taken for an anti-establishment character unless he was indeed sympathetic to the cause—and if he was, it would explain his apparent withdrawal from the church between 1841 when John Feargus was registered but not, apparently, baptized and 1847 when John and four younger children were baptized together in Wakefield. Now we know that the Fosters were attached (or re-attached) to the church within a few years of the Chartist incident but this still leaves a question-mark over Edwin's schooling for a short period of his childhood.

There were two other well-regarded public schools in Halifax, one for the Wesleyan community and the other, the Lancastrian school, was undenominational[31] and, it so happens, near to the Fosters' home in Foundry Street and a clear option for the children's schooling at this time. The policy of the British and Foreign School Society who had founded this school was to insist on the Bible and put aside the use of catechisms or human creeds or arguments,

> thus throwing open the door as wide as possible to every denomination that is content to drink at the stream of life at its pure and original fountain.[32]

Some of its sponsors and about one-fifth of its pupils were, in fact, Church of England but there is, of course, no way of knowing whether this group of apparently open-minded well-doers were any more sympathetic to Chartism than the Church of England seemed to be.

And there we must leave this question until Edwin Foster emerges in the public records as a pupil-teacher in Wakefield at Holy Trinity National School in 1848, having been there, presumably, for a year or two beforehand, if not since 1843 when the family moved from Halifax.

As described in Chapter I the Fosters settled in Kirkgate and William Foster conducted his business as a clog and last-maker from a shop in this busy street. In 1843, according to the Baines survey[33] there were thirteen public schools in this town—more than in Halifax although this was a smaller place—but only three of these were Church of England. The Parish schools were north of the town centre and the St Andrew's schools way out to the east. There was a small free Grammar School teaching Latin and Greek and offering scholarships to the ancient universities but this, it seems, did not appeal to the Fosters' ambitions for their son—or was felt to be out of reach. The rest of the public day schools were attached to nonconformist chapels.

At some point after their arrival the Fosters apparently sent Edwin, with his younger siblings as they came of suitable age, to Holy Trinity school either when it was newly-built in 1846 or even earlier when it was located in some rooms belonging to a factory. The incumbent of Holy Trinity church, Revd William Tait, soon after his own arrival in the town, became dissatisfied with this makeshift arrangement and in 1845 he consulted with Her Majesty's Inspector for the area, Revd F. Watkins, about the possibility of building a new school with Treasury aid. Together they visited a site next to the churchyard and Watkins pronounced it 'convenient, dry and airy'.[34] The school was built the next year at a cost of about £700, the managers receiving a grant of £225 from the government and £100 from the National Society.

According to the Trust Deed of 1847[35] this was to be a school for the 'labouring, manufacturing and other poorer classes in the parish of Wakefield' putting it, socially, on a par with those in Liverpool and Halifax already described. The Deed went on to say the school should be conducted 'always in union with and upon the principles and in furtherance of the ends of the National Society', leaving no room, here, for questions about the use of the Catechism as part of the school's religious instruction. Thus Edwin Foster found himself, like his two future friends in Liverpool, established in a conventional, lower-class church elementary school with all that implied by way of opportunity or restriction in the future.

This chapter has focused on the origins of just three such schools. A description of the life and work of two of them—and the roles of William Barnes, John Crosfield and Edwin Foster therein—will follow in due course. We have seen how the moving spirit in each case was the incumbent, making plans, raising money, performing the role of correspondent and chief manager. None of them was in a rich living and financing the schools was a never-ending task for all three men—the Revds Gratrix, Ould and Tait. In Halifax perhaps was the stoniest ground for the advancement of church education and even Revd Ould's windfall from a local campaign in Liverpool did not generate a regular income for his school. For the time being, these, with a host of other schools built with Treasury aid after 1833, were obliged to maintain themselves from local sources; annual grants would not come until later.

Meanwhile the National Society, for those managers who chose to affiliate their schools, bestowed the occasional grant and kept a watchful presence in the background. Nationally, as we have seen, they spoke for the Established Church in all matters

Figure 3. *Westgate, Wakefield in 1853. Note 'Speak's Shoe and Clog Mart' (Colour lithograph by Revd Thomas Kilby)*

of state policy for elementary education. But they were not wholly united among themselves, nor representative of all factions within the church and the particular biographies traced in this book will lead us later on to three effective but quite different 'church' schools none of which was a National school in the limited sense. It will thus become clear how the influence of the church on the community was even wider and more complex than the activities of this official Society would suggest.

As for the boys themselves, they grew up to be potential wage-earners just as the state began to encroach upon voluntary preserves in education but enlarging the potential everywhere for teachers and taught. From whatever pattern of causes—and these we cannot fully unravel—the boys were at first held back from manual occupations and then directed into the church sector of the schooling available. Thereafter, we can follow their careers as they unfold parallel to the expansion of state influence and the constant renewal of church initiatives in response to it.

Part II

THE PROFESSIONAL LADDER

III

Apprenticeship

For three quite ordinary boys in the north of England reaching what would now be the end of primary education—then the conclusion of all normal schooling for the working classes—new opportunities were presenting themselves in the 1840s. As we have seen, the provision of elementary education, though still voluntary, was no longer entirely private. There was now a system which channelled public funds into the schools; inevitably, concern about standards was public and acute. School managers complained they were ham-strung by lack of effective teachers and parents, too, were objecting to the youth and inexperience of the older pupils who were put in charge of cohorts of children in the schoolroom. Common everywhere, this was the old but well-tried monitorial system of the pioneers Revd Andrew Bell (of the National Society) and Joseph Lancaster (of the British and Foreign School Society). And there were difficulties, too, for the existing training institutions, dependent on the unpredictable flow of competent students who could also pay. Fortunately there was now a corps of full-time officials, the 'generals of the education army', who could articulate these problems.[1]

These were Her Majesty's Inspectors working for their Lordships of the Committee of Council for Education; from 1844 there were five, all clergy, for the church schools and two for all the others in receipt of Treasury grants.[2] Each year these men published in the annual Minutes a series of remarkable reports—eloquent, searching and as time went on, confidently prescriptive. Revd Frederick Watkins, whose domain stretched from Cumberland and Lancashire on the west to Yorkshire and

Durham on the east, with something like seven hundred church schools, made a powerful statement in 1845 on 'the state and prospects for education in that great and populous district'. The essential problem he said, was 'lack of pecuniary means' but, he went on,

> the greatest practical evil in our elementary schools is the want of well-qualified properly-trained, earnest and religious teachers. We want men for our machinery. We must have educated men to teach the uneducated.[3]

The government, not without some difficulty, responded with measures in 1846 to bring financial help to the colleges, to encourage, train, certificate and pay teachers already in service who could pass some basic tests, while opening a new and attractive way into the profession through pupil-teacher apprenticeship.[4] The resulting surge in expenditure, new burdens on the administration and new provocations to sectarian rivalry ensured for these timely and constructive reforms a rough passage in the Commons and elsewhere. But Her Majesty's Inspectors were pleased and as time went on there were many who were glad to acknowledge the wisdom of these new provisions. In 1853, a writer in the *Edinburgh Review* was moved to say:

> by the celebrated Minutes of 1846 the question of the education of the people of England was at length placed beyond the possibility of question or doubt... They have sent the schoolmaster on his mission.[5]

So let us now see what these Minutes had in store for William Barnes, John Crosfield and Edwin Foster, at school, then, in Liverpool and Wakefield. As from 1847 there was the chance of a five-year apprenticeship as pupil-teacher from thirteen—a worthwhile extension to the role of monitor which had been open to them since the age of nine or ten. As pupil-teachers they would be paid a small annual salary—direct from the Treasury; they would be coached to a higher standard in order to qualify for a year or more at training college. Meanwhile it was the teachers with the new certificates who were qualified to take apprentices and they stood to gain financially by doing so.

The government's insistence on good standards of school provision and teaching as prerequisites for grant was matched by an equal care in the selection of children as apprentices. There was, first, the question of age; boys and girls were usually allowed to progress from monitors to pupil-teachers at thirteen. Edwin Foster was apprenticed in Wakefield in late 1848 at just fourteen. John Crosfield and William Barnes were taken on together with three other boys in Liverpool in February 1848; while John was thirteen and a half, William had just turned eleven, his birthday falling in January. Inspectors often refused candidates who were too young so this boy must have presented himself as remarkably mature and capable and the whole future course of his life confirms that he was, indeed, unusually gifted, energetic and determined.

Further checks followed. There was an enquiry into home circumstances and certificates were required

> from the Clergyman and the Managers that the Moral Character of the Candidates and their families justify an expectation that the Instruction and Training of the School will be seconded by their own efforts and the example of their parents.[6]

It was not enough, however, that the home should be respectable. Church schools required good evidence of loyal adherence and William Foster at this time had so far failed to present any one of his five youngest children for baptism. His, possibly doctrinaire, reasons for this were mentioned earlier (in Chapter II). Now, in June 1847, with Edwin's career at stake, he took his son John Feargus and four of his daughters to Holy Trinity church to be christened, thus bringing the family into line.

Returning now to the apprenticeship procedures, after the initial selection the Inspectors moved on to test each candidate according to a formal schedule. Thus, each young person was required to:

1. read with fluency and expression
2. point out the parts of speech in a simple sentence
3. write in a neat hand with correct spelling and punctuation a simple prose narrative slowly read to him

4. write from dictation sums in the first four Rules of Arithmetic, Simple and Compound, and work them correctly and know the Tables of Weights and Measures
5. show an elementary knowledge of Geography[7]

Pupils in church schools were asked to repeat the Catechism, show they understood its meaning and that they were familiar with the outlines of Scripture history. Finally, each candidate was set to teach a junior class while the Inspector looked on.

Once the authorities were satisfied the pupil-teacher would make a reliable apprentice—and the family were agreeable to the conditions set for their co-operation—a Form of Indenture was drawn up and presented to the interested parties for signature. These were the pupil, his father, the schoolmaster and the school managers. In these Indentures were a number of items common to all such agreements for working youngsters at this time. Specifically for the pupil-teacher it was laid down that he should

> faithfully and diligently serve the said...in his business as schoolmaster in the...school...and shall not except from illness absent himself from the said school during school hours and shall conduct himself with honesty, sobriety and temperance and not be guilty of any profane or lewd conversation or conduct or of gambling or any other immorality but shall diligently and obediently assist in the instruction of the scholars...and shall regularly attend Divine Service on Sunday.[8]

At the same time, his parents were bound to provide him with 'all proper lodging, food, apparel, washing, medicine and medical attendance'. The schoolmaster, in turn, agreed to teach the apprentice 'the business of the school', 'afford daily opportunities for practising the art of teaching' and 'devote one and a half hours a day to his personal instruction'. Much the same would be required in craft apprenticeships but here, notably, no premium was paid to the 'master'.

So much for the ground rules. Once launched, the pupil-teacher was examined at the end of every year and each time a little more was demanded of him by the Inspector. By the end of the fifth year, at eighteen or so, the young teacher could expect to be examined on 'Syntax, Etymology and Prosody', on the 'Rudiments of Algebra' (or the 'Practice of Levelling and Surveying'), on the 'Use of Globes or the Geography of the

British Empire and Europe as connected with the Outlines of English History' and 'more completely than before' on Holy Scripture, Liturgy and Catechism. By this time, the female pupil-teachers were let off with decimal arithmetic in place of algebra or surveying. They were, however, expected to show 'developing skills in sewing, knitting and cutting-out clothes'. Then there were some other options; Euclid for boys and, for both, vocal music and drawing.[9]

Day by day, week by week, a pupil-teachership was hard work to sustain, for boy and for master. For the pupil-teacher there was the special difficulty of his new relation with his peers and those very little younger than himself—in William Barnes's case, perhaps older. The Inspector could well ask whether, after a year's practice, it had produced, as it should:

> a respect on his part towards his former fellow-pupils and a respect on theirs towards him...When he speaks, is he attended to?[10]

The teacher, too, was in danger of finding he was out of his depth, forced to prepare ahead in a syllabus as unfamiliar to him as it was to his pupils. It is true that in Church of England schools the parson would often take the burden of religious instruction from the master but this could still leave the master with much new ground to cover on his own. Fortunately, the authorities were ready for this; they welcomed the element of mutual education and they even allowed selected masters and mistresses to take on pupil-teachers before certification if they seemed competent to stay a week or two ahead. Pupil and teacher were urged to buy books and it was clearly stated that the gratuities they received were to be used for this.[11] For the pupil-teachers it was a long day, an hour and a half extra before or after school, then homework for these lessons. Girls, especially, found it taxing for they would be expected to continue their domestic chores as before; in fact it was regarded as important that girls should be competent to pass on these skills to their pupils as future wives or servants.

Of all the conditions set for these new pupil-teachers, the salary and its method of payment were the most problematic for families thinking of putting their sons to this work.[12] The new grants of 1846 brought to a pupil-teacher the equivalent of a weekly wage of 3/10d at thirteen, rising to 7/8d at eighteen. But there were numerous trades at which a boy could earn 4s or more at thirteen and much more at eighteen. According to Revd Watkins HMI (in 1856) colliers in the north of England, for example, could bring home 9/6d a week at the age of fifteen or sixteen. There were other considerations, too. Wages were paid weekly; a pupil-teacher's salary came only at the end of the year and was then conditional on a good report, so the child would need maintenance for the whole of the first year and a careful husbanding of resources on his behalf from then on. All this tended to limit recruitment from the lower social classes, as did the common assumption among parents who were manual workers that pupil-teaching was not really 'learning a trade'.[13]

However, for those who stuck to it there was the regular if not over-generous £10 per annum rising to £20 over five years. At the end of this time the apprentice was finally tested and, if satisfactory, he could apply for a certificate of completion which he could then use to obtain a post as assistant teacher or in some other field. For a while, the government actually offered posts in the Civil Service to ex-pupil-teachers but changed their minds when the numbers were not as great as they had hoped.[14] The way forward for the more aspiring was through the Queen's Scholarship examination. This led on to a year or more in a training college and to all the advantages of certification.

These then were the prospects for Barnes, Crosfield and Foster as they worked through their apprentice years. We can now look more closely at the two schools where they served their time, the daily life in them, their teachers and their place in the local community. As Edwin Foster came up to thirteen his family had been settled in Wakefield for several years. The new school for their local church, Holy Trinity, was built next to it, in George Street not far from the junction with Kirkgate. The site, 25 ft by 50 ft, was just large enough to accommodate the small compact building, stone with a slate roof, two classrooms each about 20 ft by 40 ft, girls above and boys below—far from ideal but no doubt an improvement on the premises used before (Fig. 4). When the school was visited in November 1847, open six weeks, the Inspector noted that the ventilation was 'only moderate in

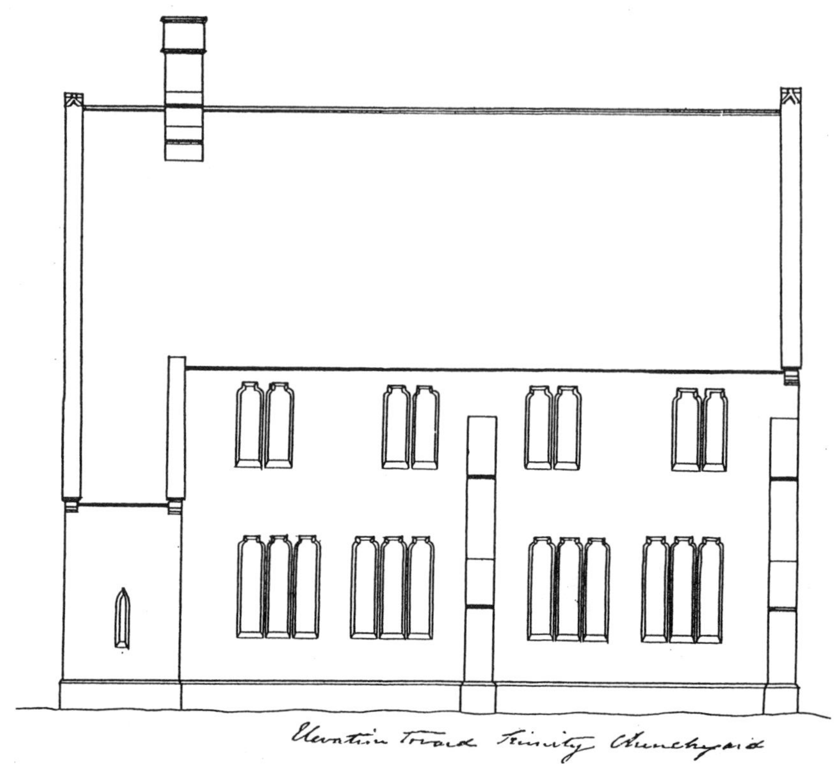

Figure 4. *Holy Trinity School, George Street, Wakefield c. 1840*
Architect's elevation

either room' and that the situation of the 'offices' was very inconvenient. He considered them 'insufficient on every respect'. He also commented on the absence of a playground other than the narrow street. However, Revd Watkins went on to say in his report that 'the master seems to be an intelligent man' and 'the school promises to be very useful'.[15]

It was here that a year later Edwin Foster, just turned fourteen, was apprenticed to the schoolmaster, John Kitchingman[16] with another lad called Bell. By this time, into the second year of the new government scheme, St Andrew's school in Wakefield already had three pupil-teachers but there were none at the parish schools of All Saints until 1851—nor any in the nonconformist schools until much later. Why was this town so much slower to take up these new, free classroom assistants than, say, Halifax? By 1848 the Halifax St James school, alone, had six pupil-teachers and there were more than a dozen in the town as a whole.[17]

One possible explanation can be found in a letter written to the Education Department by Revd Bowditch of St Andrews a couple of years earlier. He complained that

> the best monitors we can get are worse than ridiculous owing to the utterly deficient character of the education given throughout the town... The monitors so dislike the task of teaching as to perform it most sulkily and at the change of the lesson...beg permission to return to the class.[18]

Bowditch, a man of energy and intelligence,[19] was one of many clergy to realize that the solution was to pay these juvenile helpers a reasonable wage and there were already schemes to do this in a few dioceses. But why were the Wakefield schools so backward? Could it have been that there was much less rivalry here between church and dissent, less competition for youngsters to fill school places or church and chapel pews?

Then again, the Established Church in this smaller town was much less united than it was in Halifax under Archdeacon Musgrave at St John's Parish Church, a strong evangelical. The vicar of Wakefield had high church sympathies, enough to explain his reluctance to take government aid for his schools and his lack of influence with other clergy in the town many of whom were evangelical like the Revd Tait and the independent trustees of Holy Trinity.

Be that as it may, Tait was clearly doing his best for his own school. Revd Watkins called there again in September 1848 (a couple of months before Edwin Foster was formally apprenticed) to make a detailed report.[20] On that autumn day there were about a hundred boys present, some at the parallel rows of desks at one end of the room, others sitting on the loose benches and others standing. There were five classes, graded roughly according to age and ability, at least four of these taught by monitors. For some reason, Holy Trinity was, then, a very young school. So we note that about half the children were learning arithmetic no further than 'Addition' and nearly half were still on 'Letters and Monosyllables'. Only 39 boys were using paper to work on; the rest had slates. At the other end of the scale, there were 41 boys learning geography and two (perhaps Bell and Foster?) whose arithmetic was extended to 'Fractions and Decimals'. There was no other mathematics taught in this school, at this stage, nor any drawing.

As to the methods of instruction, the Inspector described them as 'individual', that is to say with the pupils addressed one at a time within a small group, the basis of the monitorial systems of both Lancaster and Bell. With most of the teaching assigned to the older pupils both method and content were restricted by the failure of these youngsters to handle the more advanced subjects or larger groups effectively.

However, it was the policy of the Education Department, then, to encourage 'simultaneous' teaching. Apparatus grants in 1843, for instance, were given for sets of parallel desks to accommodate groups of twenty to forty children—more than a monitor would usually be expected to cope with. But in the late 1840s most schools had adopted a mixture of methods (Holy Trinity already had suitable desks) and pupil-teachers would be trained for 'simultaneous' teaching in due course, for their final examination. Watkins, it should be remarked, was chary of too much of this method in which there was a tendency to rely on mass answering of questions while lazy or less confident pupils were overlooked.

On this day in 1848 Watkins had some further complaints. He mentioned again the lack of a playground, and repeated that the boys' privy should not have had its doors by the main entrance of the school; a year later he was quite outspoken about 'the stench at the master's desk'. John Kitchingman, though painstaking, he considered 'not a good disciplinarian'—and he was a little put out that the clergyman was not present for this prearranged visit.

What was Kitchingman's status at this time? He was clearly a diligent man, as Watkins had noted. Born in 1828, he had applied unsuccessfully for a Ripon Diocesan Board Exhibition to the college at York when he was about fifteen[21] but he had some training there between 1844 and 1846. By 1847 he was under pressure to apply for certification so in August that year he sat the new examinations at York. Out of 25 candidates on that occasion, 21 were successful and Kitchingman's certificate, third class Division One, showed he had reached a good standard in basic subjects.[22] In 1848, when Foster was first apprenticed to him he was still only twenty years old and living with his widowed mother in Denby Dale Road.

From 1848, arrangements were made for serving teachers to be examined at centres in the major towns and it is interesting to note in passing that the first of these sessions took place in Wakefield at Easter that year.[23] Revd Watkins was asked to make a special report. There were ten days of examinations—for men who had never been tested on paper before, in their lives—and 85 teachers were present from Yorkshire and the north-east. Watkins and Revd Bowditch who helped him, were both impressed by the earnestness of the candidates though, in the end, no more than half of them passed.

The outlook, however, was good for Kitchingman and his colleagues who achieved this new status. There was the prospect of a salary rise at once plus the bonus they could now earn for taking on pupil-teachers. For Kitchingman it worked out like this. With his third class certificate he was guaranteed £18 a year from the government, provided that the managers could pay him at least twice this sum as salary, supply a house rent free or money in lieu. The new Holy Trinity school was built without a master's house so either rent was paid for him or he received an allowance of £10 a year.

Now, in July 1848, Kitchingman's salary was £70 per annum. By that Christmas he was a certificated master with two pupil-teachers. In 1849, therefore, his salary could have been raised by the government augmentation of £18 and £9 for two apprentices to a total of £97—or, if the managers reduced their contribution to the legal minimum of £36, to £63, without rent. Let us hope they were more generous than this to compensate their school-master for the work and cost of certification, for the extra hours spent each day with the pupil-teachers and for maintaining the basic standards in the school on which the grant itself depended.[24]

Two more yearly reports on Holy Trinity school appear in the published Minutes of the Committee of Council on Education before such details, school by school, disappear from these annual volumes. In 1850 and 1851 numbers in the boys school rose to 130 and fell back to just over 100. It is difficult to imagine so many boys taught at once in such a room. Even with 90 present the Inspector considered the accommodation 'straitened'. Nevertheless, discipline continued to improve and by the end of 1851 the teaching was said to be 'intelligent and fairly successful'. It was still chiefly monitorial, in small groups, but Watkins noted a scripture lesson given by the simultaneous method in parallel desks. There were two pupil-teachers, still, but Foster's colleague was now John Speak, son of a shoemaker in Westgate (shop in Fig. 3) while one of the two girls' school apprentices was Sarah Kaye from another household in this trade, both these shoemakers using William Foster's lasts, perhaps.[25]

During the period mentioned above, about the middle of Edwin Foster's apprenticeship, Revd William Tait arranged a public function to raise money and encourage local interest in the school. He was clearly concerned about the large numbers he was admitting, particularly the hordes of younger children, so, with plans for a new infant school in mind, he invited the well-known expert on infant-school method, Samuel Wilderspin, to hold one of his demonstrations.[26]

In over twenty years of travelling and campaigning, Wilderspin had succeeded in putting infant schools on the official map and he was instrumental in founding the (evangelical) Home and Colonial Institution for the training of infant school teachers in London. He had been resident in Wakefield since 1848. Now, two years later, it was announced in the local press that on 28 November, 11.00 a.m., Mr Wilderspin would attend at the Music Saloon, Wood Street, to conduct an Examination of Infant Scholars. Tickets were sold at 1s each for adults and 4d for children. The object of the exercise was 'to show the power of Mr Wilderspin's system when rightly applied to the Training of Children' and 'to assist in defraying the necessary expenses incurred in the establishment of these schools'. A 'highly respectable audience' was gathered in the hall to be instructed, entertained and milked for funds.

A group of infants from Holy Trinity school were chosen—no doubt the cleanest and brightest. On the morning of 28 November the reporter from the *Wakefield Journal* was surprised to see 'with what rapidity the young children could enumerate numbers extending as far as hundreds of millions'.

They were also, it seemed, well-acquainted with 'certain portions of Holy Scripture'. The morning's session was enlivened with the singing of short hymns and after their performance the children were rewarded with currant buns 'which seemed to please them as much as either geography or songs'.

Was Edwin Foster there with his parents? It seems likely in view of his future ambitions. Perhaps the other children came too; Mary went on to become a pupil-teacher herself and Susan aged five might well have been with the other infants on the stage. Mary, in fact, returned to this school as a young widow for a spell in the early 1870s. Untrained, she was then in charge of the 'Infant Department' which was still, in spite of Wilderspin's efforts, part of the main school.

Shortly after this Edwin Foster completed his apprenticeship and the life-stories of the three potential schoolmasters converge in York. Let us, therefore, return to Liverpool to see how John Crosfield and William Barnes have fared, meanwhile, at the Christchurch school in Christian Street.

The frenzy of Protestant excitement which had prompted the building of Christchurch and some other church schools in Liverpool in the late 1830s and early 1840s has been described earlier. The practicalities for Revd Ould and his trustees were as follows. Two pieces of land were bought on the east side of Christian Street for £500 and £750.[27] The land came with 'messuages' including a cow-house and stables and two dwelling-houses together with the 'use and enjoyment' of the yard-wide common passageway running behind the property. The whole plot measured about 21 yds back from the street with a frontage of about 16 yds. The school when built had three floors, a schoolroom on each and there was a small yard behind with the usual 'offices', a passageway along the side and what appears to be a separate entrance at the back for the girls and infants who were on the first and second floors. The boys schoolroom was a semi-basement.

Opposite and to the sides of the school, within a radius of fifty yards or so, were two taverns and two wine vaults. Behind the common passage ran Spring Place with a couple of dozen tiny workmen's cottages and two sets of six back-to-backs while both Hunter Street, with the church, and Christian Street itself had some large terraced houses with gardens. The immediate surroundings for the new school were constricted and drab but the trustees were, perhaps, lucky to find a site so near to the church and accessible to the children of this poor neighbourhood.

An approving early comment on the school was quoted in the last chapter. A run of much fuller Inspector's reports is available from 1846 by which time we can be certain that William Barnes and John Crosfield were both in the school. Revd Watkins HMI, still then responsible for the whole of the northern district, inspected the school in 1846, boys, girls and infants, in April and May.[28] Of the boys he said they were in a good state of discipline under a master (Robert Andrews) trained at the National Society's Institution at Westminster, a man of 'much experience and good attainments'. However, there were some two hundred boys present, divided into eight classes, in a room which was ten feet below ground level. At about 50 ft by 27 ft, it gave the requisite six square feet per pupil but it was dark, ill-ventilated and poorly equipped. Nor did Watkins approve of the several 'masters in training' who, presumably shared the classes with the monitors. 'They were' he said, 'of questionable value to the school'. There was a similar arrangement in the girls' school under a less-than-competent mistress (Andrews's wife Martha). The infant mistress who had been trained at the Home and Colonial Institution in London, had a paid assistant and, again, some trainees.

It was unusual for an elementary school to set itself up in this way as an informal training centre particularly one in such an area without the best of physical amenities but it suggests a purposeful attitude on the part of the managers. If the trainees were paying their way it would explain, too, the apparently generous level of the master's salary, £110 per annum with £60 for his wife.[29] For the infant teacher, £70 was also high but all this changed when the government pupil-teacher system came in after the Minutes of 1846.

In Liverpool as elsewhere, here was a chance for bright working-class boys and girls to plan for a salaried career. In February 1848 no less than six boys were apprenticed in the school—Barnes, Crosfield and four others. The girls' school already had one pupil-teacher and a year later acquired five more.[30] This would seem to reflect the kind of enthusiasm already seen in Halifax but a significant local factor, here, could be the relative absence of paid work for children. We could also note by way of comparison with Wakefield that the schoolmaster's certificate was not awarded until Easter 1848 and was thus still pending when these boys were signed on. Andrews sat the examination in Chester but achieved only a third class certificate Division III, the lowest on the scale. This would have gained him the minimum government bonus of £15 per annum[31] which, with fees for six pupil-teachers would have raised his salary to over £150—unless of course the managers cut back their payments as trainees were replaced by apprentices.

Let us continue with accounts of the day-to-day work in this school. A report in February 1849 from Revd Kennedy, now HMI for the north-west, confirmed the previous assessment of a school in good hands but with deficiencies of accommodation.[32] Kennedy doubted whether pupil-teachers should have been introduced at all into this 'low and ill-ventilated room'—thus questioning seriously the judgement of his predecessor. He went on, 'at least so many children should not be allowed to attend the school'. There was, in fact, a large turn-over of pupils[33] an all too common problem even for the better elementary schools at this time.

On this day in February the Inspector noted there was 'nothing unusual' in the teaching methods in the Christchurch boys' school. But he gave a very complete breakdown of the numbers and ages of the pupils and the subjects taught. Unlike Foster's school in Wakefield this one had 50 or 60 boys aged twelve and over, a quarter to a fifth of the average attendance (and this was usual in the neighbourhood). Boys at the upper end of the school were studying history, grammar and geography; a select nine pupils were learning algebra; 48 did vocal music. At the lower end of the school a quarter were aged under seven; 94 pupils were still on 'Letters and Monosyllables' and 82 on basic arithmetic up to 'Addition'. The Inspector was assured that a quarter of all the boys could read the Holy Scriptures. Most of the pupils were given paper to write on but slates were in use as well. All this took place in the hubbub of one large room—as many as 250 boys under one adult and a group of six apprentices aged twelve to fourteen, plus some younger monitors. No wonder 'the master's health was suffering from excess of work'.

This was the nature of the school environment in which young Barnes and his older friend Crosfield were trained. Between 1849 and 1853 when they graduated from their pupil-teacherships some slight improvements were made. In 1850[34] the ventilation was better and a reduction of pupil numbers to around two hundred was seen to improve 'the quality of the instruction'. Andrews, now considered 'a very competent school-keeper', had instituted a system of rewards for his pupils, giving tickets of merit and redeeming these for cash, a practice which cost him about £6 a year. Finally, the year before Barnes and Crosfield left for college, Revd Birley (Assistant HMI) described the Christchurch National Schools as 'creditably conducted'. He went on, 'the master's heart appears to be wrapped up in his work'.[35]

It is a pity that we have no record of the progress of these three young men week by week or even year by year. Inspectors were so busy that pupil-teachers were rarely mentioned in the official reports except as features of classroom organization and even in the written report left in the school for the managers it was usual to note only the shortcomings, problems and failures of individual apprentices if there was some action to be taken. While a number fell by the wayside for one reason or another, we know that Barnes, Crosfield and Foster all came through to their final examinations without delay or set-back some time in 1853.

This crucial test could become an ordeal if it was conducted semi-publicly in the presence of parents, managers and interested outsiders—a common practice in these early years.[36] There were two stages to it, the theoretical examination whose main content has been mentioned earlier and the practical exercises in teaching. By this time, young men and women with this rudimentary secondary education were expected to be able to write coherently and correctly about their daily work; as the Inspector waited each candidate laboured to produce an essay on some aspect of 'The Art of Teaching'. Finally, on this day of trial, there were two demonstration lessons to be given, the first with the top class of the school 'in any subject chosen by the Inspector' and the other a 'simultaneous' or 'gallery' lesson presumably with younger children.[37]

But society, the Education Department and the Inspectorate had greater expectations still. Not long after the start of the new scheme Revd Thurtell HMI spoke for them all when he hoped that these new sponsored men and women would

> carry with them the principles and powers, the influence of which cannot but be beneficially felt by the community. They will have been really educated, educated moreover in the control of their lower nature, in the diligent application to duty and in the fear and love of God.[38]

And these were no afterthoughts. Regulations decreed that every year and most importantly at the last examination it was up to the pupil-teacher to convince the authorities of his maturity and moral earnestness. If all had gone well he could ask the managers for a certificate of good conduct, the master for one confirming diligence, obedience and attention to duty and the clergyman to certify good churchmanship.

William Barnes, John Crosfield and Edwin Foster passed these exacting tests and were ready for the next stage of training by the end of 1853. What had the last five years done for them? For a start this was hardly a normal adolescence for a working-class boy; teaching, in the common view, was not a real trade or a man's work and while in all apprenticeships there was an element of social and moral control a pupil-teacher in the classroom endured a suffocating regime of alternate work and study with, at least yearly (and preceding payment), a minute dissection of his character and skills. Not only he but his family were required to keep up standards of decent and orderly behaviour and to show their attachment to the church and its observances. To set against these heavy demands a school apprenticeship involved no premium and, because public authorities were involved, there was good protection from exploitation.

In return for his efforts the pupil-teacher received with a regular wage a genuine extension to his elementary education—enough to open doors for him into other occupations than teaching. For teaching itself there was the irreplaceable five years of classroom practice—of learning by trial and error—at a time when theoretical instruction in school method and management was poor even in most training colleges. The quality of all this experience, though, was dependent on the calibre of the schoolmaster and the wisdom, energy and skill of the local clergy. Could it be said that these boys in Liverpool and Wakefield were fortunate in these respects?

From this later perspective it is clear that the original differences between the ventures of school building in north Liverpool and central Wakefield in the late 1830s were as nothing compared to the shared managerial problems of maintenance, staffing and intake of pupils thereafter. For the children, the pupil-teachers and the masters in these schoolrooms there was little to choose between Christchurch, Christian Street and Holy Trinity, Wakefield. Both were tied to the old plan of one large room in which the need for order was paramount. Both these schoolrooms were overcrowded even by the standards of the day with all that involved by way of mental distraction and physical discomfort. The schoolmasters were qualified but only to a minimal level. The Liverpool school covered more of the normal range of elementary school subjects while Holy Trinity was handicapped by a crowd of younger children. But these two schools with all their disadvantages were typical of those welcomed by Her Majesty's Inspectors as making conspicuous efforts to fulfil a local need. At any rate they were good enough to set a number of youngsters like Barnes, Crosfield and Foster on the next rung of the professional ladder which now stood before them.

IV

The Training Colleges: Access and Choice

In the last chapter the narrative was brought forward to the end of 1853. With five years apprenticeship completed this second batch of government-sponsored pupil-teachers were girding themselves for the next stage of their careers. Some would opt to stay on as assistant teachers but for the more ambitious there was the challenge of the new Queen's scholarship examinations and a year or more at training college. William Barnes, John Crosfield and Edwin Foster were now ready to move forward on this course and into the mainstream of their chosen profession. First there was the examination to pass, then there were college places to be found.

The existing colleges acted as centres for the scholarship examinations and until this year it was assumed that candidates boarding there for the examination were applicants for that college alone. But from Christmas 1853, faced with a very unsatisfactory distribution of students around the country, the authorities said that choice would be open until after the results were published. So pupil-teachers were free to sit where it was convenient and we can be sure that while Edwin Foster went to York, Barnes and Crosfield travelled down to their diocesan college at Chester.[1]

In each case, arrangements were made with the college by 'friends and patrons' of the candidate—not, be it noted, by the young man himself, now (usually) eighteen years old, nor by his parents. These sponsors, including the incumbent of the parish, consulted with Her Majesty's Inspectors to decide, first, if the candidate was up to this further test of his intellectual abilities and if so whether he was also suitable for further training. The papers were set and marked by the Inspectors, a considerable extension to their previous duties and their content gives the best picture we have of the academic level expected of these apprentices at the end of their five-year stint.[2] For male pupil-teachers of 1853 there were nine subjects, five of them compulsory; in church schools these were Holy Scripture, catechism and liturgy, history and geography (combined), grammar, arithmetic and school management. Papers for female candidates were separate and the examinations held at different centres.

The Inspectors who planned the examination justified this choice of basic subjects as being those already taught in the elementary schools; they did not wish to upset the managers of the schools by making changes. It would, in any case, have been wholly impractical to increase the demands on a partially qualified corps of teachers. However, there were extra optional subjects, a choice of not more than three from Euclid, algebra, mensuaration and mechanics, or, for girls, domestic economy. A candidate answering really well in the compulsory subjects was awarded a second-class scholarship of £20; with one or more optional papers done well the candidate could win a first-class scholarship worth £25—sufficient to cover the average college fees for a year. The emphasis was on the thorough mastery of a few subjects—all concerned were told that poor attempts at a larger number would not win them any credit.[3]

Most of each paper tested elementary skills in computation or in the memorizing of notes or lists but here and there were more searching questions—on population changes in the history paper, for example, and a philosophical passage for paraphrase under grammar. It seems clear, too, that for the authorities at this time detailed dissection of the English language was regarded as an essential drill for school teachers, a substitute perhaps for the kind of mental training that for the upper classes came through the study of Latin and Greek.

Then there was the all-important school management paper. It was clearly intended to supplement the live demonstration of teaching skills; the candidate was given a choice of topics on which to show he could describe and discuss the fruits of his experience. What were the merits of different plans for correcting exercises, for example; how would the candidate use a blackboard, keep the registers? The questions went on:

> How would you check conceit in a clever and painstaking child who at an early age had reached the higher part of a school?
>
> Describe the means you would adopt for engaging the attention of a class before beginning a lesson and for maintaining or restoring it as the lesson proceeded?
>
> In arranging the several classes in a schoolroom how would you guard against interruption from their overhearing each other at work?

How indeed, when the main obstacles to skilful teaching—large numbers and lack of space—were still the norm?

In religious knowledge the candidates had further scope to show their intellectual worth. Following a first, easy request—to draw a map and put on it 'certain towns and rivers in the Bible lands'—came two questions on links between the Old and New Testaments and then some (for these young Anglicans) on 'confession', 'litany' and 'communion'. The words of the catechism were to be used to explain 'the parts of Baptism' and 'the parts of the Lord's Supper'.

With such a mix of intentions behind the questions set in these papers—and with open choice as to which or how many were answered—it is difficult to conceive how the papers were fairly marked. It seems that each subject was allotted to one Inspector who graded the papers on impression and the results of these gradings were then grouped to give a final mark.[4] In 1853 the pass-level was simply defined as that which allowed through the number of candidates to match the total number of vacancies in the training colleges (after places had been taken up by paying students).[5]

The final lists were published in order of merit, men and women separately.[6] In 1853, 705 male apprentices completed their five-year stint (in all kinds of school). Of these only 304 competed for Queen's Scholarships and 248 were successful including William Barnes, John Crosfield and Edwin Foster. How were they placed? Edwin Foster came out best, towards the end of the first fifteen male candidates, and he was therefore high among the first 109 who won first-class scholarships of £25. The other boys did less well; William Barnes was placed near the top of the second-class category, Crosfield somewhat further down.

But all who passed were members of a new elite, distinguished from their peers in their choice of a scholastic career (albeit a humble one) and they were now moving on to join the few hundred who qualified for further training at public expense. Between 80 per cent and 90 per cent of these potential trainees came from parish or National schools—so great was the command of the Established Church over this territory at this time. We should ask in passing, though, whether the grades achieved by Barnes, Crosfield and Foster were in any way affected by the quality of the particular schools in which they were apprenticed. Why did Edwin Foster perform so much better than the other two?

The simplest explanation is that in his school the schoolmaster had time to coach him in the optional subjects which were a precondition for a first-class scholarship. Perhaps the state of the larger and still more crowded schoolroom of the Christchurch school precluded any attempt to cover any more than the basic subjects for Andrews and his group of five or six boys or perhaps they tried and failed. Barnes, though bright, was, of course, very young and there were other hazards, like illness, to affect the smooth flow of these careers.

We now turn to the all-important and complex questions of the choice of training college. All three young men went to York, the diocesan college for Edwin Foster but foreign territory for Barnes and Crosfield. The work of these institutions was so central to the success of the new state-funded elementary schools and so important for individual careers that a reason must be sought for the migration of the two Liverpool boys into Yorkshire. Looking at the colleges from the consumer's point of view there was first location to consider, then teaching method, academic record, religious tone and, of course, availability of places.

To start with there was the straightforward option of the college built for and by the diocese; such were available at Chester, Culham (Oxford), Durham, Exeter, Saltley (Worcester),

Winchester and York. In fact such a move was expected of Queen's scholars and special arrangements were needed for church school boys to enter diocesan college somewhere else. But among the inspected Church of England colleges for men were several more with an open recruitment policy. These were the National Society's colleges at Battersea and Chelsea (St Mark's) and the college at Cheltenham under its own committee. These were the largest colleges for men, with room for 70–100 resident students, but this did not mean they were easy to get into. When the scholarship list was published late in 1853 the Secretary to the Committee of Council on Education took care to announce in a circular to the Principals of colleges that Battersea and Cheltenham had on their lists more successful applicants than they could take. All the other colleges had less.[7] We cannot therefore assume that York was the Liverpool boys' first choice—nor even Foster's, come to that, although he was so near.

As the friends and patrons of these successful Queen's scholars were deliberating over the best college for their protégés they might also have known there was something of a league-table in existence. Revd Moseley HMI, in his report on the Church of England colleges in 1853, gave some statistics on provision, expenditure and success in examinations.[8] The most telling of these were a series of pass-rates based on the whole number of students completing the course that year. In Moseley's table three colleges emerged as best—Durham, Battersea and Culham, each with a pass-rate of over eighty per cent. The lowest group (forty per cent to fifty per cent) included both York and Chester and Cheltenham appeared with sixty-one per cent. So York could not have been chosen on these grounds.

These yearly reports also contained the Inspectors' views on college organization and method. It appears that teaching was based either on the elementary school model of oral teaching—question and answer in small groups—or on the university and public school model of lessons prepared from books and tested orally or in writing. In 1851 Moseley had praised the colleges at Battersea and Cheltenham for 'the perfection of their oral teaching' and also their use of demonstration lessons.[9] Though by 1853 he was recommending a mixture of these two methods[10] both these colleges maintained high reputations and it was, perhaps, the Inspector's comments of 1851 which ensured their popularity at this time.

With reports such as these it was possible for clergy and schoolmasters to form opinions on the relative merits of the colleges available for their potential students. There was also comment in the religious press including, of course, the monthly papers of the National Society and personal views were regularly exchanged within the vast network of church acquaintanceships, lay and clerical. Ex-students, now teaching, could add their observations based on direct experience. It is easy to see why, on considerations of this sort, William Barnes and his friends from Christchurch National school in Liverpool were not sent to the diocesan college at Chester. We have noted how this college came low in the Inspector's league table in 1853 and Revd Moseley already had some reservations about the emphasis there on manual skills.[11] The schoolmaster at Christchurch, Robert Andrews, went there in 1848 to sit the certificate examination and he would have seen something of the regime.[12] It had its admirers but it was not strongly academic and with young William Barnes the vicar of Christchurch and his schoolmaster had something of a phenomenon on their hands.

As a Queen's scholar at the end of 1853 Barnes was not quite seventeen. He had been taken on as a pupil-teacher in 1848 a full two years short of the regulation age of thirteen. A few years later, his aptitude for teaching confirmed, he was all set for a successful career but if his patrons were anxious to give him the best possible chance to develop his unusual powers then Chester would hardly have been their first choice of college for his teacher training.

We do not know how strongly this consideration presented itself for Crosfield and another Queen's scholar, William Bradley Jones.[13] Perhaps it was simply felt desirable that the boys should travel away from home together. If Chester were out, the two nearest colleges were Saltley and York with nothing obvious to recommend either of them. Cheltenham, however, not much further away was a centre of evangelical education and churchmanship[14] and this college might well have been Revd Ould's first choice. But Cheltenham, as we have seen, was oversubscribed. Another possibility was St Mark's Chelsea, known to take young students of a scholarly bent and in many ways an obvious choice for Barnes.

Revd Moseley had spoken warmly of this college in 1846:

> Its founders were men in earnest; they had a confidence in the principles they have embodied in it and have laid its foundations deeply. Its system appears to me to be based in a profound sense on the sacredness of the office of the teacher, a just appreciation of its responsibilities and a firm faith in its destinies.[15]

The Inspector went on to say that the influence of the daily services of the chapel was, in his judgment, priceless. Several years later he declared that St Mark's was

> in advance of public opinion in the standard which it affixes to the qualifications of the teacher and in its estimate of the importance of his mission.[16]

This praise was echoed by Revd Watkins HMI (that same year) when he referred to 'the great training schools of Battersea and St Mark's'.[17] Maybe London was considered too far away but there were powerful reasons why this particular college would not have been acceptable, just then, to the managers of Christchurch school. To understand these concerns and to weigh up the remaining pros and cons for York we must turn back to look more closely at that most important feature of college life, religion as taught and practised.

One need not look far, in the mid-nineteenth century, for resounding statements on the importance of religion in the education of the common people. When the Venerable Archdeacon Musgrave, vicar of Halifax, went to Wakefield in 1852, for example (when Foster was a pupil-teacher there), he said to the townsfolk:

> It would be an abuse of the sacred cause of education to dissociate religion from secular teaching...or to make religion anything less than a primary and all-pervading element in the training of the young.[18]

Consensus on this broad principle was almost universal and if the school day were to be permeated by religion so too must the teacher's training. When the first certificate examinations were held in Battersea in July 1847 the assembled schoolmasters were reminded by the Principal of this college

> of those high motives to the successful discharge of their duties which are supplied by a religious appreciation of their external bearing and immeasurable responsibilities.[19]

The same kind of exhortations could be heard whenever teachers were gathered under the auspices of any one of the Christian denominations. So it is hardly surprising that when the church itself was riven with conflict, supporters of the various parties should be found among the promoters and the staff of the training institutions and that each could be labelled to some extent 'high' or 'low' in its churchmanship. In fact the high church element in teacher training was uncommon but where it existed—or was suspected—evangelical reactions were set off like a trail of gunpowder. By the time Foster, Crosfield and Barnes were on their way to college there were just two institutions which were the target of violent Protestant feeling. One of these was St Mark's Chelsea; the other was York.

The St Mark's affair was the more dramatic for taking place within the National Society whose internal problems and disputes with the church hierarchy were receiving national coverage. A small but vocal high church faction led by Revd Denison of East Brent was campaigning to stiffen the Society's response to the conditions set by the government in its distribution of grants. Some clergy went so far as to repudiate all government aid as a matter of principle[20] and inevitably there was an evangelical backlash. In May 1852 at the Society's Annual Meeting a memorial was presented by those who 'resisted the agitation for some years past prevalent in the Society' and to protest against the high church party's attempts to 'hinder the cordial co-operation of the Government and the Society'.[21] It was this group who were also demanding that all church services in their training institutions should follow the model adopted 'in well-ordered Parish Churches...recently recommended by almost all the Bishops...to the Parochial Clergy'. Quite specifically, they insisted there should be

> vigilance in Catechetical Instruction to students and scholars to prevent the apparent sanction of any doctrine or ceremonial not

> strictly in accordance with the Articles and Formularies of the Church of England.

But the implied criticisms of the training colleges were brushed aside, the Committee asking for evidence of these grave accusations. Meanwhile the evangelical party renewed their attack; the following day a large deputation waited on the Archbishop of Canterbury and the Bishop of London armed with a set of objections to the conduct of St Mark's College, Chelsea. These focused on, first, the chapel services—the music, the candles, the altar and the clergyman preaching in a surplice—and, secondly, on the appointment in 1851 of a certain Mr Daymond, a man described later in an evangelical pamphlet as 'among the worst Romanizers of our degenerate days'.

All this took place in Barnes's and Crosfield's penultimate year of apprenticeship as pupil-teachers. In 1853, their final year, matters in the National Society came to a head.[22] Two or three hundred evangelical clergymen marched out of the Annual Meeting in London to form a society of their own and this move was quickly followed up in Liverpool[23] where on 23 June a public meeting was called

> for persons interested in the Education of the Children of the Poor in the Protestant and Evangelical Principles of the Church of England.

The zealous evangelicals who met together on that day formed themselves into a Liverpool Auxiliary Society for the main breakaway group, the Church of England Education Society. As might be expected Revd Ould was among those present and this new society functioned for many years alongside the old, concentrating on the maintenance of schools rather than building and with a more flexible attitude than the National Society's to the teaching of the catechism. It helped many schools in the town which were too poor, initially, to qualify for government grants.

In some ways, this new round of Protestant campaigning in Liverpool could be seen as the natural continuation of that which led to the collection of money and the building of Christchurch, Christian Street and other schools in the 1830s. It was hardly likely in the circumstances that these clergy and laymen would consider a college like St Mark's for their young charges. The situation at York was altogether more complicated.

The York dispute was throughout a more local affair but symptomatic of continuing public unease with the growth of Tractarianism. The trouble started in 1845, rumbled on for several years until a conclusion of sorts was reached in 1854, the first year that Barnes, Crosfield and Foster were all students at the college. In August 1845 when the students were still using the local church of St Michael-le-Belfry, a group of parishioners took exception to the way the Principal, Revd William Reed, was conducting the services.[24] A parish meeting was called and Revd Reed was forbidden to use the church for college worship. Local papers took up the issue:

> There are doubtless degrees in departures from Protestant principles...the laity do not, however, draw fine distinctions...but view all who entertain Tractarian sentiment to be on a sloping roof and verging in various degrees from the Reformation until too many drop into the gulph of Popery.[25]

Revd Reed was summoned to a special meeting of the two Diocesan Boards of Education (York and Ripon) told to revert to 'normal practices' in church and to send a letter disclaiming all Tractarian sympathies to the college authorities and to the local press. This he did[26] and by 1849 the college was treading a careful evangelical path.

To understand what happened next it is necessary to turn back to current preoccupations with the Church of England's Thirty-Nine Articles—those early statements of post-Reformation doctrine—and in particular the one which purports to explain the meaning of baptism. Between 1847 and 1850 the church nation-wide was following intently the course of a doctrinal dispute over the meaning of 'baptismal regeneration' in Article 27. This argument between Bishop Phillpotts of Exeter and a cleric seeking appointment in his diocese was taken all the way through the ecclesiastical courts to a final judgement by the Privy Council in 1850.[27]

Revd Gorham, questioned by Phillpotts, stated the Calvinist view that such 'regeneration' of the soul could not be guaranteed by the mere performance of a church ceremony—Almighty God, he believed, chose the elite in his own good time. This interpretation challenged the high church view of the efficacy of the sacrament and though there were already shades of opinion current within the church, for Bishop Phillpotts this was one he could not allow to be promulgated within his diocese. The Bishop refused Gorham his preferment but the Privy Council eventually found in Gorham's favour in 1850. How was the church to understand this decision? The lay judges of the Privy Council took pains to make clear they were not, themselves, deciding a matter of doctrine; they had merely established that (in their opinion and on the best authority they could muster) the Established Church should be prepared to contain such diversities of opinion—as it had always done. But Gorham had clearly 'won' and those who later grumbled against the Privy Council decision were identified with the Phillpotts position and with the 'high' faction of the church as against the 'low'.

This final judgement of the Privy Council stirred up even sharper controversy than the wranglings which had led up to it and public opinion on such matters was raised to fever pitch when the Pope moved suddenly in late 1850 to re-establish the Roman Catholic hierarchy in Great Britain. As the newly-appointed Cardinal Wiseman declared in October, 'Catholic England has been restored to its orbit in the ecclesiastical firmament'.[28] Triumphant Catholics now joined English high-churchmen as the perceived enemies of the Reformation church.

Clergy everywhere strained themselves to ensure that their congregations were enlisted on the right side of this great divide. Baptism, familiar to even to least attached of their people, was the subject of impassioned sermons. In Liverpool (where Barnes and Crosfield were two years into their apprenticeships), Revd Francis Power of St Alban's Bevington, neighbour and ex-curate of Revd Fielding Ould, wrote a Tract in answer to the persistent questions of his parishioners'. The excitement caused by the Gorham case', he said, 'has reached all classes of society'.[29]

In Yorkshire, clergy of the Rural Deanery of Wakefield, led by Revd William Tait of Holy Trinity (manager of Edwin Foster's school) passed a resolution deploring the action of the Privy Council in presuming to pass judgement on church doctrine. That was in March 1850. Later that year Revd James Gratrix of St James, Halifax, claimed that the Church of Rome was not merely schismatic but, he declared, 'antichrist did now sit on the city of the seven hills'[30] and he joined in a further resolution deploring Romish practices within the Church of England.

Such was the background of fervent religious crusading as three pupil-teachers worked their way through the final years of their apprenticeships in two different parish schools. It is not surprising that while all this was going on Revd Hodgkinson, Reed's successor as Principal of the training college at York, should feel impelled to instruct the young people in his charge on the tricky matter of baptismal doctrine or that his words should provoke some angry reactions. He could hardly have pleased everyone, whatever he chose to say.

In a sermon to pupils in June 1850 Hodgkinson made a statement on baptismal regeneration broadly taking the Phillpotts line and, his accusers said, condemning the judgement of the Privy Council. A group of evangelical subscribers to the college called a meeting in York on 12 November and sent a memorial of protest to the Diocesan Board. From there it was passed on to Archbishop Musgrave who summoned Hodgkinson to his residence. No public statement was issued but the Principal was told it had been unwise to raise that particular topic just then. Evangelical mutterings continued this time from Robert Baxter of the Doncaster Board of Education and in May 1852 they sent a resolution to the college authorities deploring the prejudice they observed in the community against the York Training School and 'the public view of the Principal' which they saw as its cause.[31]

In 1853 when Barnes, Crosfield and Foster were preparing for the Queen's scholarship examination, local evangelicals were still sniping at Revd Hodgkinson and in October that year they grouped themselves into a local branch of the Church of England Education Society. (It will be remembered that a Liverpool branch was formed in June.) Faced with new accusations against the Principal of the Female College, located nearby,[32] the York Committee of Management asked the Archbishop to set up an enquiry. A formal report took over six months to prepare and was finally presented in September 1854; each charge was dealt with in turn and though there was the occasional word of warning the Committee agreed unanimously that:

> no proof has been established that the doctrines he (the Principal) inculcated in his pupils are other than such as may be held by a pious and faithful minister of the Church of England.[33]

The female Principal, Miss Cruse, was also exonerated.

The result of all this was that, for a time at least, the college had two sets of enemies; those who thought they had sniffed out evidence of Popery and deplored it and those who were put off by the sternly evangelical line eventually taken by the college authorities. Among the latter group were, possibly, the vicar of Leeds, Dr Hook (of whom more in due course)[34] and the vicar of Wakefield, both known to have Tractarian sympathies. So clergy in Liverpool anxiously weighing up the benefits of the different colleges, would have found opinions of this one in Yorkshire somewhat mixed.

If we now follow the actual movements of Queen's scholars in the huge York and Ripon catchment area[35] we can see that many clergy were in fact steering their protégés elsewhere. Although the college was nearly full in 1854 with 52 in residence and places for 55 there were at least ten outsiders including the three young men from Liverpool. For example, in that year only five Queen's scholars came from Leeds out of the fourteen who went to college somewhere. In Halifax there were eleven Queen's scholars and not one chose York. No student entered that year from York itself, nor Ripon, and none from Bradford (out of a possible eight).

Where did all these potential teachers from Yorkshire go to be trained if it was not their own diocesan college? The answer is Cheltenham which not only featured well in the league table mentioned earlier but was attractive to many evangelical clergy as an institution set up

> to instruct pious persons as Masters and Mistresses upon Scriptural Evangelical and Protestant principles in accordance with the Articles and Liturgy of the Established Church.[36]

In 1854, this south of England college took no less than nine Queen's scholars from Halifax, three from Huddersfield and three from Leeds, but Yorkshire students (male and female) also went to Battersea, Oxford, Lichfield, Salisbury, Whitelands and the Home and Colonial college for infant teachers in London. Very nearly all these students came from church schools.

In view of the York troubles over religion which were coming to a head just as the crucial decisions were being made for that year's Queen's scholars the pattern described above is what might be expected. It seems unlikely that students were sent there from either the parish of Christchurch, Liverpool or Holy Trinity, Wakefield without some misgivings. In Edwin Foster's case these were clearly not strong enough to overcome the advantages of a diocesan college some 25 miles away. But even then it might not have been Revd Tait's first choice and, as for Revd Ould in Liverpool, he would surely have preferred Cheltenham once it had been decided to avoid Chester. Ould must have received some assurance from his evangelical colleagues in York that high church heresies could be dealt with before Barnes, Crosfield and Jones were sent on their way.

Meanwhile, the government which was still paying out large sums of money for teacher-training at this time, became aware of the problems in a college pecking-order. Perhaps it was HMI Moseley's fault for publishing league tables or simply the back-biting within the church that made some colleges less popular than others but the complaints that came in from Principals of under-subscribed institutions were firmly set aside in 1854:

> the Committee of Council cannot undertake any correspondence whatever as to the selection of one Training School rather than another by the friends and patrons of successful candidates.[37]

In fact Revd Moseley, in praising St Mark's that year, was careful to distance himself from current religious controversies. His opinion, he said,

> should be received without reference to those questions which at present divide the Church. My judgement has been formed, I trust, irrespective of them...it would ill become me to carry into the business of inspection...any allusion to my own views in respect to them.[38]

A few years later the government was still trying to distance itself from the mere suggestion of inequalities:

> the emptiness of some colleges [is] not due to inferiority. The question of the college in which he may have been trained is never again mooted by my Lords (of the Privy Council) in determining his rank or estimation as a certificated teacher.[39]

The Inspectors, of course, knew better and claimed to be able to identify a schoolmaster's alma mater almost at once from his style and competence. For better or worse, Edwin Foster, William Barnes and John Crosfield spent this crucial time at York. The next chapter describes the college, outlines the nature of their experience there and considers the value of this training to these young men at this important stage in their careers.

V

Two Years at York

Just as William Barnes, John Crosfield and Edwin Foster were fortunate to be born in time for the first national scheme of teacher apprenticeship, so too they were lucky to be eligible for the newer residential courses. These promised not only the cachet of the trained and certificated teacher but also the elements of a cultural education which, Her Majesty's Inspectors claimed, would offer in one year 'a parallel to the first examination of undergraduates in the Universities'.[1] And all this in a setting where a young man from a working-class background could learn something of the manners and deportment of a gentleman. As the Secretary to the Committee of Council wrote to Her Majesty's Inspectors in November 1853:

> These young persons are drawn for the most part from very humble homes; they have learnt the routine of teaching and a few elementary subjects in the day schools where they have served their apprenticeship, but the first, and often the last, point in their career at which they are brought into intimate or domestic contact with persons of superior cultivation and are obliged to conform to higher standards of manners and habits, is in a normal college.[2]

In 1854 the concept of formal training for elementary school teachers was far from new but all the earlier arrangements, dating back to the National Society's Central School of 1812[3] and the Borough Road (Lancastrian) School of about the same time, were based on the simple plan of observation and practice under an experienced master. The idea that teachers of the poor should extend their own education grew more slowly but by the 1850s there were colleges, more commonly known as training or normal schools, which tried to do just this. They took a whole range of men and women from different backgrounds and occupations and introduced them to regular academic study and from the start these included serving teachers hoping to improve their status and prospects in the profession.

For the careers of Barnes, Crosfield and Foster an important step was the spread of government funding into the maintenance of these institutions after 1846, and with the funding, inspection, and eventually control of the syllabus and examinations. By 1854—the year that all three started at York—the students were nearly all of the new, young, ex-pupil-teacher breed and most of the larger colleges had been absorbed into what was now, effectively, a national system of training and certification. For the young men themselves it was the start of a 'prolonged trial of character and conduct',[4] costly in time, effort and money but with long-term rewards for those with stamina and ability.

Some time has already been spent in discussion of the various Church of England colleges at work in the early 1850s and the possible reasons why Edwin Foster from nearby Wakefield was joined at York by two Queen's scholars from Liverpool. The story of the long drawn-out dispute between the Principal of this college and some of his local critics, described in Chapter IV, can now be set aside while this chapter concentrates on the history of the college, the students' daily lives and the content of the course and examinations.

The diocese of York had a 'central school' from before 1840[5] in which teachers could receive some training, but in 1842 it was decided that

> the Ripon Diocesan Board will unite with the York Diocesan Board of Education in establishing an Institution in the city of York for the training and instruction of Schoolmasters and Schoolmistresses to be called the York and Ripon Diocesan Training Schools.[6]

If there was any doubt that this was to be a church institution it was settled by the composition of the management committee; the Archbishop of York, the Bishop of Ripon, the Archdeacons and Rural Deans, the clerical and lay secretaries of the two Diocesan Boards (already supporting schools) and 28 persons to be elected by each Board annually. By the summer of 1851 the governors had planned and paid for a handsome range of new buildings in Lord Mayor's Walk for 50–60 male students; there was separate provision for women nearby in Monksgate.[7]

In York, as elsewhere, the college was beset with financial problems. At first they were dependent on subscriptions and on a steady intake of students who were sponsored or could pay their own way, but as soon as the first pupil-teachers arrived in 1851 there were pro-capita grants from the Exchequer and some help towards staff salaries.[8] In 1853, the college at York had 46 resident students of whom 11 had been pupil-teachers qualifying for entry as Queen's scholars. The next year there were 36 Queen's scholars out of 52 students, but even then, because the money was paid to the college retrospectively, the Committee's minutes were full of complaints that it was difficult to balance the books.[9]

However, a small Yeoman School for 'the sons of clergymen, farmers, tradesmen and manufacturers', conducted alongside the college from 1847,[10] brought in some additional income and over the years the governors were able to finance improvements and to aid those students who had come in on second-class scholarships. Barnes and Crosfield and many others in this position fell behind from time to time in the quarterly payments by which they were expected to make up the £5 difference between their scholarships and the fees of £25. The Quarterage book for 1854 and 1855 shows these debts finally settled but does not make clear whether these two young men paid off what they owed or were granted remission by the Principal under a special arrangement made in February 1853.[11]

It is clear that even with government grants these training schools still imposed something of a financial burden on the parents of these younger students. Not only was income foregone—£40 or £50 a year perhaps, which an uncertificated ex-pupil-teacher could earn—but Queen's scholars at college still had to find money for travel, clothing, books and so on.[12] What were the students offered in return for this outlay and commitment? The new college building stood on the north side of Lord Mayor's Walk just outside the city walls. The accommodation included a large common-room and dining-room and two class-rooms for the first and second year students.[13] There was no lack of space in the dormitories where

> for purposes of private devotion and other deep considerations it has been deemed advisable...to allot to each pupil in training a separate sleeping apartment.[14]

These were, in fact, cubicles, each with its own window, an expensive arrangement and one granting more privacy, surely, than most of the students would have experienced up till then. From 1853 the dormitories were lighted by gas and a bath had been installed for the use of the pupils in 1844. By the time Barnes, Crosfield and Foster were in residence there was 'gymnastic apparatus' for their use and a tennis court.[15]

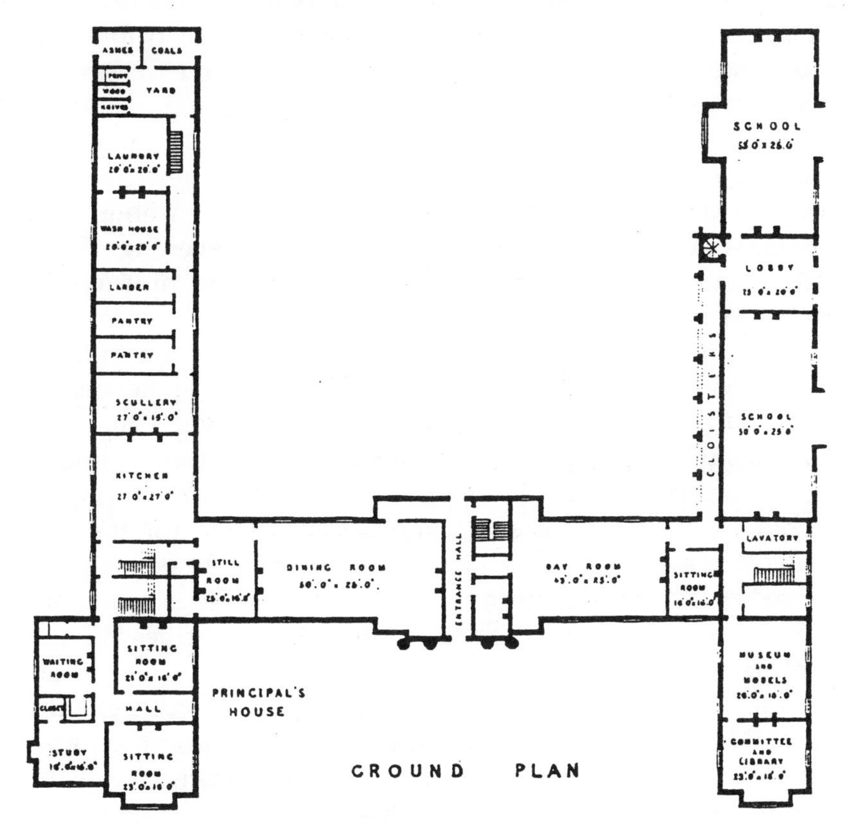

Figure 5. *The College of York and Ripon. Ground floor plan as reproduced in the Minutes of the Committee of Council on Education 1847–48*

As for the daily regime, there are two accounts. One dates from 1849 when Principal Hodgkinson was in charge[16] and the other from 1860 when his successor Revd H.G. Robinson made his report to the Royal Commission in Popular Education.[17] Robinson took over at the end of 1854 and the following details are taken from Hodgkinson's account; there is, in fact, very little difference between them.

The day started with morning prayer from 7.00–8.00 a.m. and closed with evening prayer from 8.30–9.30 p.m. while two hours were set aside for 'leisure and industrial occupation in the grounds and gardens'. In 1855 the Principal encouraged the students to take up gardening by giving them plots of land.[18] Domestic drudgery—making beds and serving at table—was demanded less of the students by the end of the decade.

Formal classes and teaching periods were arranged for three hours in the morning and three in the afternoon, each session being divided into three or four lessons. Within these hours was the time allotted for the students to take a tour of duty in the Yeoman School. They were expected to do three quarters of an hour private study before morning prayer, half an hour after breakfast and a further two hours during the evening. There were mid-week and Saturday half-holidays and nine weeks vacation a year.

In two respects this routine would have changed a little by 1854. A chapel was built in 1851[19] saving the time needed to assemble the students at St Maurice church, several hundred yards away. Secondly, the Yeoman School, though it continued to operate for the benefit of the community (and to bring in funds) was not, in the end, considered suitable for training students in elementary school method and in 1849, soon after he arrived, Revd Hodgkinson arranged for students to use the York National School for practice while urging the authorities to build a separate Practising School.[20] This they agreed to do and it was completed as an extension to the college in 1850; here the Normal Master gave weekly demonstration lessons. Work in the somewhat artificial atmosphere of the Practising School was the only practical experience students had during their training but of course most of them would already have had five years of the real thing as pupil-teachers.

Turning now to the structure and content of the training college course we find it well-documented for 1854 for it was the first year of the new centralized arrangements made by Her Majesty's Inspectors under the Committee of Council for Education. Revd Moseley HMI explained the rationale for these changes in his report of that year.[21] He started by reminding their Lordships that up till then a separate examination had been set for each college, the Inspectorate recognizing 'in the studies of these institutions whatever subjects might be deemed by their promoters expedient to be taught'. Later he explained how each had its own dominant subject; 'classical literature prevailed in one, higher mathematics...in another and in a third, Church history' with the subjects of elementary education treated as accessories. But Moseley observed a consensus emerging, 'as elementary education began to be better understood', so that when the scale of teacher training expanded and the conduct of separate examinations became impossible, it was not too difficult to draw up a common syllabus and obtain support for it. It was on this syllabus that the Christmas examinations of 1854 were based. These were the first papers sat by Barnes, Crosfield and Foster, the test by which they were judged to be minimally trained, fit to leave as schoolmasters, if they wished, or to continue with a second year at college.

Moseley's aim was to base the college course firmly on the subjects as taught in school. These he listed as religious knowledge, reading, arithmetic, English grammar, geography and English history to which he added penmanship and vocal music.[22] He also included physical science (from the second year) explaining that while it was not usually a subject of instruction in its own right, it figured prominently in school readers and should be dealt with in a course of teacher-training. A scientist himself, he had decided views on the value of science in the training of mind and faculties.

At some length in this report of 1854, Moseley explained that the basic subjects, as normally taught and as presented in school books did little to 'develop reasoning powers or the exercise of intelligence'. It was therefore the task of the teacher to 'place them under forms better adapted to his use,' selecting facts so as to illustrate 'cause and effect'.[23] He envisaged in the training course a 'higher study' of the subjects of elementary instruction, so that teachers could draw from pupils 'all that such subjects are capable of yielding to the profit of poor children'. However, a careful look at both syllabus and examination papers for this particular year suggest that this new and powerful instrument for sharpening the impact of elementary education for the masses was not, in practice, likely to cause a revolution in the nation's classrooms.

For example, in geography, where the scope for the exercise of reason is wide, the first year syllabus for the training colleges simply asked for knowledge of 'outline maps' of the quarters of the globe and of each country in Europe.[24] At the same time, the 'outlines of the History of England' were to be 'known thoroughly'—hardly possible unless severely condensed. The questions set for the end-of-year examination in these two subjects exactly and fairly covered the ground indicated with not one that invited thought or reflection or the connection of cause with effect.

However, among the others were some papers more testing of the intelligence.[25] In English grammar, for instance, students were asked to display some grasp of the language's more obscure rules. The various papers on religion—Old and New Testament history, catechism, liturgy and ecclesiastical history—did contain items that called for mature understanding but most were, again, simple tests of memory. One section out of six in the arithmetic paper asked the student to 'give a reason for each step in working'; the rest were simple exercises in computation.

It is true that first year students were required to offer an additional subject, either Latin or higher mathematics, but there was no scope here to demonstrate the power to 'extend' the ordinary subjects as demanded by Revd Moseley in his statement of aims; whenever the course was more demanding it was markedly less relevant. It was thus left to the school management paper to test the students' most essential progress and at the end of the first year's training they were questioned quite searchingly on their understanding of the teaching methods and techniques they had learnt in college or earlier. When it came to demonstrating their practical skills, however, the only test was a single lesson delivered in the presence of the Inspector. Moseley himself had serious reservations about his colleagues' ability to maintain consistent standards in judging these performances and he doubted whether, in any case, the student had a real chance to show what he could do.[26]

For what it was worth, then, this one-year college course was the basic measure of a student's competence in 1854 and his fitness to proceed to certificate status. Though the salary prospects were poorer for the one-year trained, nearly half the 1854 York students left at this point. Barnes, Crosfield and Foster were among the nineteen who remained for a second year.[27] What were they to find that was new, useful or more relevant in the programme for 1855?

By this time the authorities were clearly trying to make the two year course the norm. To promise a higher rate of salary augmentation was one inducement; widening the syllabus was another.[28] So we find, for example, that geography in this second year took in commercial and political aspects, history some reference to 'the progress of the people...their manners and customs' and elements of what we would now call 'citizenship', while mathematics was extended to include compound interest and logarithms. In parallel with the other subjects, school management now became more demanding, the examination paper covering the control and organization of a school as well as the practice of teaching. At Christmas 1855, for instance, questions were asked on the ways to divide a school into classes, to make use of desk, floor and gallery space—and how to deal with fights. It is worth noting that this particular year Her Majesty's Inspectors had a special concern for the keeping of registers and they tried to use the college examination machinery to bring about some urgent reforms.

That some of the so-called trained teachers, even after two years, were unprepared to have full charge of a school had been a matter of complaint for some time. The results of a late 1855 spot-test on 'scholastic book-keeping...the accurate calculations of attendance, age and payments',[29] confirmed the authorities' worst fears and vindicated the decision they had made earlier to introduce a couple of years probation before certificates were granted.[30] At least now they could withhold certification if a teacher proved incompetent when left in sole charge of a school for the first time.

So how did William Barnes, John Crosfield and Edwin Foster emerge from all this? They had spent two laborious years in college and worked for two sets of examinations. The results of the first round at Christmas 1854 were published in February 1855.[31] Of the 536 who were tested, then, in the various Church of England colleges for men, 411 were successful; at York 34 out of 40 passed. Of these, only one was graded first class and he was William Barnes; Edwin Foster was among the five who achieved second class and John Crosfield was in the large third-class group. At the end of the following year, Foster joined Barnes in the first-class category while Crosfield stayed among the thirds.[32]

The serious question of what these results meant, as official labels or as real measures of ability, we can pursue later as we trace the details of each mature career stretching ahead for the next twenty or thirty years. In the immediate future for Barnes, Crosfield and Foster lay the need for employment and managers were looking for more than examination passes. What did people at the time think of these elaborate college courses for elementary schoolmasters? What was their value in the market-place?

There is no doubt that by the time the products of the 1854/55 course were offering their services to the community—and Barnes, Crosfield and Foster were in the first batch of the two-year trained—public opinion had settled in favour of the new, professional teachers; they were undeniably a superior breed. But some hands were raised in horror at the cost and there were complaints, too, that the money was ill-spent, giving these educators of the poor altogether too much book-learning. Nor were all managers satisfied with the attitudes of their new employees; some of them were much too sure of themselves, it was said, while lacking the earnestness expected of men in their humble station.

Even the providers of the new courses—officials of the Education Department, the Inspectorate and the Principals of the colleges—were ready to admit there were failures. Revd H.G. Robinson of York was one of the chief witnesses to the Royal

Commission on Popular Education in the late 1850s and he gave full and frank details of his own experience as Principal of the college. Those giving evidence in this field had been asked:

> Is the training given to masters and mistresses in normal schools and training colleges well adapted to its object?[33]

Speaking in late 1859 and early 1860, Robinson felt able to say that in the main the colleges were producing 'a valuable and right-minded body of teachers'.[34] But he shared some of the public misgivings about the content of the course; in fact he was critical of just those aspects of the syllabus which Revd Moseley HMI had been most anxious to reform.

In Robinson's view not only was there far too much lecturing and book-study in proportion to classroom training—there was only three week's teaching practice, for example—but much of the work was 'routine and mechanical'. The students, he complained, were emerging with 'full but languid and unbraced minds' and with a distaste for further study. Inevitably, 'as the master has been crammed himself...so he crams his pupils'.

All this in spite of Moseley's efforts to reform a system which, Robinson admitted, was earlier governed by 'a kind of instinct to the usage of the Universities'[35] and in spite of persistent efforts to keep the cumbersome machinery on its new rails. The Inspectors went on to issue a revised syllabus in 1857 including some minor changes, but with it, discreet pressure was put on the colleges to change the emphasis of their teaching. Principals were told that

> a large proportion of the marks assigned to any paper will depend on the degree in which the candidate shows himself capable of applying the subject of that same paper (whatever it may be) to the purposes of elementary education.[36]

Robinson and his colleagues were also sensitive to criticism of the attitudes and character of the teachers they had trained. Students at York, the Principal claimed, were decent enough men, capable of 'generous emulation, devotion to study, heartiness and sympathy'.[37] Whatever their previous habits, their 'general tone and spirit and deportment' were creditable and he was sure that any 'gross or immodest conversation' would be checked in the common room by the 'better men'. Nonetheless, he felt the colleges should check the growth of 'fine gentleman airs'. He could see that new teachers were liable to forget they had come from humble backgrounds and that 'all their acquired culture was owed to public provision'. Even the five years as pupil-teacher tended to generate 'a somewhat pretentious manner of thinking and acting'. As Revd Cowie HMI sternly warned, about this time:

> They cannot be too often reminded that the difficulties of their calling...are aggravated by any attempt on their part to step out of their position.[38]

Finally, as expected, the clergy Principals of the Church of England colleges were deeply concerned about the impact of the religious element in the syllabus. They had always done their best to produce good churchmen and Robinson assured the Royal Commission that he noticed 'some leaven of religious principle' among the students. However, he went on, 'anyone looking for any settled habits of devotion or any great religious earnestness'[39] would be disappointed. To some extent he blamed the clergy for this; they had the pupil-teachers under their charge for five years—what could a college do in one year or two? Even with the parish clergy watching over and reporting back on students after each short break at home (a common practice) they could not guarantee any great advance in godliness.

Some of this concern was, naturally, directed towards the encouragement of the right kind of churchmanship—whatever that might be in the eyes of the college. But recollecting the climate of feeling that has produced the York row earlier it is significant that the authorities were now trying hard to discourage any such partisanship. Nevertheless, part of the second-year syllabus in 1854 and 1855 was devoted to a detailed study of the Reformation with questions concerning the life of Martin Luther and the times of Henry VIII; students were asked 'What three great principles of the Reformation were established in that reign?'[40] Back in 1849 a York college paper on Scripture Doctrines had asked the students to list all references to 'Romish errors' in the Thirty-nine Articles but now, in the nation-wide examination, though the tone was evangelical, Tractarian views were no longer directly targetted. And Revd Robinson, Principal in 1860, was generous enough to concede that 'the spirit of reverence' was commonest among those with a high church upbringing'.[41] For students like Barnes, Crosfield and Foster from evangelical backgrounds there was here, perhaps, their first chance of relaxed and informal contacts with colleagues of different views.

Looking back over their two years at York, these young men would have known that, with all its deficiencies, there was no better preparation to be had just then for their chosen vocation. By the mid-1850s the new state system of training had absorbed the fruits of many years experience, transmitted from clergy, managers and teachers to Her Majesty's Inspectors on their tours around the country. If the best of the new ideas were slow to take root in college or school, this was only to be expected. The 'intelligent teaching' that HMIs admired would always be difficult in the ordinary noisy and crowded schoolrooms of town or village; teachers were only human and managers, inevitably, were tempted to settle for old-fashioned drill. From now on, it must have been clear to these three young teachers that to distinguish themselves in later years they must set their own sights high. Wider choices for those with ambition would indeed present themselves as time went on and we shall see in due course how Barnes, Crosfield and Foster made use of them.

VI

Teachers on Probation

Through the mid-forties to the early sixties young schoolmasters with a vocation to teach the poor enjoyed a buoyant period of state encouragement and support. When Barnes, Crosfield and Foster had completed their two years at college at the end of 1855 certificated teachers were still in demand for the church schools and employment prospects were good.[1] To start with, however, their field of choice was limited; students leaving the diocesan colleges were expected to serve in the diocese or, coming from elsewhere like Barnes and Crosfield, to return home for their first post.

In fact it was usual for these early appointments to be made through the college Principal or a local committee of clergy, partly to safeguard the student's own interests and partly to ensure that the diocese saw a return for its money. Thus we find that of the students leaving York at the end of 1854, 1855 and 1856 most went to parish schools in Yorkshire, a few to Durham, Lancashire or Nottinghamshire into which county the vast diocese of York extended at this time. It was also expected that students would go into elementary schools but there were exceptions. In 1857 a very able student, William Hugill Thompson (later ordained) went straight from college to Helstone Grammar School in Cornwall.[2] It is not clear why this was allowed; in 1854 another clever student was actually recalled from an appointment as assistant master in Louth Grammar School where he was serving under the ex-principal of the college, now headmaster there.[3] Barnes, Crosfield and Foster, though, made no challenge to the authorities and moved into conventional posts.

William Barnes and John Crosfield both went back to Liverpool, Barnes to their old school in Christian Street and Crosfield to St Thomas, Toxteth in south Liverpool for a few months then on to the Holy Trinity National school in Birkenhead. Edwin Foster, meanwhile, responded to an advertisement for a school in his old home town of Halifax about fifteen miles from his family in Wakefield. Under the new scheme for a term of probation, masters were expected to show two years continuous service in one school and Crosfield probably delayed his certification by moving during this period. Up to this time, though, in early 1858 all three men were entitled to claim certain minimum salaries, just as their own teachers had done earlier (Chapter III).[4]

Under the current rules, Crosfield stood to receive at least £30 a year—£10 from the Treasury conditional upon £20 from the managers—Barnes and Foster, £45 each. Beyond this, managers were expected to provide accommodation or £10 in lieu. Over and above these minima even probationary certificate-holders were in line for another important source of government income. Unless the school was very small and isolated they would be likely to have pupil-teachers and/or stipendiary monitors under them and they would be paid to instruct such apprentices at the rate of £5, £9 or £12 for one, two or three. From what we know of the various schools it would be fair to assume that each had three or more such youngsters to help in the schoolroom. On this basis we can set a minimum first-year income for Barnes and Foster of £57 and for Crosfield at £42 (plus accommodation in each case). Foster's actual salary, as will be explained later, was considerably more than £57, the other two comparable, possibly.

Let us now turn to the schools in question. The origins and particular circumstances of the Christchurch school in Liverpool have already been described; the difficulties and discomforts of location and premises are unlikely to have changed much while Barnes was away—nor, to be fair, the popularity of the school and the constructive attitude of the managers. However, we have no details of Barnes's period here as a schoolmaster, nor of St Thomas school where, it appears, Crosfield took over briefly from his old schoolmaster, Andrews. The Birkenhead school, though, is fairly well documented until just before Crosfield arrived.

By 1856 Birkenhead was an important seaport, market town and centre for shipbuilding.[5] For some at least the town appeared 'a clean well-ordered healthy place' and many of Liverpool's merchants and businessmen chose to live there. Holy Trinity church was built in Price Street in 1837, surrounded by working-class terraces and when John Crosfield came to the town this church, under Revd Joseph Baylee, had associated with it two National schools. One, next to the church, was run as a free or 'ragged' school; the other, half a mile away in Trinity Street, was a normal day school for boys, girls and infants. It was to this school that Crosfield came in 1857.

The school was built in 1843–44 as a result of the same kind of initiatives that Revd Gratrix was exercising in Halifax. Baylee, like Ould, Gratrix and Tait made use of all the help he could muster from the National Society (Fig. 6) and from the Treasury, and like these men he was 'a champion of evangelical truth'.[6] However, while there were anti-papist riots in Birkenhead (later) in 1851 and a local Protestant Association was active[7] the business of school building was not, at this time, caught up in the cross-currents of religious politics. Nor did Baylee apparently feel challenged by the nonconformists. Indeed he claimed in 1855 that of the population in his own district, two-thirds were already in the fold of the Established Church. So while his task was substantial he was not held back by religious tensions or antipathies.[8]

What is more, the financial burden of the undertaking was eased from the start when John Laird, the shipbuilder, donated land in 1842. He gave it then

> as a site for a school for poor persons...and as a residence for schoolmasters and schoolmistresses,

the school to be

> in union with the National Society and conducted according to its principles and in furtherance of its aims.[9]

The various proprietors of this new school, once it was built, put their heads together and drew up a separate Deed,[10] a most unusual document, binding the incumbent of the parish to work

TERMS OF UNION

TO BE SUBSCRIBED BY PARTIES DESIROUS OF UNITING THEIR SCHOOLS WITH THE

National Society

FOR PROMOTING THE EDUCATION OF THE POOR IN THE PRINCIPLES OF THE ESTABLISHED CHURCH THROUGHOUT ENGLAND AND WALES.

We, the undersigned, being desirous that the School ~~at (or to be~~ established at) Birkenhead ~~near~~ *in the County of* Chester *and Diocese of* Chester *should be united to the* NATIONAL SOCIETY, *declare that*

1. "*The Children are to be instructed in the Holy Scriptures, and in the Liturgy and Catechism of the Established Church.*"

2. "*With respect to such instruction, the Schools are to be subject to the superintendence of the Parochial Clergymen.*"

3. "*The Children are to be regularly assembled for the purpose of attending Divine Service in the Parish Church, or other place of worship under the Establishment, unless such reason be assigned for their non-attendance as is satisfactory to the Managers of the School.*"

4. "*The Masters and the Mistresses are to be members of the Church of England.*"

5. "*A Report on the state and progress of the Schools is to be made, at Christmas in every year, to the Diocesan Board, the District Society, or the National Society; and the Schools are, with the consent of the Managers, to be periodically inspected by persons appointed either by the Bishop of the Diocese, the National Society, or the Diocesan Board of Education.*"

6. "*In case any difference should arise between the Parochial Clergy and the Managers of the Schools, with reference to the preceding Rules, respecting the religious instruction of Scholars, or any regulation connected therewith, an appeal is to be made to the Bishop of the Diocese, whose decision is to be final.*"

Signed, Joseph Baylee Clk — Percy Matthew Dove
L Gladstone — R. W. Richard
Wm Richardson
~~[illegible]~~

Dated, 13th April 1846

To be signed either by the Minister and Managers in conjunction, or by the Minister alone, stating that he is sole Manager; or by the Minister alone, declaring that he is empowered to sign both for himself and for the Managers.

In the absence of the Incumbent of the Parish, it is requested that the Officiating Minister, who signs the above, will state whether the Incumbent approves of the application for Union.

The above form, when properly filled up and signed, should be transmitted to the Secretary of the Society, who, when the Committee have received the School into Union, will send an official Certificate to be hung up in the School-room.

Figure 6. *The National Society's Terms of Union as signed by the managers of Holy Trinity School, Birkenhead in 1846*

with a lay committee, which met every month to run the affairs of the school. Members of this committee (other than Baylee, his curate and the churchwardens) were elected at a General Meeting once a year by all the school subscribers and there were very detailed rules on the appointment of staff and the daily conduct of the school. Crosfield, expecting the usual informal instructions from the incumbent, would have found himself part of an ordered machine. As to the school's effectiveness, year by year, we have some Inspectors' reports and they give an impression of effort without, at first, very much success.

Revd Norris HMI in 1849 and 1850[11] described the master (then) as 'zealous and painstaking'. The school, he thought, could be 'efficient and prosperous' though it shared 'the general depression of everything connected with Birkenhead'. But even in these working-class areas he saw the potential for better things. By the summer of 1852 he had homed in on the problem of capricious attendance. He took note of 'labourers without any regular employment' whose children filled the ragged school but he saw other work-people with real aspirations for their children. These, he judged, would respond to a greater emphasis on 'writing and accounts'.[12] Norris then suggested that the 2d a week fee was 'quite too low' for this section of the community and he advised the managers to charge an admittance fee of one shilling and make the children pay for their books.[13]

By 1855, shortly before Crosfield's arrival, the school must have been achieving some of the success predicted for it, because Baylee that year made an application to the National Society for a grant towards the building of an extra classroom,[14] to accommodate about 30 boys. The secretary to the managers was able to tell the Society that the average daily attendance was 'steadily and rapidly increasing'. Already there were 200 boys in the main schoolroom (60 ft by 18 ft)[15] but, happily, on this site there was room for expansion. Other schools, like Christchurch Liverpool, were less fortunate.

The use of separate classrooms was now officially advocated,[16] not just to relieve pressure but to bring variety to the school day and as a base for more concentrated simultaneous teaching. From this point of view, at least, it seems that Crosfield at the Birkenhead school, catering for the upper echelons of the working-class, had found himself a less demanding post than his friend Barnes in Liverpool—or, as we shall see, than Foster in his Halifax part-factory school at this time.

It is a little surprising, however, that both Crosfield and Barnes chose to marry before their two years' probation was completed—not that their competence was in question but with full certification at the start of 1858 (a bit later for Crosfield?) they would be free to move and could reasonably expect a rise in income. But it seems they had formed attachments to a pair of sisters. John Crosfield, the elder of the two, married Caroline Sarah Feast, one of three daughters of a milk-dealer, in the church of St John the Divine, Fairfield, Liverpool on 1 January 1857. Once married John and Caroline had the use of the master's residence in Birkenhead; this appears to have been a small terraced house facing out on to the traffic of Beckwith Street. Here they were provided with three bedrooms, parlour, kitchen and scullery in a typical 'two-up, two-down' with small back extension.[17] Their first child, Lilian Edith, was born here that autumn.

Within six months of the Crosfield wedding, William Barnes, still a minor, married one of Caroline's elder sisters, Margaret Jane Feast. William's mother had died a month before the wedding and it is possible that the young couple took in Richard Barnes (his father) and the only other surviving child of the family, seven-year old Sarah Ann, for the short time they were to remain in Liverpool. When they left, not long after, Sarah went with them and Richard Barnes spent his last four years as watch-case maker residing with a sister-in-law at an address off Bold Street in the town centre.

With relatives or not, it seems certain that William and Margaret would have been sharing the roomy house they were allotted in Clarence Street. This pleasant road was a whole mile north of the school in Christian Street, on the upper slopes of Everton and its clientele was a respectable one. In 1851 and 1861 there were several book-keepers and accountants, some retired men and women and at least a third of the households had living-in servants. Some of the young people in the road were apprentices but all to white-collar or the cleaner manual trades such as tailoring. The houses were each two rooms deep, possibly three storeys high, with a ground-plan of about 15 ft by 30 ft and those at the older end of the street where Barnes lived had small back extensions allowing for a scullery and perhaps a room or two above. Each had a tiny front 'garden' about 10 ft by 15 ft and a yard at the back. A few years earlier the Christchurch schoolmaster, Robert Andrews, occupied one of the newer, smaller houses in the road with his wife, six children and three lodgers. A short-lived son, William, was born to the Barnes couple in 1857 and a daughter, Helen Barbara, in 1858.

Compared with the Crosfields' home in Birkenhead this one in Clarence Grove was altogether more desirable but in return for social distance and fresher air William Barnes had the inconvenience of a mile's journey through the streets—a significant factor for the schoolmaster whose every working day finished with an extra hour and a half tutoring his apprentices. When Edwin Foster moved to this school later he met with the same problem of the long haul home but from a different address.

Let us now bring Foster's life up to the time of his full certification; in doing so we introduce the last of the ordinary urban elementary schools these three teachers were connected with before 1870. The building of it was foreshadowed in the earlier activities of Revd James Gratrix in Halifax and, as with the Liverpool, Wakefield and Birkenhead schools already described, it was started before the great extensions of government aid in 1846.

In fact it was in 1843, the year the Foster family moved to Wakefield that Revd Gratrix decided to extend the church schooling he had already built up in his part of Halifax. His mood now was optimistic; he declared in a sermon that

> perhaps the most pleasing feature in the present day is the facilities which are afforded to us for communicating religious knowledge to the rising generation. It has been said that our hope for the Church is bound up with the young and I may go even beyond this and say that our hope for genuine religion is derived from them.[18]

As for so many of his colleagues, the aim was to create schools to serve the church but the incumbent of St James did not shrink from the mundane problems of running a good elementary school. By this time his combined infants, girls and Sunday schools in Victoria Street was full and the only other National school in the town—that based on the Parish Church—was overflowing. Older boys from St James infant school could only transfer to the nearby Lancastrian school—if they stayed at school at all. But Gratrix was also planning ahead for the hordes of factory children who, under the forthcoming Act of 1844, would be limited to half-day working and who would be free—indeed compelled—to attend school for a whole morning or afternoon. These were the new 'half-timers' and in these plans Gratrix was helped and encouraged not only by the Vicar of Halifax, Ven. Charles Musgrave, but also by the Bishop of Ripon and the local factory inspector, Robert Saunders.

By the early 1840s the prospects for elementary education in Halifax were good. Not only would the new legislation make it possible for ordinary schools to accommodate factory children within the normal timetable, it seemed there was 'an increasing desire by the working-classes to see their children educated'.[19] So Revd Gratrix wrote to the National Society in August 1843 (as he had in 1837) with his proposals for a new school and by November of that year he had pulled in a National Society grant of £300 and a government grant of £432 plus local subscriptions of £77. According to Saunders, the local millowners were shortly to embark on the half-time system. He mentioned one mill employing 130 children 'which will, I dare say, have nearly 200 in the next three months'.[20] Gratrix, in turn, was buoyant: 'We are already doing a great work...we have already one-tenth of the population in our schools'. But the way ahead would not be smooth.

The main difficulty was the old one in the West Riding towns of competition from the nonconformists. In the autumn of 1845 when the school had been open a few months, Saunders wrote to Revd Kennedy HMI as follows:

> ...in no part of my district have (the factory children) been worse provided for in Church of England matters than in Halifax and its neighbourhood. This has given the dissenters a great advantage... They have upwards of 300 factory children attending one British school and as many more in different establishments and the Revd James Gratrix has other claims on his funds...and...but few

> factories in his own district...he is most desirous to recover some of the ground we have lost.[21]

Note at this point how Saunders, a public official, identifies himself wholeheartedly with the interests of the Established Church.

Gratrix, of course, had seen these problems coming. He wrote to the National Society in October 1844:

> If the part-timers can be got their payments will defray much of the cost. Without help in the beginning, and liberal help, the success of the school will be doubtful as the millowners are for the most part dissenters.[22]

Later in 1845 he was still complaining that 'the millowners keep their children from me'.

St James Crosshills was opened in January 1845. Situated on a slope at the north end of the town it overlooked the factory area across the North Bridge. The site was an awkward one with a twenty-degree slope which made building a great deal more expensive than had at first been anticipated. It was, however, the choice of the factory inspector who had advised that it should be nearer the factories than the church.[23] A schoolmaster's house was included; there were two separate yards, each with a double privy, the girls' opening into the lower schoolroom, the boys' by a flight of outside steps to the upper one. Each room measured 36 ft by 36 ft, designed for 216 boys and 216 girls and while attendances were below these figures space was more than adequate[24] (Fig. 7).

In 1844, as the building rose from the ground, Gratrix made enquiries for a schoolmaster. He consulted the National Society:

> Do you think I could get a pious and clever master from the Battersea institution...? He must be a man of piety and ability as a teacher, for many of the millowners are adverse and it is only by holding out the prospect of superior instruction that I can hope to prevail...[25]

In a further letter he insisted he must have 'a pious, clever and active man. I could not keep one of Tractarian sentiments'.[26]

This latter point is interesting, coming when it did, for it was September the next year when the Principal of the York Training School, charged with Tractarian sympathies, was first called upon to answer to his governing committee. Would such rumours in the district have explained Gratrix's approach to the National Society, rather than his own diocesan college, for a schoolmaster? In the event he did accept a York man, Ralph Close, as did his successor, Revd John Allen, some years later—and after much more local controversy—when Foster was appointed. It seems that neither incumbent with a school of this kind, even when new, was in a position to be highly selective.

Records of the school in the intervening years show well the difficulties it encountered. In 1848, for instance, the number of children in attendance 'was much diminished by the badness of trade and the closing of some of the mills'.[27] Even in good times there was a large turn-over of pupils.[28] However, the managers were quick to respond to the new pupil-teacher system of 1846; by 1852 there were six apprentices in the boys' school and three in the girls'[29] and that in a town where there was work for adolescents at better wages than a pupil-teacher could command.

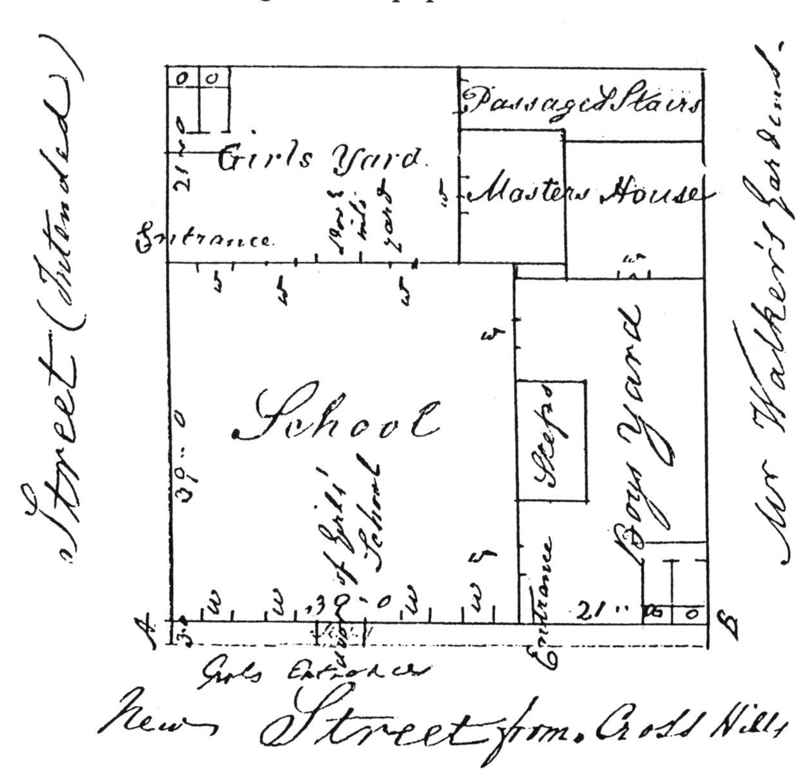

Figure 7. *Plans for St James Crosshills School, Halifax c. 1844*

In the early 1850s pupils began to drift away from another cause—the opening of first one and then another factory school nearby. Income from fees was precariously maintained, on the advice of Revd Watkins HMI, by a rise for the older boys from 2d to 4d.[30] Then, in 1855, the master, Edward Stevens, decided to move on and Revd Allen placed an advertisement in the National Society's *Monthly Paper* for 'a certificated master and mistress, married couple preferred'.[31]

Now, St James Crosshills was not the most promising of schools for a young man to take over in his first two probationary years. Apart from the threat to numbers there was the regular difficulty of timetabling for a mixture of part- and full-time pupils, but there were also points in its favour. The managers were conscientious and committed; their other school, St James Victoria, received consistently good reports.[32] Then it seems that Halifax had one of the earliest Church of England teachers' associations and Foster's predecessor had been an active member[33]—another sign of good morale in the area.

When, in due course, Edwin Foster was accepted for this post he was offered £62 a year with 'half the pence received above this amount'—a common enough formula. On top of that he could expect £15 from the government and perhaps £12 for three pupil-teachers. With around £6 from the children's pence—a sum calculated from data in an HMI's report—his salary would have come to £95, more than the local average of £88 for certificated masters at that time.[34]

The managers were also obliged to cover the cost of his accommodation and they were clearly hoping for the economy of a married couple who could occupy the master's house together, but Foster was still a bachelor and his colleague for the next two years, Miss Maria Norris, lived in this house, alone. Accommodation for Foster in the town, though, would have been a simple matter with all his family connections there (see Chapter I and the Foster family tree in the Appendix). We know that, in the end, whatever its comforts or discomforts, Foster looked back on this period working in the industrial town of his birth as one of useful experience.[35]

We can now move on to consider prospects for these three young men ready to be assessed for full certification, Barnes and

Foster, at least, at the end of 1857. Schoolmasters would not even be considered for the next stage without good Inspectors' reports for the last two years and even with these a brief, final check was made, each man required to 'perform the exercise of teaching in the Inspector's presence'. The question, then, of whether he was entitled to a certificate and, if so, of which class was decided

> by the tenor of the two reports and by the result his examinations previous to quitting the training school.[36]

With full certification, two-year college students could now reap their reward; a move up the government augmentation scale meant they could demand a larger sum from managers who wished to employ them and they now had a 'parchment' on which the exact level of certificate was recorded—first, second or third, with sub-divisions.[37] Just how Barnes, Crosfield and Foster stood at this point is conjectural; we have to work back from later records. Thus, Barnes was right at the top of the scale by mid-1864, with a first-class certificate, division one,[38] but even he was not selected for the special honour of a first-class certificate on completing his probation for he was only in the second-class division two, in 1863. So he was probably entitled to a minimum salary of around £76 in 1858. John Crosfield (with a second-class certificate, division three, in 1863) might have claimed £72 and Edwin Foster (whose career is less well documented for this period) perhaps at Barnes's level in 1863.

Now we have already seen that Foster was earning more than £90 in 1856–57 during his probation in Halifax and the fact is that managers of the larger, more efficient schools in the towns were offering well above the statutory minima to attract good qualified teachers. If Barnes and Crosfield were paid at average town rates in 1856–57[39] and if none accepted a cut thereafter, how would these earnings have placed them socially at the start of their independent careers in 1858?

The answer seems to be, in a position no higher than that of a medium-grade clerk, a skilled artisan or even—as Revd Watkins, ever the teachers' champion, pointed out—that of 'a day labourer in some of our Yorkshire ironworks'. But, he went on, the schoolmaster with his 'intellectual attainments and professional skills' who was expected to 'dress and conduct himself like a gentleman' deserved a great deal more.[40] In practice, therefore, Barnes, Crosfield and Foster could look forward to positions of modest status in the community while dependent, always, on the generosity of the managers in the task of maintaining a household to match these middle-class expectations.

Part III

Schoolmasters and Family Men

VII

William Barnes at Farnley

Happily for the qualified schoolmasters making their first independent choice of school in the late 1850s, these products of the new government-sponsored teacher training were still in demand. Some took advantage of the sellers' market for their skills to trail, dissatisfied, from one post to another, but most of these men—and surely their wives—were looking for continuity. Though William Barnes, John Crosfield and Edwin Foster all moved in 1858, by 1862 they were all settled for periods of six to ten years.

It was early in 1858 when Barnes and Foster achieved full certification, Crosfield possibly a few months later, and it looks very much as if Barnes's new appointment triggered the changes for all three. In March, or possibly earlier, he was engaged as schoolmaster for the Iron Company's school at Farnley near Leeds.[1] At this point Edwin Foster moved across the Pennines from Halifax to take Barnes's place at the Christchurch school in Liverpool and sometime in the next couple of years John Crosfield (from Birkenhead) joined his brother-in-law for a brief spell in Farnley. By the end of 1862, though, he was back in Cheshire. With these movements in mind and to do justice to all three from now on we must allow the narrative to branch, following separately the careers and family life, the choices and fortunes of each man through the 1860s and leading on, for each of them, to a phase of continuous employment after 1870.

Let us start with William Barnes. His move to Farnley took place just as the managers were completing a programme of extensions and looking for a master to shoulder a set of unusual responsibilities. The origins of this school, the nature of the management and the routine there will all be described in due course but this was no ordinary replacement of one teacher by another and the special circumstances in Farnley require some explanation.

There was nothing inherently surprising when the Armitage brothers of Farnley Hall decided to convert what had been a boys school with some provision for girls and infants into a full, conventional three-department elementary school in the autumn and winter of 1857–58. They were, it is clear, benevolent and generous employers. But they had taken on as recently as the previous August a new certificated master, Thomas Ryder, to work alongside a Mr and Mrs Morgan who had been there some time. By March 1858 this master was on his way elsewhere and Barnes had been appointed to replace him.[2]

Was Ryder one of the footloose variety of schoolmaster or were the managers dissatisfied with him? Possibly neither for it seems that the new, ambitious plans for the school were brought forward, if not first thought of, when William and James Armitage agreed to take on the care of three young children from London named Margaret, Mary Ann and Alice Tweedy. Why these three working-class girls were sent all the way to Yorkshire without their parents starts to become clear when we see that two of them were registered at birth as 'Armitage Tweedy', their father one James Armitage Tweedy, himself presented for baptism in 1812 by a single woman. Of his own father, all that James A.Tweedy would reveal on his marriage certificate was that he was a 'gentleman'. Can we escape the conclusion that the girls were grandchildren of James Armitage of Farnley, the result of a youthful indiscretion on his part, in London, in his late teens?

As for the break-up of the Tweedy family, we know they lost an infant son in the autumn of 1857 and that James himself fell ill that winter or soon after and died in the summer of 1858. Whether or not James Armitage had been in touch with them all along, it seems likely they appealed for help at about this time. If at this point he shied away from the idea of taking these three young cockneys into his own rather grand household, he could perhaps be forgiven. How could their presence have been explained to friends and neighbours? Both James and his brother

William were getting on in life with married sons of their own. To select a superior schoolmaster, capable, discreet and married and ask him to foster the girls was one obvious solution. It was then a simple matter to proceed with the extension of the school; a large extra room had already been built in 1857 to take an expanding church congregation.[3] As for Thomas Ryder, no worse need be said of him than that he did not fit these requirements.

But there was more to the Farnley school than this. From early on the Armitage brothers had arranged for their young male employees to attend classes in the evenings and when Barnes came in 1858 the plan was for a regular three-session day and two certificated masters to work a shift system. Who better than John Crosfield to come and assist his friend and brother-in-law William Barnes? So it was that these two Merseysiders came back into Yorkshire while Edwin Foster, no doubt ready for a move himself, made his journey from Halifax to take up the vacant post at Christchurch school in Liverpool. Looking ahead for a moment, John Crosfield did not stay long at Farnley and the course of his life in his next post—and Edwin Foster's career in Lancashire—we can follow in due course. We must, first, complete the story of the Farnley school and Barnes's time there until his departure in 1868.

We have seen how the Farnley managers hand-picked their new schoolmaster but why, out of numerous worthy young men, did they choose William Barnes? The simplest explanation is that he was recommended by the college at York, directly or via the network of local clergy, but there may have been a more personal link. Back in the last couple of years of his pupil-teachership in Liverpool, in 1852 and 1853, young Barnes of the Christchurch school was probably known to the new curate at nearby St Bartholomew's, Revd John Ellison.[4] The problem of finding good apprentices was a common preoccupation of clergy with schools to run and no churchman in the north of Liverpool could have been unaware of Revd Ould's remarkable protégé. By 1857, the year before Barnes came to Farnley, Revd Ellison had moved from Liverpool and was established in the post of chaplain to the iron works. He was the obvious person to be consulted about the choice of a new schoolmaster and his role in Barnes's career was to be even more significant later.

Meanwhile, the Iron Company's school at Farnley presented a range of interesting challenges to an ambitious young man. The setting was more rural than industrial but this was neither an ordinary village school nor a factory school in the usual sense. The pattern of its daily life will be described later but it can be viewed, first, as one of a pair which the Armitage family set up in the 1840s to educate the children of the local working-class. The Lords of the Manor, as the Armitage brothers sometimes called themselves, were relative newcomers to this estate[5] and when they arrived at Farnley, Methodism was already strong among the local people. One of their schools ran into difficulties over the religious issue; the other, Barnes's school, had an easier passage.

The smelting of iron in the new works began in November 1846 and it was sometime that year or the next that the proprietors started to build a school in the growing village of New Farnley[6] expressly for the children of the iron workers and nearby households. The prime mover for the other school was the curate of Farnley, Revd George Trevor;[7] he told the National Society in 1846 that he was concerned about the absence of church schools in the area and feared (like Revd Gratrix in Halifax)[8], 'the incursion of Socialism, Chartism and infidelity'. He was even prepared to work with a local nonconformist who had already tried to set up an infant school under the auspices of the British and Foreign School Society. The Armitage brothers promised their backing and the school was half built when Trevor left[9] and was replaced by Revd Henry Jones. This cleric chose to object to the Trust Deed[10] on the grounds that it allowed dissenters a place in management—an uncommon concession, it is true—and a long dispute followed involving the National Society, the bishop and the secular authorities. As late as February 1848 Her Majesty's Inspector was complaining that the 'handsome and convenient building' was still not in daily use.[11]

Compared with the National school in Old Farnley village the Iron Works school had an altogether more promising start. It was built, financed and managed by the proprietors of the works with none of the hazards of a search for grants or the framing of

Figure 8. *The Farnley Iron Company's School near Leeds.*
Note the classrooms to the rear and the two 'school-houses' right and left.
(Sketch from a photograph c. 1970)

a Trust Deed. No approach whatever was made to the National Society and it was ten years before this school came under government inspection. Then, too, it had a captive clientele; competition from small, local nonconformist or dame schools was negligible. But while the managers were free of outside interference they also lacked the stimulus of inspection. The Morgans, mentioned above, were not trained or certificated. The next appointment, Thomas Ryder, had spent a year at the Cheltenham Training College[12] and he was certificated but he did not come to the school until mid-1857. Although the managers then decided to apply for government grants the school was still in poor shape when Barnes arrived the following May.

The circumstances of his appointment have already been discussed. Let us look now at the accommodation provided for him. From 1857 it is clear there were two good school-houses; in that year one was occupied by the master, Thomas Ryder, apparently without family. The other was occupied by Mr and Mrs Morgan, now 'Infant master and mistress'. The main teacher's residence had parlour, kitchen and scullery and three bedrooms (one 14 ft by 19 ft and two half this size).[13] Probably these two dwellings were '45 and 46 Gainsborough Place' both described as 'school-house' in the 1861 census and they can be seen to the right and left of the school in the sketch made from a modern photograph (Fig. 8). How exactly they were occupied in 1861 is not so clear.

By that year Barnes and his wife had a sizeable household to manage. There was a daughter Helen Barbara, born in Liverpool, another, Eva Mary, born in Farnley and the only remaining member of William's own family, a younger sister Sarah Ann now aged ten. To help them they had one servant and a nurse and there were five boarders, the three Tweedy children already mentioned and two certificated schoolmistresses both, like the servants, from the Liverpool area. In the other house was George Hoyland certificated schoolmaster (appointed March 1860) and his wife.[14] The census thus listed the two 'households' but it seems likely that the sleeping accommodation, at least, was shared out more equitably between numbers 45 and 46.

The school itself was a modest L-shaped building, one-storey, with two large schoolrooms each about 20 ft by 70 ft and two small classrooms.[15] The 'hall' with the Gothic windows on the right in the sketch could be the extension built for church services in 1857. With only 80 boys in one room and 60 infants in the other, teaching space was generous by the standards of the time. The regime in 1857 appears to have been that of a 'morning and evening school'—boys and infants in the morning, some girls taught sewing in the afternoons with older boys and young men attending in the evenings.

When Barnes came in 1858 there were further important changes to the school. Soon after his arrival he supervised the setting up of separate girls and infants departments each under a certificated teacher. The Morgans apparently left with Thomas Ryder and Barnes had the field to himself from then on. With Crosfield beside him, at first, Barnes advertised for, and sometimes travelled to interview, new staff for all sections of the school. It seems more than likely that his young sister, his two daughters and the three Tweedy girls all passed through the infant and girls departments in due course.

At the end of the year the Farnley Iron Works school was inspected by Revd Watkins HMI and he reported as follows:

> Girls The Girls are now in very good order and considering the circumstances, in a creditable state of attainment. The mistress has only been here four months and is doing her work very well.
>
> Infants The Infants are in very fair order under a mistress who teaches them with energy and fair method but seems to need assistance for the lower classes.
>
> Boys There is considerable improvement here since Mr Barnes came, both in discipline and attainments which he reports, with truth, to have been very low when he came.[16]

Barnes and his wife and the Armitage brothers at the Hall must have been well content that Christmas. Barnes, still only twenty-one, with a deal more responsibility than most schoolmasters of his age, was proving equal to it. The managers, we can suppose, were congratulating themselves on an excellent appointment.

At the end of each successive year, 1859, 1860 and 1861 Inspectors' comments tell us that the New Farnley school continued to prosper and from the end of 1862 the school log books give a much fuller picture of its progress and also of the difficulties and setbacks which Barnes had to deal with. The detail, of course, relates to the boys' school as the girls' and infants' departments kept their own records. However, a full set of Inspectors' reports enables us to keep an eye on all three day schools and also the night school which became increasingly important while Barnes was there.

Here we should pause for a moment to take a wider view for it is remarkable that in these particular records of school activity in the late 1850s and early 1860s we shall find no hint of the great upheaval about to take place in the nation's elementary schools. The Royal Commission on the State of Popular Education set up in 1858 under the Duke of Newcastle was to stir up, yet again, all the painful questions about the public funding of education which had been turning over and over since 1833, and now not only schools but the teachers and the colleges were under scrutiny. When the Commission's work was done the government issued a brand-new set of directives, the so-called Revised Code of 1862.[17]

Ignoring an essential half of the Newcastle recommendations—that a local rate should provide a grant for schools—and taking up the other, for a Treasury grant based simply on attendance and progress in the 'three Rs', the Education Department set to work its team of sixty Inspectors testing pupils and calculating yearly grants in shillings and pence. The impact of this new, mechanical 'payment-by-results' on the curriculum, on the teachers' working habits and on the income of most schools during the 1860s was to prove dramatic.

Aspects of these radical changes will be revealed as we follow the regime in the Farnley school but we shall see nothing of the trauma. Here was a school confident in its aims, well-funded and competently run by a schoolmaster who was free to follow his best instincts. Barnes was fortunate; dependent as never before on the goodwill of managers, he found himself with employers who could command the resources to offer a reasonable wage even without the old government 'augmentations' now swept away entirely by the Revised Code. His pupil-teachers, too, would be making independent contracts with the managers under the new rules; these will be described in the next chapter which follows Crosfield's career in the 1860s. The third man of this trio, Edwin Foster, also escaped the worst anxieties and frustrations of this period by moving into a school which had never sought government aid and therefore had nothing to lose.

With these considerations in mind we can now turn to the daily life of the Iron Works school, its teachers and the Barnes household. First, a question to which the log books fail to give a complete answer. Who exactly were the children using this school? We can say with confidence that most of them were not themselves employed in the iron works. For one thing, this kind of industry did not provide much in the way of openings for boys and none at all for girls and even when it did—there were 'forge-boys', for instance, as young as nine—there was no compulsion on employers to release them for education. In any case, the Iron Works school took no pupils part-time during the day.

However, the Armitage brothers also ran quarries, collieries, a fire-brick manufactory, a cotton mill and they farmed 200 acres;[18] in 1861 they claimed to have nearly 800 children in their direct employ. So where, if at all, were these youngsters educated? Many could be accounted for as half-timers at the Armitage mill in nearby Wortley, at school there under the factory legislation already mentioned in Chapter VI. There were also special rules for colliery boys under twelve who could not read or write; the way they were catered for in the night school will be described later. So it is clear that Barnes's day pupils could only have been the sons and daughters of Armitage employees plus children from other local households such as shopkeepers or independent artisans.

In the years 1862 to 1868 the number of children and young men using the Iron Works school fluctuated around the four hundred mark, dropping slowly over this period as the families of the earlier incoming workers matured perhaps. There had been a substantial rise, though, in Barnes's time, with the reorganization of the school in 1858. By 1864 there were over 130 infants as compared with half that number earlier and the boys department expanded from 80 to over 100. Here, as elsewhere, there were fewer girls in school and when the other Farnley school ran into difficulties in 1866 there was a sudden influx of boys and some infants only.

Naturally these children paid fees—free schools were only for the very poor—but there is no mention in the log book either of the rates of payment or of problems in collection. However, a yearly total entered in May 1864, at £46.12.11 for an average attendance of 99 boys for, say, 40 weeks, suggests a weekly fee of 2d or 3d, a quite ordinary charge.[19]

What were these children taught? In terms of subjects the curriculum looks much the same as it would have been ten years earlier, here, and for the schooldays of Barnes and his colleagues. That is to say, in this school of about a hundred boys, there were four or five classes and all had a basic diet of scripture, reading, writing and arithmetic. From class three upwards they were taught geography and the top one or two classes, English history and grammar.

There was nothing new about this emphasis on the 'three Rs'; it had always been so, but the framers of the Revised Code sought to concentrate the minds of teachers and managers on achievement in these basic skills throughout the school.[20] Hence, the division of the new annual grants into a section based on average attendance and another based on the individual examination of pupils in reading, writing and arithmetic. For this latter purpose 'Standards' were defined, one to six, and the levels to be arrived at were briefly described for each. Thus, children to be examined in Standard I (the lowest, at about the age of seven), would be expected to read 'a narrative in monosyllables', by Standard VI, 'a short ordinary paragraph in a newspaper'.[21] Teachers were free to group their pupils for examination into Standards as they wished, cutting across the normal class divisions where appropriate and there were no strict demarcations by age for either. But failures were penalized in the calculation of the grant and there was a rule which prevented a teacher from entering a child more than once in the same Standard. Beyond this, the payment of the whole grant was dependent on a range of other conditions, including the general state of the school and the level of staffing.

Revd Watkins on his rounds in the north of England in 1863 noted a wide variation in pass rates. Within any school he regarded 93 per cent as good, 50 per cent as poor. Teaching within this framework held no terrors for William Barnes; year after year his pupils achieved pass rates of nearly 100 per cent. What is more significant, he was praised for just those qualities in his teaching which Her Majesty's Inspectors had been calling for earlier. Revd Watkins, reporting on the Farnley Iron Works boys' school in 1866, said:

> The school continues in an excellent state of order, discipline and attainments. The viva voce answers show that the boys do not learn mechanically or by rote but in such a manner as to enable them to show that they thoroughly understand what they have been taught.[22]

Nor were the 'higher subjects' neglected. Even before a new grant was offered in 1867 to promote their teaching,[23] Watkins could say (after the usual praise of the school):

> The answers to questions on the Catechism and Holy Scriptures evinced great intelligence as well as careful training, while [the boys'] knowledge of grammar, geography and history was quite as great as could possibly be desired.[24]

Here and there the log book gives a hint of the informal way in which Barnes tried to extend the education of the older pupils. In November 1864 they were shown a 'microscopic exhibition' in the Reading Room (part of the night school).[25] The following year James Armitage came into the school to give a lesson on 'Astronongraphy'.[26] Older pupils, both boys and girls, were taught drawing and fifty of them were examined in May 1866 under new regulations of the Department of Science and Art.

Plainly, William Barnes was an exceptional schoolmaster and we shall return in due course to enlarge on his personal role in the success of the Farnley school. Let us meanwhile review the whole question of staffing, the comings and goings of Barnes's assistants and his duties in relation to them. It was mentioned that, right from the start, Barnes had the task of organizing and hiring staff for the whole school and though we cannot suppose that he had an entirely free hand, entries in the log book suggest that only the most general directives were issued by the managers at the Hall. It was up to William Barnes to decide upon and implement the best tactics for staffing the school efficiently under the varying conditions of the decade he was at this school.

When Barnes came to Farnley in 1858, the rules were simple and prospects for school improvement were good. The pupil-teacher system under which he and his friends had been trained was still operative and generously financed by the treasury. The certificated teacher in charge of a school received his bonus from the government and extra pay for taking on apprentices. It was very unusual, then, to employ a second certificated teacher but managers could make use of ex-pupil-teacher assistants plus monitors who were, of course, much younger and often unpaid. According to Sir James Kay-Shuttleworth, first Secretary to the Committee of Council on Education, the Minutes of 1846 set out to encourage the appointment of one pupil-teacher for each 25 pupils after the first 25.[27] This was, in fact, the maximum number of pupil-teachers for which the government would pay but it set a norm; a schoolroom of 100 children, say, with one schoolmaster and three apprentices. This would allow a regular division into four classes and with an assistant teacher and/or monitors the groups could be smaller.

Under the Revised Code all this changed. Staffing levels were redefined. If the school was not able to provide at least one pupil-teacher for each 40 pupils, or assistant teacher for 80 after the first 50, the grant would be reduced.[28] This was to set a new norm, based on many more pupils per teacher and though managers could employ as many as they liked, they now had to pay them out of such grant as the children could earn, school fees and other funds. Nation-wide, teachers' pay went into decline and pupil-teacher numbers dropped for the first time since 1846. Overall, pupil/teacher ratios increased, but the proportion of adults serving in the schools increased also, swelled by a new category of the 'provisionally certificated'—ex-pupil-teachers who were allowed to move straight into rural schools at the age of nineteen or so.[29] There were serious consequences for the numbers and quality of entrants to the training colleges.

For William Barnes at Farnley there was a dual task. He had to staff his day schools efficiently throughout the period of change and forward, under the new dispensation, and, at the same time, he had to provide for the three-shift day in the boys school, with male teachers to cover the evening work. A glance through such notes of staff appointments as can be gleaned from the log book and the Inspector's reports, shows that there were always more adult teachers than apprentices in the boys school during this time and we need to look beyond the national trend, as described above, for the explanation.

There was indeed a dramatic slump in pupil-teacher apprenticeships among the brighter, older pupils after 1862 but, if the managers were prepared to pay at the old rates or higher, they could be found. It seems more likely that Barnes insisted on a mainly adult staff and that he was supported in this by the managers. We know that he started with one certificated colleague, John Crosfield, possibly replaced by George Hoyland in 1860. Between that year and 1862 we do not have lists of staff but from the end of 1862 a fairly clear picture emerges.

In the six years 1862 to 1868 Barnes had no less than twelve assistant teachers on the pay-roll at one time or another. He seems to have aimed at a complement of four, two at least to be above the new 'fourth class', just emerged from college or recently examined. Such a team allowed him to teach most days of the week in the night school, half days in the day school and still to ensure there would a responsible master on the premises. Probably there was at least one pupil-teacher in the day school, most of the time, plus monitors. But there is no doubt that Barnes, for all his zeal and efficiency, had great difficulty both in finding teachers and keeping them and we need to ask why. Events gradually unfolded as follows.

At the end of 1862 the boys day and night schools were run by Barnes and Hoyland (both certificated), Thomas Nield (probationary) and James Christian, an ex-pupil-teacher assistant, together with one fourth year apprentice.[30] Problems started the following year. Nield acquired his certificate and left at the end of 1863. In the previous June ten applicants came forward for the vacant post—none was deemed suitable. That August, Isaac Priestley came as assistant from a school near Halifax and Nield acquired his final certification. In the following year Hoyland left but Christian gained a certificate by examination. He had been in the school since 1861 but Barnes seems to have had a low opinion of his capabilities for he engaged two new masters straight from the college at York in January 1865 to be his second and third masters while he designated Christian as 'fourth' with Priestley as assistant.

Throughout 1865, 1866, 1867 and into 1868 Barnes continues to tell us, in his log book, of the changes in his staff, month by month, of their competence, their demands upon him and of the duties laid down for them. Christian left in October 1865 dissatisfied with his pay and following a reprimand for absenting himself from duty in the Sunday school. Priestley took a post elsewhere; a new assistant stayed three months. Two of the best-qualified teachers were offered extra pay in 1866 but both had moved elsewhere by the end of the year.

Even in 1867, his last full year, Barnes could not relax. Two masters left in September—one of them to work for the certificate examination. A new appointee threatened to leave almost at once but was persuaded to stay with the offer of a salary rise. At the start of 1868—in the run-up to Barnes's departure—the school had four teachers, all appropriately qualified, but one was brand new, two had a year in the school and only one had two years.

Barnes decided that his replacement should be F.W. Dickenson appointed in 1867; he was to be responsible for the boys and the night school only, and he was offered £100 per annum plus 15 per cent of the grants in these two departments. He also had the use of a house rent-free (less one bedroom and a sitting-room). Now Barnes himself had oversight of all sections of the school and he continued to visit as 'manager' for some months after he had moved elsewhere. What is more, his certificate had been raised to first class, division one, in August 1864[31] and teachers of this grade were uncommon. His own salary, therefore, must have been considerably above Dickenson's—perhaps £150 plus extras. Arranged privately with the Armitage brothers Barnes's own salary was not something to be confided to the log book.

Looking back, was Barnes in any way to blame for this unsettling turnover of staff? True, he seems to have maintained the quality of teaching in spite of it but it must have been a source of concern to him and to the managers. Was the Farnley school simply reflecting the general atmosphere of malaise in the world of elementary education generally? A 'Yorkshire clergyman' writing in 1861 prophesied a time of 'much activity, general restlessness' would follow the new grant regulations[32] and he was right. Most Inspectors reported a drop in the level of salaries and, to make matters worse, by 1863 there was 'overstocking of the teachers' market'; Watkins had come across schools receiving 'a hundred applications for one post'.[33]

So while Barnes was unlikely to run out of candidates he was still, in trying to employ a team of adult teachers, running a greater than average risk of meeting the disaffected. The pressures seem to have been less acute for women teachers; it is noticeable that the girls and infants schools had a serene and untroubled passage during these years, with only a succession of apprentices to contend with. It was natural that such groups of male teachers should be unstable when there was no tradition of adult team work in elementary schools and each man was looking forward to the satisfactions and rewards of his own final independence.

Then, finally, it must be admitted that work in this school was not easy, with the stifling pattern of duties, days, evenings and Sundays. The pupils were a rough lot, most of them. Barnes had reason to punish for cruelty to animals, rudeness to the girl pupils, blasphemy and bad behaviour in the toilets. And he may not have been an easy man to work with—if not a slave-driver by intent, he was clearly a perfectionist and something of a visionary with enormous reserves of energy; not an easy taskmaster for ordinary mortals to work under.

That said, we can now turn back to some other aspects of William Barnes's work, his family life and the development of his own career during his years at Farnley. While Barnes and his wife were at the schoolhouse they had several more children. Twin girls were born in December 1859 and they were baptized in Farnley church together with the Crosfields' daughter, Louisa Augusta, born about the same time. Of the Barnes's twins, though, only Eva Mary survived. Then a son, Horace William, was born in 1861 and after him two short-lived babies in 1864 and 1865. William's young sister Sarah Ann served as a pupil-teacher in the girls' school, completed her five years but died at the age of eighteen shortly before the family left in 1868. So in ten years the Barnes's household expanded and then contracted again to five.

When William Barnes came to Farnley he may or may not have had a plan in his mind to seek ordination. It was not unknown for able and earnest college students to head in this direction and, conspicuous for his academic abilities, he may have had the idea put to him by someone at York. But he was clearly cut out for teaching and there would have been immense practical abilities in training for the ministry once he had a family to support. He was, in any case, very young when he came to this post. Ordinands were not accepted under twenty-three.

In Farnley, though, several things happened at once. He was able to demonstrate his powers of leadership and he found himself with employers who were also friends and patrons, ready to encourage, tutor, advise, offer financial help and generally clear the way for him to prepare for this new role. He also had a model in the person of John Ellison, the much-loved evangelical parson who was chaplain to the Iron Works during Barnes's first few years. Ellison was one of three remarkable brothers, sons of a Cheshire bricklayer, all of whom became Church of England clergymen (see n. 3).

We should note in passing that, with these abilities, he may have considered the role of Assistant to Her Majesty's Inspector, open to schoolmasters from the mid-sixties.[34] As early as December 1864, for instance, William James Armitage sent him to 'examine' the Roundhay school in Leeds[35] and later he went further afield to the Clergy Daughters school in Casterton to test the pupils there.[36] Even with his own staff he sometimes adopted an inspectorial tone; of Mr Hobson, in 1867 for example; 'With some desire to please he shows very little intelligence in his work'.[37] But it was perhaps his contribution to the life of the night school that finally convinced everyone he had the makings of a clergyman.

The Armitage brothers opened this school for their employees in 1850 and it was conducted, at first, for about thirty or forty boys and young men with an unqualified master in charge. From 1858 it was placed under government inspection and the numbers started to increase to around a hundred for most of Barnes's time there. Revd Pickard HMI chose to make a detailed report on this school in 1866 and he explained the character of its pupils as follows:

> From the nature of that occupation (iron workers and colliers) one might easily imagine that the scholars would be extremely rough before they came to school and that their moral and religious condition would naturally be low. Besides, some begin to work before they are eight years old and soon throw off the little parental control to which they were previously subject. Many of the apprentices, too, are hired by the workmen from a distance, often from workhouses and from these little good can be looked for. The general character of the boys and youths, if not restrained by the influences brought to bear upon them by the Company, may easily be inferred.

And further,

> the scholars come tired with their hard day's work, perhaps inclined to rebel against discipline which has to be carried out in a different manner from that in the day school, since the night scholars come of their own accord and possessed of the self-will and intolerance of restraint characteristic of self-supporting youths. Thus to interest them in their work and to preserve good order...requires peculiar energy and remarkable ability on the part of the teachers.

Barnes described his task thus:

> ...the first duty of the teacher is to eradicate indolent and vicious habits and to implant feelings of self respect, to call into existence and stimulate the better feelings of humanity—to change, in fact, the whole character.[38]

This mixed assemblage of pupils was divided into about five classes and they were schooled in the 'three Rs' and examined for grants like the day scholars. However, to make the work more interesting, Barnes and his colleagues, aided sometimes by James Armitage, gave 'oral lectures' on history, biography, travels and voyages and Armitage encouraged them with prizes for reading. It was said that some knew hundreds of lines of poetry by heart.

The managers and teachers made special arrangements for the colliery boys under twelve who were required by law to learn to read and write. As many colliery owners were realizing, if they sent these boys to day schools for the requisite two sessions of three hours per week, these few attendances would not qualify them for a grant.[39] In any case it was difficult to teach this kind of boy in the ordinary classroom within the normal timetable. On the other hand, a three-hour evening in the night school could only be worked if one teacher came an hour earlier for these boys—and this was done at Farnley. Thus Barnes hoped they would acquire the habit and continue even when they had their certificate of basic skills and were free to leave. This night school was constantly praised by the Inspectors and picked for mention in several of their general area reports. When Barnes left in 1868 it was said of him that:

> The influence for good which he has exercised over the young men in the Night School may be expected to bring forth fruit after his departure.[40]

Then, finally, in all this reportage of Barnes's mature influence on the schools and their pupils we can see evidence of his special interest in and aptitude for religious instruction. Though never associated with the National Society the Iron Works school was clearly run on Church of England lines. The pupils were taught, separately, Old and New Testament Scripture and the catechism, the older ones liturgy also and after 1862 it was a precondition for grant that Her Majesty's Inspector should approve the religious instruction, generally. Not only did Barnes teaching, here, meet with approval, it was the object of many an interested visit from outside clergy. For example, in June 1865, James Armitage brought Revd Nichol, vicar of Wortley 'to hear the children examined in Scripture knowledge'. In October 1866, Revd John Gott of Bramley 'was present at the Scripture examination'—and so on.[41]

There were also visits without a stated purpose; from 'Revd E. Jackson (of St James, Leeds)[42] and two clerical friends' in November 1866 and, more significantly, from James Armitage's son Revd Francis Armitage in October 1865 and again in May 1867.[43] On this last occasion Revd Armitage was accompanied by Revd Pickard HMI who was paying an unofficial visit to oversee Barnes's examination of pupils in the upper two Standards in Scripture. The cumulative impression of all this clergy interest is of something beyond the managers' understandable desire to show off their star teacher. When we see that the Bishop of

Carlisle was in the school in March 1867 'to observe the Scripture examination'[44] it is clear that for several years the Armitage brothers had been summoning up their resources to persuade the church authorities to approve this young man as a candidate for ordination. As early as 1864 the Bishop of Llandaff had called at Farnley[45] but it was in Carlisle that William Barnes was eventually accepted and it was Revd Francis Armitage, then at Casterton, who took him on as a curate in 1868.

Ordained deacon in the summer of 1868, Barnes was priested in 1869.[46] In all he had two years in Westmoreland, in some ways an interlude but a period of intense activity while he found his way into a new role and a new profession. But at no time did he let drop his interest in education. His introduction to Casterton had been through the Clergy Daughters School and the regular examinations he had made there since December 1866.[47] Once ordained and resident in Kirkby Lonsdale he no doubt kept a benevolent eye on the church elementary schools there and in Casterton village.

And here he might have stayed but an invitation to take up a parish in Leeds came his way in 1870. His new patrons, the Marshall brothers, flax-spinners of Holbeck, were faced with a vacancy, suddenly, when their incumbent at St John the Evangelist died in the summer of 1870.[48] That William Barnes's name was put forward by someone is not surprising; the Marshalls were part of an extensive church and business network in Leeds and they also had residences in the Lake District. So it was that the whole Barnes family moved back into Yorkshire by the autumn of that year to start a new life in yet another challenging social environment for this couple and for their children.

VIII

John Crosfield at Knutsford

Of all the school locations which our three schoolmasters experienced the most congenial was probably the small market town of Knutsford where John Crosfield took up residence in 1862. Moving there, he was regaining his independence after a spell as William Barnes's second-in-command at Farnley. Ahead of him lay the challenges of the new, stringent Revised Code, but the Knutsford Parochial School presented none of the difficulties which he and Barnes had faced with the working population of Farnley. Here was a settled and diverse community and Crosfield soon established a niche for himself within it.

When the Crosfields arrived with their second, surviving, baby daughter, the town of Knutsford held about 3000 inhabitants plus a few hundred in the separate village of Over Knutsford. The town was situated 'in a delightful part of the country with many good shops and genteel houses'. The 'opulent gentry' residing in the neighbourhood supported local trade and agriculture and were the benefactors of some of the town's institutions including the two Parochial Schools and the church of St John the Baptist. Other religious denominations, including Roman Catholics, were represented, too, and there were chapels for Independents, Methodists and Unitarians.[1] There was some light industry but the inhabitants of Mrs Gaskell's 'Cranford' enjoyed clean air, prosperity and good facilities in this busy but respectable mid-Victorian town.

Did the Crosfields have any personal reasons for moving here? Both had contacts, still, with Liverpool. John's elder brother Thomas, a joiner, was still there, married with a young family and Caroline's parents (John and Mary Ann Feast) were still in the 'milk-house' in Kensington with her grandmother and a third, unmarried sister. A young brother was somewhere in the area, too. But all this was thirty miles away. Other possible contacts were Revd Fielding Ould (late of Christchurch Liverpool) now a country parson in Cheshire and, most likely of all, relatives and friends of Revd John Ellison of Farnley, earlier in Liverpool, who had been born in this county. But we should not exclude the possibility that Crosfield picked up the appointment through more usual channels.

As might be expected, Knutsford was the kind of town where it was profitable to run small schools for the middle-classes and where there were gentry with the means and leisure to provide also for the children of the poor. In 1860 there were six schools, at least, in the town. A small Free Grammar School had been there since the time of Edward VI; the Misses Holland ran two private infant schools, there was the Parochial School for boys and another for girls and a few girls were trained for domestic work at Lady Egerton's school near the entrance of Tatton Park.[2] None of these schools was attached to the National Society at this time though all were church-oriented, but in the late 1850s three of them applied for government grants and came under regular inspection, with all that implied by way of increased status and efficiency.

One of these was Lady Egerton's school opened in 1810. By 1859 it was 'in good order' in the hands of a certificated mistress.[3] That year, too, the Girls Parochial School acquired a qualified teacher for the forty girls housed in an old Baptist chapel in Tatton Street. However, by the end of 1859 there were only 27 girls in average attendance and the Inspector's report was lukewarm.[4] Meanwhile the Boys Parochial School was flourishing.

It had come through a bad patch. In 1851 the schoolmaster was the parish clerk, Thomas Pollitt, untrained, uncertificated and aged 55. That year the vicar of Knutsford, Revd Clowes, invited Revd J.P. Norris HMI to come and inspect the school and advise on its future. It was not at all unusual for clergy to call on the Inspectorate in this way; though public servants, these clerical HMIs also represented the power of the Establishment and, as we have seen, they were the natural allies of parish incumbents who cared about their schools. On this occasion, in October 1851 (while Crosfield and his friends were still pupil-teachers elsewhere) Norris set the boys at Knutsford the task of writing out the fifth commandment: 'Honour thy father and mother that thy days may be long in the land which the Lord thy God giveth thee'.[5] Out of 48 boys only eight could do this 'imperfectly'. 'Except for some fragments', Norris continued in his report, 'the school is without books'. Even then, the managers were slow to respond but the breakthrough came in 1855 with the appointment of Henry Newland, trained at Battersea and with experience in London and Wolverhampton.

When Newland came to Knutsford there were only fifty boys in attendance but the number had risen to eighty by the time the Inspector called in November 1858 and two of the boys had been officially apprenticed as pupil-teachers. According to Revd Norris, the school which Newland had found 'very inefficient', was now 'one of the best in the county'[6] and this was how Crosfield took it over in January 1862. Newland, the same month, took his skills 'up-market' and opened a private school of his own in Manchester Road beside the Heath.[7]

In their first few years at Knutsford the Crosfield family occupied a house in King Street, the main shopping thoroughfare of the town. A second daughter, Helen Maud, was born here in July 1862 and a son, Harry Arthur, in March 1865. Harry was christened in the parish church—a matter of routine, one might have supposed for the parish schoolmaster—but Helen was not presented there. Instead, at the age of two, she was taken to Liverpool and baptized at St Peter's where John's brother Thomas had taken three of his children in the previous few years. When the Crosfields had another son, Walter Harold, in January 1868, it seems he, too, was baptized elsewhere.

While at King Street the Crosfields were a few minutes walk from the Parochial School but in January 1866 they moved out to a quieter residential road on the north-west side of the town.[8] Here, in Queen Street, Crosfield was half a mile or so away from his work, no great distance, of course, but many schoolmasters (like his two friends at this time) were supplied with houses on the school site. However, to have been near the school would have isolated this family from the nucleus of the town, the school in its original location at the junction of King Street and Brook Street becoming separated from the town after 1864 by the building of the railway.

The Boys Parochial School, built by Lord Egerton in 1830, was the usual, plain one-storey, one room structure, 24 ft by 42 ft with a small porch at the front (Fig. 9). Said to have been built for 200, by Crosfield's time the school's average intake was about half that number giving more than ten square feet per pupil, a good allowance of space for that time. Indeed there seems to have been no complaint about the school accommodation during the 1860s.[9]

For the greater part of John Crosfield's first year at the school no records remain but a log book was started in 1862 and the first volume to have survived opens in December that year. As required by the new rules Crosfield copied into this book the report of Her Majesty's Inspector that autumn:

> The master has shown considerable skill and spirit in the instruction but should cultivate a less noisy and fatiguing method. The religious knowledge and reading are fairly good. The writing and arithmetic are good, dictation fair, discipline pretty fair.[10]

There are no further comments on Crosfield's 'method' in later years so we can assume he took the Inspector's hint. It is worth noting that the assessments here are made within the old categories of 'poor', 'fair' and 'good', applied by each Inspector according to his own personal scale. Mechanical testing under the Revised Code, giving numerical results, was introduced gradually in Cheshire during 1863. So by November 1864 we find the Inspector reporting as follows:

> This is a very good school. The examination in elementary subjects has been most successful. The intelligence of the boys has been thoroughly called out and a very considerable amount of information has been imparted to them.[11]

The testing had taken place on 1 November with 112 boys present; seven were absent. Only 96 were examined, the others failing to qualify through poor attendance, perhaps; the requirement was 200 morning or afternoon appearances in the past 12 months. There were no failures in any subject so, assuming there were no deductions for shortcomings in religious education or in the premises or equipment, we can calculate the grant earned on this occasion and its contribution to the burden of maintenance.

The total was probably around £50 to £60, made up from capitation at 4s per pupil and 8s per head for all the pupils successfully examined.[12] This sum, though a useful addition to the school's income, was nowhere near enough to sustain the school for a whole year—not even enough to pay the schoolmaster, at say £80 plus house rental.[13] The balance must have been derived from school fees and subscriptions.

Figure 9. *Knutsford Parochial School for Boys*
(Sketch from an early twentieth-century photograph)

Without seeing the accounts we cannot be sure how much was raised locally, or donated by Lord Egerton himself. We can, though, make an estimate of fees income. In 1855 the boys were being charged at 2d a week.[14] Without an increase in the meantime this would have brought in a yearly income of £35 to £40. Now it was up to the managers to ensure that the local element was at least equal to the level of the grant—or the grant would be reduced. Remembering that by 1863 the managers were paying the wages of all their pupil-teachers at £10 to £15 a year (if they kept to the old rates),[15] it is doubtful if the good folk of Knutsford would have been called upon for less than about £50 a year for this one school. Such an estimate helps us to evaluate the true role of government funding during this period.

Crosfield himself does not complain anywhere in his log book of difficulty in the collection of fees. He does, though, cast an oblique light on the poorer class of pupil in this following anecdote and comment (October 1870):

> J. Kennerly punished for truanting...afterwards ran out of school...confirms me in a long-formed conviction that children who are paid for by others than their parents are the most irregular and troublesome.[16]

Around this time, the Guardians of the Poor for the Altrincham Union were insisting that the children of parents on outdoor relief attend school, so the pupils that Crosfield complained of were receiving either public charity (out of the poor rates) or private charity of some kind. Moreover, it was quite within the powers of the managers to have excused some poor children their fees and this may have happened, too.[17]

Whatever the precise pattern of funding, it appears that this school was kept on an even keel, financially, and in its daily work it came up to the expectations of the church, the managers and the Inspectorate. Thanks to the log book we can now look more closely at life within the school and the role of the teacher and pupils in the community. In the years 1862–71 Crosfield tells us something of how he organized the boys in the schoolroom and how he designed the timetable to ensure their good performance in the yearly tests.

Crucial to the success of the school were the pupil-teachers and monitors with whom Crosfield shared the work and responsibility for the pupils' well-being. After his time at Farnley, Crosfield was back in an ordinary schoolroom with no adult colleagues or assistants and when he started here the pupil-teacher arrangements were as he and his friends had experienced them since 1848. But significant changes were made soon after and the lads working for Crosfield were apprenticed under rather different rules.

As explained earlier, when Barnes, Crosfield and Foster were boys, this kind of apprenticeship was a promising new alternative for the intelligent thirteen year old wage-earner. These three in 1848 were among only the second batch to be appointed nation-wide; they were directly on the Treasury pay-roll and the teachers who instructed them also received a government bonus. The system was a success but the cost to the Exchequer rocketed between 1847 and 1858, the year when the Newcastle Commission began to collect its evidence. Change was inevitable.

Since 1839, when the Committee of Council distributed a total grant of £30,000, the annual published cost of elementary education to the nation had risen to £800,000 of which over half went towards the training of teachers.[18] The system, it was pointed out, 'contained the germ of indefinite expansion'.[19] Moreover, there were those who thought the state system, both in range and content, pretentious and extravagant:

> in relation to other classes in the community, the teacher is placed in an exceptional and highly favoured position, and it may be confidently affirmed that there are no other persons in any rank of life who receive from the State so large a sum as £150 towards their education and maintenance between the ages of thirteen and twenty.[20]

However, the Royal Commission was assured by witnesses up and down the country that the schools had spectacularly improved since 1846. Matthew Arnold HMI declared that the pupil-teachers were 'the sinews of primary instruction' and he begged the Commissioners not to recommend a cut-back in their maintenance; 'Entreat Chancellors of the Exchequer to lay their entrenching hands anywhere but here' he said.[21]

But in spite of warnings from experienced and committed workers in the field, all direct payments to teachers and pupil-teachers ceased under the Revised Code of 1862. No-one for a moment considered dismantling the pupil-teacher system altogether but it became very much harder to find and keep suitable young people to work in the schools and to persuade them to spend a further two years in college. The new profession of elementary school teacher had lost some of its earlier appeal.

One might reasonably ask why the government did not shed the cost of screening and examining pupil-teachers altogether when it shed the cost of paying for them. But this would have been to remove the first stage in what we would now call professional accreditation. Standards had to be maintained if pupil-teachers were to be considered qualified for the existing options; to become assistants; to be examined for entry to college; if over 22 to sit the certification examination without further training; to be provisionally certificated to take charge of small rural schools or, finally, if they wished to take some other employment, to apply to the authorities for a testimonial.

We therefore find the rules of admission unchanged. The school still had to meet the criteria set out in 1846 and the candidate's moral qualities and home background had still to be verified in certificates from managers and clergy. The age qualification—no entrants under thirteen—was re-emphasized.[22] The young William Barnes might have taken some other route to professional and social advancement in these stricter times.

A new, simplified form of Agreement between the manager and the parent or guardian of the boy replaced the old form of Indenture and the term 'apprenticeship' was dropped. The idea of a pupil-teacher apprentice was always somewhat anomalous. No premium was required and the 'master' to whom he was apprenticed did not pay his wages. In fact the earlier form of indenture made no mention of wages at all. By 1862 things were very different. Shortly after John Crosfield came to the Parochial School he took on a lad called William Peel and the 'Memorandum of Agreement' drawn up for him between his guardian, Joseph Woodfine, and the managers of the school has been kept. It almost exactly follows the official wording.

The essential terms of this agreement were as follows. Peel was to serve under 'a certificated teacher' but for 'not more than six hours per day or 30 hours per week' and for the five years between 1 November 1862 and the last day of October 1867.

Instruction from the schoolmaster out of normal school hours was now to be only five hours a week as compared with one and a half hours per day, previously. As before, but in more general terms, it was clearly stated that a pupil-teacher could be dismissed for 'idleness, disobedience or immoral conduct of a gross kind' but he was no longer required (by these rules) 'to attend Divine Service on Sundays'.

As for wages, the government now decreed that they were to be fixed

> at the discretion of the parties having in view the local rate of wages and the advantages of the school as a place wherein to learn the business of a teacher.[23]

No doubt these pupil-teachers received their wages cash-in-hand from the managers. Earlier, when the money came through from London, once a year, it was sent as a Post Office Order and the managers were told to ensure that a parent or guardian went with the apprentice to collect it.[24]

William Peel at the Knutsford school was paid at the old official rate, £10 in the first year and increasing by £2.10s in each of the succeeding four years. In this respect he was lucky; not all managers were so generous. But what about the old problem of payment-in-arrears? The Agreement had a clause allowing the managers to withhold all or part of the yearly increment but only on the report of the Inspector who required three certificates; one of 'good conduct' from the managers; another of 'punctuality, diligence, obedience and attention to duties' from the master; and the third from the clergyman that the boy had been' attentive to his religious duties'.[25] The wording of this Agreement suggests that any loss of earnings would be imposed at the year-end inspection and dating from any misdemeanour during the year. In other words, young Peel was having to work a whole year satisfactorily before receiving any pay at all. Pupil-teachers elsewhere—perhaps half, nationally—were being paid half-yearly or more often at this time.[26]

This Memorandum of Agreement, 16 December 1862, was signed by Lord Egerton of Tatton, Lord de Tabley and Revd Robert Clowes representing the managers. Joseph Woodfine, a prison watchman, the boy's guardian and 'surety', signed as agreeing with all the provisions including his own obligation to 'clothe, feed and watch over the said pupil-teacher'. Peel himself signed and J.D. Crosfield also, not as a party to the Agreement but as a witness.

Like the pupil-teachers of Crosfield's own generation, those of the 1860s followed a detailed syllabus of work in which they were examined year by year by Her Majesty's Inspector. The new syllabus of the Revised Code[27] shows that a complete overhaul took place and numerous changes were made but in view of the public outcry about the extent of this 'secondary education' for teacher apprentices it is surprising that so little appears to have been cut back. Admittedly it is sometimes difficult to be sure what was implied in these yearly items of content but there does seem to have been a certain amount of narrowing and redefinition. For example, geography at the end of the second year was now expected to cover only 'The British Isles', omitting 'Palestine' as previously. History (which started in the third year) was limited to 'The succession of English Sovereigns...' in place of 'Outlines of English History'. Second year grammar was succinctly defined as 'The pronoun, adverb and preposition with their relations in a sentence' in place of 'Syntax and Etymology'.

However, in some respects the syllabus appears to have been broadened. For instance, Latin grammar could be offered as an alternative to English grammar in all five years and 'Writing and Composition' from year two onwards included a memory test; up to 100 lines of poetry and 80 lines of prose. But this is to ignore perhaps the most striking feature of both old and new versions—the careful distinctions between items for boys and girls. These demarcations were somewhat fewer post-1862 than before. Latin, mentioned above, was not an option for girls, nor were they apparently expected draw maps when tested in geography. But the sharpest discrimination was to be found in mathematics, the myth already established that girls could not be expected to handle figures with any degree of confidence.

It is surprising that nearly fifteen years of experience with female pupil-teachers did not reveal to the authorities that there were no inherent disparities of intellect, but it may be that girls consistently performed less well. They were much more tied to duties at home and, in school, compulsory needlework, sometimes every afternoon, meant they were bound to fall behind. These are points to bear in mind when comparing William Barnes's experience as a pupil-teacher with that of his young sister, Foster's with his sister Mary's, and Crosfield's with his two daughters' a few decades ahead.

In Crosfield's time at the Knutsford Parochial School there were half a dozen pupil-teachers, all working under the new dispensation and paid by the managers. Did Crosfield find these boys satisfactory? It seems they performed adequately, passed their examinations and received their certificates, but like Barnes with his assistants, Crosfield had his problems with them. In December 1862 two were taken on,[28] William Peel (already mentioned) aged thirteen and Thomas Mullin, somewhat older. Within a couple of weeks Crosfield was absent for a few days and the school was 'carried on by the pupil-teachers'. They were left in charge again in June and September the next year and in November 1864 though, as mentioned later, the curate was visiting regularly that year and acting as stand-in for Crosfield on occasion. These youngsters were not always reliable without supervision. In June 1863,

> William Peel left in charge of boys retained in the school amuses himself by playing with them and racing up and down the school. I have repeatedly cautioned him about the same conduct.

Of these two boys, one went on to complete his apprenticeship in Knutsford but Mullin applied to be transferred to Doncaster. His young brother had been expelled from the school the previous autumn for 'impertinence'.

During 1865 Crosfield had to manage with only one pupil-teacher and he must therefore have had at least two monitors. These (usually) unpaid helpers tended to come and go and were rarely named in the log book. However, in May 1865 we are told that Herbert Lindsay was 're-admitted' with the object of becoming a pupil-teacher. He must have been about fifteen years old by then and it seems he was at once given charge of a class. In October, shortly before the annual inspection, Crosfield noted:

> The fourth class is too large for Lindsay to manage. I wish the Inspection was over so the class could be thinned.

Though by the close of 1866 Lindsay was officially a pupil-teacher, second year, he gave no end of trouble in the school. On 30 January 1866, when he and Mullin were both late, Crosfield threatened not to 'make an entry' (that is, record attendance) next time. Once there, Lindsay was reported to be 'striking and ill-treating the children' and further complaints of the way he manhandled his charges followed in September and October that year and February and April the next, but they cease thereafter and Lindsay completed his five year stint in 1870. William Peel finished in 1868 and was replaced by Charles Ellison who, again, was alone as fourth year pupil-teacher when Crosfield left at the end of 1871.

Crosfield had another set of problems with James Jackson in 1867. He was acting as a monitor in May that year but was 'sent to his class for misbehaving'. In August he was expelled for 'misconduct and gross insolence'. Thus it seemed that some of the older, cleverer boys who may have showed some potential for teaching, found it too constrictive an outlet for their adolescent energies.

Turning back now to the organization of the school day we can see from the log book that almost all of each day was spent on the three examination subjects, reading, writing and arithmetic, taught as such but also under the headings of dictation, spelling, notation and tables. In the lowest (fourth) class where the boys would have been about seven, coming on from infant schooling somewhere else in the town,[29] writing on slates was specified. Crosfield himself had permanent charge of class I (as was usual) and he sometimes taught class II as well. These upper classes would be examined in the top two Standards IV and V and with the older boys (ten and upwards) the curriculum was somewhat wider than the 'three Rs' plus Scripture which were general throughout.

By 1862, class I were learning grammar and geography as were pupils in all the better schools in Crosfield's own time as a schoolboy. History is mentioned for class I in 1863, again standard for older pupils for many years. The more advanced mathematics, algebra, Euclid and mensuaration were also commonly taught (they were options for pupil-teachers from 1846) and Crosfield introduced the latter two subjects in 1863. He was more ambitious with natural science in November 1863 and he even embarked on 'the elements of French' with a few pupils in August 1868. As at Farnley, drawing was taught in the school from 1865.

Thus the records make clear how an able and energetic master could, with the managers' backing, pursue the 'higher' subjects ignored in the current system of payment-by-results. However, it was not long after this that the government, under some pressure, extended the range of subjects it was prepared to reward with grants. Pupils who had already passed in Standard VI could now be examined in 'special subjects' such as history, geography and grammar provided these had been on the regular timetable for twelve months.[30] Though long overdue for many schools, these incentives simply brought for the Knutsford Parochial School (and the Farnley Iron Works school and many others) payment for work already in hand.

As at Farnley, the curriculum here was extended even further by visitors who came in to encourage or instruct. Prominent among these, naturally, were the clergy. From early in 1864 the curate, Revd E. Weddell, called in regularly. He took the occasional arithmetic lesson and he also taught music, as did Miss Clowes, one of the vicar's daughters. Revd Clowes himself gave £1 as a 'gratuity' to the boys 'as a little encouragement' in May 1863. (The log book does not explain how the sum was divided out). After Clowes died in 1864 his successor Revd H. Barnacle took over the managerial role. He examined the top class in History in May 1865, gave a music lesson that December and a demonstration of Hydrostatics a few years later. Another regular visitor was Captain Henry Hill of the Yeoman Cavalry, while he and one of the Misses Holland both took an interest in the teaching of history. Finally, just before Crosfield left, Revd Barnacle proposed a prize scheme to encourage the boys to learn algebra and Euclid.

This lively interest in the boys' secular education is worthy of comment. When schools in rural areas were so often under attack from local farmers claiming a right to children's labour and scornful of 'book-learning' why was the Knutsford school so happily free from this kind of pressure? There were several reasons and the first was the 'public spirit and generosity' of the

Cheshire landowners who kept their schools open even during the economic stress of the cattle-plague in the mid-1860s. Revd Temple, HMI for the area, commended them in his report of 1867 and his remarks were quoted in the Report of the Royal Commission on the Employment of Children, Young Persons and Women in Agriculture that year.[31]

Closer to home, Lord Egerton of Tatton, in a letter to the Commissioners, spoke of the many 'excellent schools' in his area and though he gave a personal view that in some the education went 'further than necessary' he went to explain and justify this state of affairs. 'In my schools', he said, 'scarcely one of the children of labourers return to farm work but aspire to be clerks or mechanics'. This was specially true of the boys he had employed from twelve to fourteen in a half-time scheme of his own making. Egerton clearly recognized that even unskilled workers were the better for being literate, but he also accepted 'the natural consequence of the neighbourhood of a town like Manchester' and 'the desire to rise in life which one cannot find fault with'.[32]

Added to all this was the nature of Cheshire agriculture, based on cattle and sheep in permanent ley. There was no great call for children or women (outside dairying) and much of the harvest work was done by itinerant Irish.

For these fortunate boys in mid-Victorian Knutsford, school life was further varied by a whole range of formal and informal activities, from regular annual events to the multifarious excuses for a day out for work, play or entertainment. Absence for a variety of reasons was accepted philosophically by schoolmaster and managers while truancy was severely punished. No doubt the boys and their parents could recognize the fine dividing line between legitimate and illegitimate absence even if the boys did not always respect it.

Among the official events were the May Day celebrations and outings such as the visit to 'Gilbert's Panorama of the Pilgrims' Progress' in August 1868 and, for several years running, a 'choir fest' in local centres such as Manchester and Altrincham. Sometimes the boys were released early or given a day off to amuse themselves—on 5 January 1865 'to go on the ice' for instance, and 13 February 1879, the day of the Knutsford

Ploughing Match. They also had the occasional holiday for a wedding or funeral. On 11 August 1864 the vicar's daughter was married; in March 1865, the Mistress of the girls' school; and there were two grand Egerton weddings in October 1867 and January 1870. For the former, Crosfield himself had a day off 'to organize the decorations'.

There would always be some boys missing school for the annual march of the Yeomanry through the town, for the Knutsford Races and the Stockport and Bowdon Wakes. As each season brought transitory tasks requiring unskilled labour, the absence of boys working and earning for a few days was clearly accepted. Crosfield notes, without comment, on 15 April 1863 boys away 'gardening'. In mid-May there was the movement of cattle into 'ley', hay-making in June, potato-picking in September, gathering acorns in October. Sometimes, the schoolmaster, acknowledging the nature of their home lives, simply records that it is 'the country boys' who are missing. All this adds up to a remarkably complex but relaxed pattern of work and play and a far richer one for school and pupils than for the town children that Crosfield had taught in Liverpool or Birkenhead or indeed for the children at Farnley, where the range of occupations and amusements was that much narrower.

All this would be true even without the special relationship between school and church and those activities by which the school justified its foundation as 'Parochial' in the religious sense. The managerial presence of the clergy has already been noted but without a Trust Deed or other formal statement we can only piece together the evidence for the nature of this particular school's link with the Parish Church and with the life of the Church of England generally.

While it was undoubtedly a church school it was not affiliated to the National Society until much later in the century. Nevertheless, it was sometimes referred to locally as the 'National School', the term having acquired by mid-century a rather loose general meaning. Perhaps the early proprietors had no need of grants and saw no point in complicating their task by adherence to the Society's rules. For instance, they may have planned from the start to accommodate dissenters and Roman Catholic children and, as we have seen, concessions of this kind spelt trouble with the National Society in London. Certainly by Crosfield's time the Parochial School boys included both Wesleyans and Roman Catholics; Revd Clowes, who was 'remarkable for the moderation of his views'[33] and 'lived in harmony with all denominations' allowed these children to be absent from school for their own sects' functions.

Then again, the emphasis on religious instruction was much less marked here than at Farnley where the progress of each class was so carefully checked and noted. Maybe John Crosfield, a more typical schoolmaster and without his friend Barnes's special vocation, left more of this to the vicar. We have some evidence, though, of Crosfield's practical co-operation with the incumbent in the work of the parish. In December 1863, for instance, he discussed the progress of the Sunday School with Revd Rudd and in February 1864 he accompanied the vicar to appeal against the rating of the school.

As for the children, they were taken to church on high days and holy days—to Divine Service on Ash Wednesday for instance—and they were drawn into the Church of England's ritual plea for deliverance from the cattle plague in the mid-1860s; that disease (according to *The Times*) 'coming we know not why or whence or whither'.[34] In Farnley William Barnes took his pupils to church on 14 March and in Knutsford it was 26 February; both these days, appropriately, in Lent. Despite the nation-wide petitions the plague continued for several years affecting four hundred localities in Cheshire alone.

The boys from the Parochial School also made a public appearance each year at the May Day celebrations. This ancient festival was revived in the town in 1864[35] by the vicar's daughters and it seems to have gathered in the children of the church rather than those of the dissenting schools.[36] The Crosfields, as might be expected, were fully involved; John was one of the organizers, his wife made costumes for the procession and, in 1867, their elder daughter, Louisa Augusta, was chosen to be May Queen.

In the May Day festivities, as in the daily life of the school, the role of the church can be seen as all-embracing if not rigidly exclusive, in this town. Another sphere of this influence—bringing with it work for Crosfield—came with the start of evening classes. A Parochial Night School taking adolescents and young men from the age of fourteen upwards was launched in 1868 but it seems there had been a men's night school for some time before that. On the evening of 21 February that year, a tea party was held and the long account of this function in the local paper is revealing of the church's role in educating the townspeople and of Crosfield's place in the community.[37]

The schoolroom that evening was 'very tastefully decorated with evergreens under the supervision of Mr Crosfield'. Various appropriate mottos were hung upon the walls as well as six large pictures, 'handsomely framed and glazed'. These pictures, of Scripture subjects, together with some books, were given as prizes to successful pupils. There were several speakers at the tea party. The vicar, Revd Henry Barnacle, enlarged upon the usefulness of education; how it could help a young man to 'command a higher position in life' and in his leisure hours 'study the word of God'. The aptly-named Mr Cram, teacher in the school, claimed that the progress made by his pupils was 'perfectly wonderful'. George Gallop, the prison governor, spoke of the duties of parents in the education of their children.

Then Crosfield made 'an excellent speech' in the course of which he claimed to have been present on every night the school had been opened. Not once had he to reprove for misconduct; the scholars, he said, 'seemed deeply interested in their work'. After singing and recitations the teachers were thanked and the proceedings were brought to a close at 9.30 p.m. with the singing of the doxology and Benediction from the Chairman.

About ten years after John Crosfield and his family arrived in Knutsford he was planning to move again though there is nothing to indicate he was dissatisfied. In fact his work at the Parochial School had clearly established his reputation as an experienced, energetic and capable schoolmaster and his certificate was upgraded in November 1866 from second class division three to second class division one. With one child in 1860 he now had four and the Crosfields, by 1871, were part of a more extended family group in the town. Caroline's sister Helen, still in Liverpool with her parents, married John Hulme the Knutsford postmaster in 1866. When she came to Knutsford it seems both her parents came too and John Feast, at 61, took up employment as post-office clerk under his most recent son-in-law. Still in Liverpool was a Feast brother, Arthur, who married in 1871 and set up as a grocer. Altogether there were reasons enough to keep the Crosfields in this pleasant town but John was then rising forty and perhaps he was looking for wider responsibilities and better pay.

These he was to find in his last professional move, back into Yorkshire. Local teachers had been complaining that Cheshire salaries were way below those in large towns in 1871; '£60 at least below Sheffield'[38] was perhaps an exaggeration but momentous changes were taking place since the Education Act of 1870—these will be described later—and schooling in the populous areas was now big business. So, from Knutsford, a quiet backwater by comparison, Crosfield moved his family to Leeds where thirteen new schools were about to open in 1872 and where his brother-in-law William Barnes was newly settled as incumbent of a down-town parish. Closing chapters will take the lives of these two men and their families, together, through their last two decades of professional work.

IX

Edwin Foster in Lancashire

We can now return to the question of Edwin Foster's movements in the 1860s. Like his friends William Barnes and John Crosfield, Foster had a settled period in this decade but, in all, three posts in the Liverpool area before 1870. It was mentioned earlier how Foster left Halifax to substitute for Barnes in the Christchurch National school when he and Crosfield left for Farnley in 1858. Under any other circumstances would Foster have chosen this school?

It seems unlikely, for though he was the only one of the three young men still unattached, with only his own comfort to think of, his roots were in Yorkshire and there must have been schools comparable to this one in the larger West Riding towns. Even better ones, perhaps; from what we know of the Liverpool school and its environs it would not be surprising if Barnes were obliged to offer a stand-in. When Foster was at work there in October 1859 the Inspector remarked again on the noise of heavy traffic (this time recommending 'double sashes' on the windows) while the schoolmaster himself was praised for keeping up a standard considered 'fair in all the circumstances'. The schoolroom was still very full with about 150 boys and Foster had working for him no less than six pupil-teachers.[1]

Then there was the problem of somewhere to live. The small site had never allowed room for a master's house. Barnes, and Andrews before him, had lived in Clarence Grove, a mile away in Everton. Now, Edwin Foster took a house about the same distance away to the south-east in Queen Street, Edgehill[2] (Fig. 10)—another long trek back and forth for a busy schoolmaster with pupil-teachers to instruct at the end of a busy day. But like

Figure 10. *Number 7 Queen Street, Edgehill, Liverpool.*
Edwin Foster lived in number 9 (to the right) after his marriage in 1858.
(Sketch from a photograph 1966)

the Everton house, this one was up on one of Liverpool's ridges of high ground with a good supply of the freshest air this smoky city could provide. Foster's house, 'two-up, two-down' was in one of the working-class terraces which were gradually engulfing the middle-class suburb of Edgehill at this time.[3] It was here he brought his wife in the summer of 1859.

He may have known Sarah Flockton for some time because her home was in Stanley near Wakefield, her father an engineer at the small waterworks there. He was widowed and remarried with a stepson by the time Edwin moved over to Lancashire. Sarah was one of the elder daughters, at twenty-six two years older than Foster and with some training as a dressmaker. They were married in St Peter's Church, Stanley on 21 June 1859. Sarah's brother Thomas was one of the witnesses; another was William Barnes now settled at Farnley some ten miles away. The Foster's first child, a son, Edwin Flockton, was born in Liverpool on 19 August 1860 and he was baptized a few months later in Christchurch, Hunter Street near the school.

All things considered it is hardly surprising that the Fosters moved away soon after this to what was to become their family home in the country until the late 1860s. Sometime over the winter of 1860–61 they took up residence in Melling, a small isolated village lying about six miles north of Liverpool. On a slight rise above the south Lancashire plain, it was surrounded by an expanse of open fields with no more than seven or eight hundred inhabitants the year the Fosters came. Of these about thirty were farmers some of whom doubled as grocers or victuallers and the other needs of the village were served by a blacksmith, a farrier and a wheelwright, several public houses, a tailor and a boot and shoe-maker. Many of the fields were devoted to fruit and vegetables and even the schoolmaster's house had some outbuildings and a small plot of land where the couple could grow their own produce.[4] A contrast indeed to the urban surroundings of Foster's earlier homes in Yorkshire and Liverpool.

Professionally, though, what kind of a move was this? By the end of 1860 it must have been apparent that changes were on the way—the Royal Commission on the State of Popular Education was yet to report but its brief, to recommend measures for elementary instruction that would be 'sound and cheap'[5] had an ominous ring to it, and we have seen how the new regime which came in a few years later cut away at the base of the career structure which had offered so much to the trainees of Foster's generation. Though Edwin Foster was three years beyond certification he must have been wondering about his long-term prospects. It so happened that the school he moved to at the start of 1861 was isolated, independent, non-inspected and unlikely to be affected by new legislation. Could he have chosen it for this very reason?

This seems unlikely for he went on after 1869 into more demanding posts and he could never have made such a comeback if he had deliberately chosen to opt out a whole eight years before; we can be sure that he weighed up carefully the school's career potential for himself while considering the attractions of the village as home for wife and children. It was essential, for instance, that his certificate remain valid—indeed he must have sought upgradings—and we can only assume, in the absence of log books or Inspector's reports, that the Melling village school was visited, officially from time to time and the master's performance kept under review. Though records of this kind, standard in all grant-aided schools, are missing and though this country school was too unimportant to feature in the local press, we can piece together something of its origins and the role it played in the local community from other sources.

The school in Melling was a very old one, much older than any so far described and it was supported by an endowment. Early in the eighteenth century the 'lords and charters' of Melling enclosed the commons and one acre of waste land was set aside for school. Some local men put up the money for a three-bayed stone building, part school and part master's house. Shortly after, some property was left in trust for the school and between this date and 1860 a succession of trustees managed the property, drew the income and maintained the school.[6] By 1860, however, only one trustee remained, Revd George Holden of Maghull. Whether he moved to amend the trust or whether he was under pressure from the Charity Commission is not clear but the outcome was a new Trust Deed in 1861 with four new trustees. These were Lord Skelmersdale (landowner), Revd Richard Leigh (rector of Halsall), Revd William Bolton (rector of Aughton) and Matthew Froude (of Maghull, landowner).[7]

The Melling deed of 1861 was a lengthy document which reaffirmed much of the earlier provisions, describing in minute detail the nature of the property in question and the ways in which the 'rents and profits' could be used. Alongside all this were the ground rules for the management of the school, for the hiring and firing of the master and for the instruction of 'the poor'.[8] There was nothing, however, to say how much the schoolmaster should be paid and in the nineteenth century the trust property was bringing in much too little for the salary of a master, even an unqualified one. Sums given in various reports of the Charity Commissioners suggest that income from the trust was about £35 to £40 when Foster came to Melling, rising to something over £50 after 1900. It will be remembered that Foster was earning about £90 when he was at Halifax in 1856–57. Now married, he would hardly have moved for less though his income was probably arranged with the managers as a package deal in which his stated salary would have been just one item.

Thus, he had the use of a house rent-free; he might well have had free wood or coal. For most, if not all, the time, he was at Melling a member of his family helped in the school and he must have received some allowance for this. Early on it was Foster's wife, Sarah, who taught in the school. Later, his young sister-in-law, Elizabeth Flockton, took a turn though she was only seventeen when they arrived and neither of the women had any training for the work. Possibly they alternated in the schoolroom to allow for Sarah's regular pregnancies. Then there was a younger sister-in-law, Mary Eliza, and she may have been called in, too. On top of all this, Edwin himself was appointed Parish Clerk—as were many country schoolmasters—and this imposed extra duties in church, weekdays and Sundays, but a small extra stipend of perhaps £10 a year.[9]

With his new income, whatever it amounted to exactly, Edwin Foster maintained a substantial household. Apart from his wife and first child, in 1861 there were Sarah's two sisters mentioned above and a living-in 'house-servant' aged fourteen. In the next few years two more sons were born and a daughter.

From the trustees' point of view it would have been cheaper to employ an uncertificated master, a mistress or a provisionally-certificated youngster to replace the untrained man, James Bennett, who, following his father in the post, had served since 1851.[10] But, to their credit, they chose Edwin Foster, trained, certificated and experienced. Why not take the further step and apply for government grants? There seem to be two reasons but we need to ask, first, how many children were using the school.

By 1871 an official survey revealed there were 149 pupils at Melling, rather more than we should expect for Melling-with-Cunscough, a township of a mere 800 souls, particularly with a Roman Catholic school taking 83 children within its boundaries. But the true catchment area for these schools could have been wider; it is difficult to predict how far children might be sent from isolated farms, in fact government officers in 1871 were estimating that 40 children would come into Melling from Kirkby and Maghull.[11] But it is clear the school was popular, locally, in 1861. That year nearly all the under-tens in the village were 'scholars' and about half the older children aged ten to sixteen.[12] It would therefore be reasonable to take a minimum figure of, say, one hundred pupils for most of the time Foster was there.

The trustees who took on Foster some time before the start of 1861 were perhaps wise to hesitate before signing up the school into the government system because it was only too clear then, that major change was on the way. In the event, the Revised Code which came into operation in mid-1863 would have required not just the one certificated master but, for a hundred children, an assistant with at least basic qualifications—an ex-pupil teacher fourth class.[13] Furthermore, it is unlikely that a school of this size including infants could have earned itself more than about £50 in grants and this sum would have been cut by £35 to £40, the amount of the endowment,[14] leaving too little to compensate the trustees for the weight of regulation they would have to submit to. As things were, they would have the benefit of informal advice whenever Her Majesty's Inspector called to check up on Foster's certification—the best of both worlds perhaps.

We can now turn to the school itself. The building where Foster worked dated from 1844 replacing the early school. This small edifice in the Gothic style so popular at the time had just one large room about 50 ft by 22 ft with a porch on each of the long sides.[15] In this room were taught, one can suppose, a hundred or more children aged from three or four to thirteen or fourteen. For a young man brought up in all-boys schoolrooms and practising in no other kind for ten years, this must have been a startling change. Even with the children separated into small groups with the mistress of the time, plus juvenile assistants (paid or otherwise), the planning of the school day was a complex task for which Foster had no special preparation. William Barnes at Farnley was in a similar position but with enough pupils and space to fill separate girls and infants schools he could hand over day-to-day responsibility to female teachers with the requisite training.

Nor had Foster any experience with country children who were said to be generally duller and less ambitious than their counterparts in the towns. Revd Watkins, who had visited the area some years before found the pupils at Maghull (a mile and a half away), 'heavy and slow and very ignorant'[16]—hardly surprising when one considers the limited prospects before them. In Melling itself there were only three apprenticeships being served in the village in 1861; two at the shoemaker's, one to the blacksmith. All the other youngsters employed were in farm or domestic service. Though Melling was much nearer to Liverpool than Knutsford to Manchester it seems there was no local stimulus to ambition as the Cheshire town apparently gave to the youngsters there.[17] So it was to everyone's credit that the Melling school was so well patronized at the time.

And this would finally sum up the character of the school were there not some ambiguities in its relationship with the church. To understand these we need to return to the trust deeds. It was mentioned earlier that the new body of trustees in 1861 included three local clergy and from the first there had been at least one. The deed itself, though, made no mention of religion, neither defining the school's allegiance to the church nor listing any content for the pupils' religious education. This was in marked contrast to those other trust deeds for schools in

Halifax, Wakefield and Liverpool which were quite specific on these points. This exactness was, of course, a condition of each school's affiliation to the National Society. The trustees of the Melling school made no such commitment for the same reasons, possibly, that they steered clear of the grant system; they had enough money, for the time being, and they preferred to run the school without outside interference. By the 1860s church and school were close but only by local custom, not formal agreement.

As at Knutsford and Farnley, the practical questions here concerned access for children whose parents were not church people. Catholics could use the school at Cunscough but if younger children and any nonconformists wished to attend the village school there was nothing in the rules to stop them. The teaching of doctrine and church attendance on Sundays and feast days we know nothing about but it seems the trustees were not inclined to be dogmatic on these issues. Asked in 1872 if they would be willing to operate a Conscience Clause, they said they would be happy to do so.[18]

But there is another unusual feature of this school. When three clergy were made trustees in 1861, Revd J.K. Glazebrook of St Mary's church, Melling was not one of them. Why not? Much later on when the trust was reconstituted in the early 1890s[19] there was a new rule to include the incumbent, ex-officio. At the time it was said that the clergyman had previously been 'sole manager'. If true, this could explain why Glazebrook was apparently cold-shouldered. To manage the school was a specific and quite onerous responsibility but it would have left this cleric free of financial commitment; perhaps he preferred it that way.

As for the schoolmaster it was wholly in his interests to work with Revd Glazebrook and the trustees and there is nothing to suggest that relationships were discordant. Indeed for Edwin Foster and his family the 1860s were most likely a time of placid but fruitful activity within the framework of the school's year, the church's year and the rotating seasons. But the pattern had to change. Whether or not Foster had planned such a timetable in advance, by the late 1860s it was imperative he should move if he was to climb to higher levels in his profession. With the extension of the franchise in 1867 there were already calls for better elementary education and, once again, the prospect of significant changes in the way that teachers were employed and paid.

These weighty matters apart, the Foster family had two good reasons of their own to be seeking a move away from Melling. The first of these concerned their sons. By 1868 young Edwin was eight, Herbert William was six and Arthur Edward, four. (Florence, born in 1866 was only three). Isolated at Melling there was no schooling for intelligent boys and we can be sure that Foster had academic aspirations for them.

Added to this the old schoolmaster's house in the village was falling into disrepair; in 1871, not long after the family's departure it was said to be barely habitable. Sometime that year Revd Glazebrook (for the trustees) asked a local architect to inspect the house and advise on repairs. This man, Thomas Mellard Reade, earlier resident in the village, wrote to Glazebrook as follows:

> My opinion is that it is so radically bad that no repairs will make it satisfactory. I should recommend you to pull it down and build a new one with the usual modern precautions against damp...I should hesitate before I allowed a family to occupy the house at all.[20]

The trustees responded by negotiating with the Charity Commissioners for permission to sell a portion of the trust property. They argued that no better use could be found for the money locked up this way, the Commissioners agreed and a new schoolmaster's house was built in 1875.

Who occupied this most unsatisfactory building in the meantime? When Reade declared that no family should be asked to live in it he surely had in mind that the Fosters had lost a baby son in February 1868 a few months before they left the village to return to Liverpool. So it came about that Foster's replacement was a single man of thirty with his sister to housekeep but the trustees allowed them to take five boys aged seven to thirteen as boarders.[21] With a young servant, thirteen years old, there were eight people in this rotten house for several more years. The Fosters, meanwhile, had found themselves better accommodation in the city and Foster himself was back in mainstream, government-funded education.

Later chapters will show how, by late 1870 and early 1871, as the nation gathered itself to respond to the new and sweeping demands of the 1870 Education Act, the careers of William Barnes and John Crosfield were each set on a purposeful course, Crosfield taking advantage of the demand for capable teachers in large town schools and Barnes offering his expertise, in due course, to an urban School Board from his position as vicar. Not so for Edwin Foster. Though he eventually won through to a good position with the Liverpool School Board, his first engagement back in the city, though with better prospects, was not altogether happy.

The Liverpool to which Foster returned in 1868 was still a place of dramatic contrasts. At the Christchurch school ten years earlier he had seen the drabber if not the most poverty-stricken side of city life; now he was to meet the children of the really poor but in a setting which was a landmark to this town's civic pride and generosity. In 1868 the Registrar General gave a figure for the death rate in Liverpool exceeded only by those for Manchester, Leeds and Glasgow: 'When will the north undertake the noble work of saving the lives of the people?' he exclaimed.[22] But meanwhile a local directory was assuring visitors to the town that it was a place where

> in the contemplation of works which had for their object either utility or splendour, expense has only been a secondary consideration.[23]

Such a work of 'utility' was the Kirkdale Industrial School, built for pauper children in 1845. Most pauper schools at this time were still on workhouse premises but here and there a Poor Law Union had adopted the more enlightened policy of separating the children from the adult paupers and building their schools some distance away. Liverpool's Poor Law committee, the Select Vestry, followed this course in the 1840s and the result was a handsome and substantial building two miles north of the Brownlow Hill workhouse. About five hundred children were moved there initially; the premises were designed for a thousand and often took more.[24]

The building cost over £32,000 and the style of it suggests an academic institution, a public school perhaps, rather than a place of refuge and instruction for the poor.[25] This grandiose statement of public philanthropy was followed by another in the 1860s when a huge new wing was added to ease the pressure on accommodation and to separate off the youngest children from the rest. The new architects, Messrs Picton and Son, were instructed to use the same ornate finish as for the main school. Composed of 'brick of different colours with stone dressings'[26] this new range of buildings had a frontage of 375 ft, three storeys rising to 40 ft and a central tower above that. Over the main entrance was an oriel window and two carved figures representing Charity and Mercy.

On the ground floor were day-rooms, teachers' rooms and offices and above that, the dormitories. In three wings projecting back were the dining-room (30 ft by 80 ft), the main schoolroom and a play-room of similar size and a large play-shed. The whole building was centrally-heated from furnaces in the basement[27] and the five acres of land on the site were developed later as gardens, partly ornamental and partly for the growing of vegetables. A full-time gardener had pupils under instruction working for him.

The opening of the new school was celebrated by a 'feast' on New Year's Eve 1868. Contractors, architects, parish officers and vestrymen took part, there was champagne—someone said 'too much of it'—and the Chairman of the Industrial Schools Committee made a speech.[28] At once questions were asked about the financing of this party; the costs of the building had already soared from an estimated £12,000 to £20,000 and the administration was constantly under fire, later, for what was considered extravagant use of public funds.[29] This did not mean any noticeable generosity to staff or inmates (some of whom slept three in a bed) but it seems the fault, if any, lay in the fashionable preference for large institutions rather than mismanagement.

This was the establishment which Edwin Foster and his wife considered working for when they decided to move from Melling. In some ways it was an attractive proposition for a professional man who had been in a rural backwater for nearly ten years. Here was the chance of major responsibility—Foster said later he had 500 children under his charge at Kirkdale[30]—the salary promised to be adequate and the premises, within the school or elsewhere, a vast improvement on the decaying cottage in Melling. But for the first time Edwin Foster was to find himself under the control of a local public authority, the Select Vestry, his work supervised and managed at three levels—by his immediate superiors in the school, by the Vestrymen and by their masters the Poor Law Board.[31] A contrast indeed to the freedom and informality of a small village school.

However, if more onerous, the prestige of this post was correspondingly greater. When vacancies were advertised for Infant School master and matron a large number of applications was reduced first to eight and then to three couples who were selected for interview. Edwin and Sarah Foster were chosen from these on a narrow vote of the Industrial Schools Committee and they were told to start work in Kirkdale on 21 December 1868.[32]

At first the Committee laid down that the principal teacher and matron of the new Infant School should receive a salary 'not less than £100 together with rations, apartments and washing'.[33] By the time the Poor Law Board approved these arrangements Edwin Foster's salary was set at £50 and Sarah's at £40. Edwin was also promised any excess of the Parliamentary Grant earned by his pupils over £50, and after some discussion about the size of their family, the couple were offered £25 each in lieu of rations.[34]

Would this prove a reasonable income? It is difficult to say; by Christmas 1868 there were four children in the Foster family and another on the way. Perhaps the authorities were chary of an open-ended commitment to feeding this large brood when they withdrew the earlier offer of 'rations'. Then there was another adult in the household, Sarah's sister Elizabeth, an essential helper while both parents worked. Foster himself clearly had some anxieties about money because we find him asking, in Spring 1869, for a plot of land to grow vegetables.[35] This was agreed but the presence of the schoolmaster working on part of the site caused a squabble later with the gardener.[36]

As for their living accommodation, the Poor Law Board were not keen on teachers with families living on the premises (though the Principal Master, Birchall, did throughout) and the Fosters were no doubt happy to be located elsewhere for much of their time. The Select Vestry had several small properties round the city in use for workhouse inmates of one kind or another. One such was in Mitford Street, Everton (previously Mary Anne Street), acquired from the owner some time in 1865. Known as 'the house in Netherfield Road' it was actually on the corner with Mitford Street which ran steeply uphill eastwards to connect with Northumberland Terrace. This house was one of the few remaining large villas on the upper slopes of Everton (Fig. 11) when the whole area began to decline, socially, in the 1860s. Not long before, Liverpool had been recommended for its sea-breezes and the 'villages' of Kirkdale, Everton and Bootle were singled out for praise.[37] By 1870 though, Picton, the chronicler of Liverpool's urban growth described Northumberland Terrace thus:

> The land on the east side has been covered with streets and cottages. On the west side a few of the better-class houses still stand in a deteriorated condition not having land enough to render them worth pulling down and yet quite unsuitable to the altered character of the neighbourhood.[38]

So it was in one of the vacated 'better-class houses' that the Foster's sixth child, Gertrude Eliza, was born in April 1869[39] a few months after they had arrived. When they came, the house had been serving as a small infant school but in January 1869 steps were taken to transfer all these pupils with all the furniture and 'school utensils' to the new building, together with the existing staff, matron and school mistress. From this point on it is not clear how Edwin Foster and his wife apportioned their time between their home in Mitford Street and the school half a mile away. Possibly they stayed overnight at the school on occasion, leaving Elizabeth Flockton in loco parentis; it is difficult to see how Sarah could have fulfilled her duties as matron otherwise. Edwin worked an ordinary school day, of course.

At this early stage the Fosters' home base away from the main school was inconvenient but had some advantages, not least the separation of their own young children from the hordes of young paupers who were Edwin and Sarah's responsibility at work. What were these children really like? That they were from poor homes is obvious but how were they selected for this institution?

The Kirkdale school was one of several places in which the town's most needy children were lodged and educated. In some of these the children were taught practical skills and, whenever possible, released into employment. Such schools were designated 'Industrial'; in the mid-1860s there were in this town the Liverpool and Kirkdale Industrial Ragged Schools and the St George's Industrial School all of which were run by charitable committees with some help from the town council[40]. The Kirkdale (workhouse) school, though, was a public institution entirely supported by the Poor Rates and government grants and there was an important difference in the way that children were allocated to schools of this kind.

While there was a central aim to keep pauper children out of adult institutions, secondarily there was the need to separate the deserving and uncorrupted poor from the 'morally-depraved' inmates. Easier said than done, of course, but the system was as follows. Into the workhouse schools went not only the children of adult inmates or of parents on outdoor relief but also those who were deserted, orphaned or with parents unable to care for them. Another such group were the illegitimate—if neglected for this reason.[41] The other Industrial schools also took needy children—those found begging, wandering, destitute, with a parent in prison, in the company of thieves but to these were added children beyond the control of their parents, 'refractory' in the workhouse or convicted of certain criminal offences. In these Industrial schools some or all the places were reserved for children committed to them by the magistrates. Once checked as suitable these schools were 'certified' under the Industrial Schools Act of 1866.

For Edwin Foster and his colleagues, therefore, in the workhouse school the task was to care for and educate pupils who came to them dirty, uncouth, ignorant but not necessarily practised in street crime. That, at least, was the theory, but it was quite impossible day by day to separate out 'the child of some deserving parishioner whom misfortune had reduced to poverty' from

> the child of the depraved wretch who is constantly found dragging from the schools her unfortunate offspring to return them in a week or two inbred with that poison which has so degraded herself.[42]

This writer in one of Liverpool's weekly journals identified a massive problem for the work-house school—the lack of power to hold the children there however great their need. Like adult paupers they were free to come and go while those committed to certified schools were obliged to stay. But in spite of this constant turn-over Edwin Foster claimed later that he knew all his five or six hundred pupils by name.[43]

In this situation the schoolmaster's primary task was an administrative one. With so many pupils, boys and girls together aged (Foster tells us) from three to nine, two or three female certificated assistants, a batch of pupil-teachers (in rotation from the sixteen employed in the main school) plus some monitors, Foster had to work out a daily timetable, plan the movements of staff and pupils and supervise the teaching generally. In 1869 there were six classes, in 1870 eight, in two broad 'divisions' and the curriculum was basic; religious knowledge, reading, writing on slates, spelling and arithmetic.[44] The only industrial training thought suitable for these 'infants' appears to have been the knitting described later by Foster as a popular activity among these small children.[45] It would be surprising if the girls did not also learn to sew.

By Foster's time the vexed question of religious education for pauper children seems to have been settled in this particular institution. About half the children at Kirkdale were known to be of Catholic origin—some, of course, had no identifiable roots—and by 1869 a Roman Catholic schoolmistress had been appointed to teach them. Priests were also allowed to visit while the rest of the children had the, by then, normal diet of Church of England instruction.[46] Though the 'moral training' of the pupils was always a focus of public interest and concern this aspect of the curriculum does not seem to have caused any problems for Foster and his staff.

Viewed simply as an elementary school how did this institution rate by the standards of the time? One of Her Majesty's Inspectors who was engaged in a survey of Liverpool and Manchester in 1868 and 1869 made this comment:

> ...children of indoor paupers...are better instructed than almost any other children of the poorer classes [in the area]. Education, however, is a wider term than instruction and as to the education

> of the children in these asylums interesting considerations arise which I omit.[47]

The curriculum was indeed limited and though grants were tailored to the Inspector's judgement of the school the old, pre-Revised Code categories of 'poor, moderate, fair and good' were applied to both the subject teaching and the performance of the teachers. Thus, in May 1869 Edmund Wodehouse stated:

> These are new schools and considering the short time they have been open they are in fair order.[48]

The teaching, this year and the next[49] was, at worst, 'pretty fair', the odd subject 'very fair' with 'good' appearing only twice; once for a spelling lesson with the top class where the children, up to nine years old, were out of the normal infant category—and possibly taught by Foster himself—and for 'discipline' in 1869. This final point has some bearing on incidents in June that year to be described shortly.

We turn now to the question of Foster's certification. He came to Kirkdale with a first-class certificate from the Committee of Council on Education but there was an entirely separate system of qualifications for teachers under the Poor Law Board[50] and no guaranteed transition from one to the other. When Foster was granted a certificate of 'Efficiency grade three' at Kirkdale in May 1869[51] was this a fair equivalent to his previous grade? Possibly, for we do not know at what level his first-class certificate stood nor when he was promoted to it. His two assistants had certificates of 'Competency' and below that again were two more levels, 'Probation' and 'Permission', the last applying to pupil-teachers only.[52] Then again, salary was linked to certification in a way long since dropped in the ordinary elementary schools. In 1869, Foster qualified for a grant to the school of £50 and was paid this amount. In 1870 he stood to get £5 more for his upgrading to 'Efficiency grade two'.[53]

Considering now Foster's personal experience at the school, we find that very soon after his first formal inspection he was in trouble with the Industrial Schools Committee over his treatment of the children. That his discipline was effective the Inspector had noted but his methods were now in question. A nurse in the infant school complained to Mr Birchall that

Mr Foster had 'severely punished two of the children'. This was entered in the Headmaster's journal with the comment that 'in one of the cases referred to the punishment inflicted was objectionable both in nature and degree' and the Committee were obliged to consider the matter when the journal was put before them at their meeting on 1 June 1969.[54]

As a result, Mr Foster, the Matron (Sarah Foster) and Miss Farrish, the assistant matron, were called before the Committee and 'their respective duties and responsibilities were pointed out to them by the Chairman'. Though a blow to Foster's professional pride this matter was not reported to the Poor Law Board nor—luckily for him—was it mentioned in the local press, the normal column inches devoted to this Committee being taken up just then with a financial scandal at the Blind School. Had this telling-off been a matter of public gossip the course of Foster's career might have been very different. As for the actual punishments used we have no clue as to what they were. What could have been more 'objectionable' than caning which was commonplace and accepted even for small children by most authorities at this time?

Then in the following year, 1870, came a series of changes and upheavals. One factor which began to set the Vestry's plans awry was a slow but steady decrease in pauperism, or rather a slackening in the demand for assistance. No-one seemed to know why; the Secretary to the Select Vestry, H.J. Hagger, wrote to the Poor Law Board saying that the change was 'extraordinary and unparalleled'.[55] At the time of this letter, in the winter of 1869–70, the Netherfield Road house was occupied by aged paupers and the Fosters presumably resident in the main Infants School. Within a few months their future was seriously in doubt as the Industrial School Committee tried to rationalize its use of premises and staff.

As summer followed spring in 1870 the Vestry had a new problem, an epidemic of relapsing fever, and they conceived the plan of emptying the whole of the new Kirkdale Infants wing for use as a fever hospital. After some anxious discussions with the Poor Law Board about the risks of cross-infection the Vestry were permitted to do this and in August some of the children

Figure 11. *St George's Church and the slopes of Everton, Liverpool c. 1815. The Fosters occupied one of the villas when it housed part of the Kirkdale Industrial School c. 1870. By then, terraced houses had taken over much of the area. (From an early nineteenth-century lithograph)*

were moved into the main building and others back to Netherfield Road with Mr and Mrs Foster.[56] Some cases of fever among the older pupils at Kirkdale caused a minor panic but this infection proved to be typhoid and unconnected with the temporary fever hospital next door. By the following February, 1871,[57] there were fewer cases of relapsing fever but smallpox began to make one of its periodic reappearances; that month there were 77 cases in Kirkdale and it seemed wise to keep the hospital open. The building was never returned to use as a school—with the Fosters or anyone else—a fact which, surprisingly, elicited no public comment at the time.

During that spring and early summer the Fosters lived and worked at 2 Mitford Street. The composition of this household is interesting considering the house had been until fairly recently a private home. According to the census of 1871 there were the two Fosters there with five children and a sister-in-law; seven nurses aged 29 to 64, all but two of them paupers; two male employees; two female monitors aged 13 and 15 and more than a hundred children, mostly boys, aged four to nine.

Under these circumstances the Fosters must have had the greatest difficulty keeping their own small family separate from the crowd of young paupers, safeguarding them from infections and from noise and distraction. Possibly they were sent out to school somewhere in the neighbourhood. St George's church school just up the road had a good reputation with the middle classes and there were small private establishments nearby. But they did not have this worry for very long. The drop in numbers at Kirkdale was now some 30 per cent, from 1500 to 1000 and by the summer of 1871 the Committee could see no sense in keeping a tenth of them in an annexe. So, at a meeting in August, it was resolved to close the Netherfield Road house, take the pupils back into the main school and serve 'a notice of discontinuance' on Mr and Mrs Foster 'to expire on September 22nd.'[58]

As reported in the *Liverpool Mercury*[59] the decision was made 'so that expenses might be reduced, an object which everyone had in view'. Cries of 'hear, hear' confirmed there was general assent to this proposal. Mr Hagger, though, intervened on behalf of the Foster couple. He pointed out that by this action the Vestry would be ousting them 'from what they were led to believe would be a permanent situation' though he was ready to concede the Vestry were not to blame. As a conciliatory gesture the vestrymen agreed to extend the Foster's notice to three months. Thus ended a rather unsatisfactory and unsettled three years for Edwin Foster, his wife and children.

Part IV

The School Board Period

X

Edwin Foster in Liverpool

The narrative so far has taken the lives of three schoolmasters into their thirties, men now well established with dependent families and all of them—even, in retrospect, William Barnes—beneficiaries of what had slowly become a national system of education. Not that anyone could have located a blueprint for it. The ingredients and motive power for this vast undertaking had come from a host of people in the earlier decades of the nineteenth century—politicians, clergy and, in due course, officials—men of strong personal conviction who were sometimes willing, sometimes forced to co-operate in the great work of educating the poor.

In the most recent period of stress, for example, Matthew Arnold HMI was moved to issue a diatribe against the Revised Code of 1862[1]—but in it he paid tribute to the work of Sir James Kay-Shuttleworth who had set up the Education Department in 1839 'in the face of immense prejudice, of angry outcry, of vehement opposition'. Arnold went on the praise the clergy, 'their schools dearer to them than their prejudices', whose attachment to the system probably saved it from destruction in the early years. And finally he claimed 'the country at large' now valued the practical benefits of the huge, expensive machine. It was surely this reservoir of strong public feeling which made possible a new and significant step towards state control of elementary schools in 1870.

In spite of the progress which had been made, for serious-minded Victorians the great 'education question' was far from settled by the close of the 1860s. There were still profound differences of opinion over the way money was handed out to individual schools when every one of them was a kind of religious nursery. Public support for basic literacy was one thing; incidentally financing the sects was another. That any practical decisions at all were made testifies to the unity of purpose which Arnold had seen and which underlay much of the surface bickering. Indeed as the years went by it was simply not possible to ignore the claims of the untutored poor any longer. Too much had been written and said about their human predicament, about their failings as a work-force and about the threat they would pose after the extension of the franchise in 1867. At whatever cost, by whatever means, something more had to be done.

Even then, the Elementary Education Act, produced after seven months of debate, was no master plan.[2] It had within it the weakness of a half-measure. Based on the grand new principle of universal education it failed to unify responsibility; the new 'state' schools, under local School Boards, were merely to fill the gaps between, rather than replace, the old voluntary schools and this, in turn, brought new grounds for dissension. To start with, who was to say if and where new schools were needed? Her Majesty's Inspectors made local enquiries and published figures.[3] In many small towns and rural areas provision was adequate but in the larger towns it was not and these figures were invariably questioned by rate-payers on whom would fall the burden of expansion. On the other hand, if the basic figures were agreed, the proposed number and location of the schools was not—and here the churches had a direct interest. Encouraged by the Act to extend their own coverage,[4] churchmen tried first, with collections of money and the announcement of plans, to stave off the formation of a School Board altogether. If this failed, they would try to delay, prevent or alter the Board's scheme for schools in their locality.[5]

So although there were pious hopes that the School Board era would be one of fruitful co-operation, too often there was wasteful competition and bad feeling between the providers of Board and voluntary education in the large centres of population. No-one wanted the burden of half-empty schools when government grants were still being paid in shillings and pence per child and the churches resented the Board's access to rate-income while they still depended on voluntary contributions. If, though, the

Boards used their more reliable source of income to cut school fees they were left to cater for the poorer children and, in any case, the scatter of voluntary schools across their territory made logical planning difficult. Parents did not help when they moved their children from one school to another and this was still a problem when attendance was compulsory everywhere after 1876.[6] As we shall see, for Liverpool and Leeds these were difficult and challenging times for all concerned.

It was, at first, quite possible for the working schoolmaster to ignore the education debate going on over his head in the months leading up to the Education Bill and its passage into law in the summer of 1870. His attachments were local, his employers almost certainly the leaders of religion in his community. True, there were teacher associations but these were mostly sectarian self-help groups and their public role was limited. After August 1870, though, all this changed. The teaching profession became politicized and all teachers, whether they allied themselves with the new movement or not, had to consider and assess the new options presented to them. Ahead lay the prospect of an era with more varied and better-paid work but in contemplating these new avenues of advancement Church of England schoolmasters were faced with a test of loyalty. Should they continue to offer their services to the church and its people, to the organization and the individuals who had encouraged, trained and rewarded them over the years? Or should they cross over to the new state system where the schools were maintained from public funds alone and where there were new restrictions and controls?

What had been one of the sharpest points of debate was now at the heart of the schoolmaster's dilemma. Could he detach himself from the habits of a lifetime and start to teach 'undenominational' Christianity—for this is all that was allowed in the new Board schools? Parliament had wrestled for months seeking a formula to satisfy those who wanted religion in the schools for the poor but could not allow the teaching of it to be sectarian. In the end they decided to exclude 'any catechism or formulary distinctive of any particular denomination'[7] from the schoolrooms of the rate-supported Board schools. So, for every School Board, an early task was to devise a syllabus based upon the plain reading of the Bible and a few familiar hymns and prayers. At the same time Her Majesty's Inspectors were forbidden to enquire into the teaching of religion and Boards sought ways to check up on teachers and examine pupils without offending local susceptibilities. Inevitably there was friction but teachers (from all backgrounds) and clergy (of most denominations) in most places, most of the time, did their best to make the system work.

Even in the parish schools, the master's work came under new regulations. Voluntary schools wishing to stay on the government grants list could still use 'catechisms and formularies' but when it was seen that children might be forced into these schools, regardless of sect, by the new attendance laws, there was renewed pressure to allow for opting out of these lessons. The 'conscience clause' which governments had tried for years to force on voluntary schools was now imposed by law and it was made tighter by the restriction of religious teaching to the start or end of the school day. Board schools, too, had to adopt the new 'timetable conscience clause'[8] thus opening these schools to minorities such as Jewish pupils.

Perhaps for many teachers it was not, in the end, a matter of high principle. For instance, when John Crosfield moved to Leeds as a Board school master in 1871 and when Edwin Foster was taken on as a Board official in 1872 we can see, in each case, a mixture of motives at work. For William Barnes, though, a much more public, ideological commitment was required. As vicar in a parish with a long-established school he had an immediate local interest in the plans of the Leeds School Board after 1870. In due course, he had a choice of alignments; would he join the clergy in the town who supported the new system—tentatively or wholeheartedly—or would he do his bit, along with a handful of clergy in most of the large towns, to oppose the Board and all its works?

In the next few chapters we shall follow the consequences of the 1870 Act for Barnes and his two friends as they made their choices and completed their careers in this last, eventful period for elementary education in Queen Victoria's reign. However, of the three men let us start with Edwin Foster because he, unlike the other two, experienced some local action in the run-up to the passing of the Education Act in 1870 and was personally involved in a first School Board election in the autumn of that year. The borough councils of the larger towns all agreed, with little hesitation to set their local School Board machinery in motion as soon as the law allowed[9] and in Liverpool, where Foster was working, as in the other towns, there was great drama and excitement.

As an elective body the School Board was a remarkable new invention entirely separate from the mish-mash of committees that made up local government at this time. It was hoped these Boards would have a wider and somewhat different composition from either the borough councils or the Boards of Guardians and so it was arranged that with fifteen members to each large Board, electors would have fifteen votes to apportion as they wished.[10] This gave minority candidates a chance—if they could organize their supporters to 'plump' in their favour. As in the council elections all rate-payers could take part, including women if they managed their own affairs and women could also stand for election. The ballot was to be secret, moreover, a novelty then in Britain. In Liverpool, a city of half a million, some 70,000 were on the burgess list, among them a fair number whose children would be likely to use the Board schools. Given the entanglement of religious with political and social issues in this new civic undertaking, stirrings at all levels of society were to be expected.

So we find that in a commendable display of enthusiasm, 64 candidates were nominated for the first Liverpool School Board that November. The main protagonists were the religious groups; there were 24 Church of England nominees, five Roman Catholic and five nonconformist but no less than 26 'independents'. Named in this last group was Edwin Foster, schoolmaster.[11]

It seems that during his recent time in Liverpool—and in spite of his brush with the Select Vestry in 1869—Foster had shown himself keen to work with his fellow teachers and had won their respect. When, in November 1870, the city was astir with talk of the impending election, teachers were among the groups with an eye to representation. At this point there is some discrepancy between press reports but it seems a large meeting was held in the Hibernian Schools, Pleasant Street on the evening of Friday

11 November under the chairmanship of Edwin Foster.[12] According to the *Liverpool Mercury* these teachers called themselves the Liverpool School Union; the *Daily Post* refers to the Liverpool Teachers Association. Whether two bodies or one, this assemblage was of mixed denomination and while it may have been an outgrowth of an earlier Church Schoolmasters' group in the town[13] a new sense of professional solidarity was evident among them. Foster, from the chair, declared that

> an influential section of the inhabitants of the town were anxious to record their support to the candidature of a schoolmaster.

Aware that there were rumours of a share-out of seats among the religious bodies the schoolmasters, nonetheless, continued with their deliberations and after 'a somewhat lengthy conversation between several of the leading schoolmasters present' the chairman was proposed as candidate.

Edwin Foster then confessed that 'he could not guarantee to devote proper attention to the duties ' without first obtaining the permission of his employers (still the Select Vestry). A second nomination followed, Edward Jones BA, head of the Hibernian School; a third was made and withdrawn. Finally, 'at an advanced hour of the evening' members were called upon to vote, whereupon Mr Jones said that he, too, would withdraw. Mr Foster was 'all but unanimously elected for nomination' and the meeting passed a resolution pledging members to use every effort to secure his return.

However, when the *Daily Post* listed the final nominations both Foster and Jones were there.[14] Foster had done as he promised and consulted with his employers but their reply, asking him to withdraw, apparently came too late for the list to be corrected. It is interesting to note in passing that the objections of the Vestry were based on more than the size of the schoolmaster's workload. One of the vestrymen spoke for the Industrial Schools Committee. It was undesirable, he said, for

> a paid official like Foster to be on a Board where he would probably come much in contact with his employers such as members of the Committee.[15]

In fact there was no direct overlap between membership of the Vestry and that of the School Board at any time but the underlying, social message was clear. Liverpool teachers took the point, and though their union increased in power and influence (as a branch, later, of the National Union of Teachers) they never again put forward a candidate for a School Board election.

Maybe some useful lessons were learnt from all this but the rumours of a denominational share-out proved correct and no election took place. Leading members of the community agreed on the division of seats—seven for the Established Church and four each for the Roman Catholics and the nonconformists. All the independent candidates including Edward Jones were asked to withdraw.[16] Though later elections were contested—there were 70 candidates in 1873—much of the work of the Liverpool School Board after that was conducted in a spirit of gentlemanly co-operation. In Leeds, as we shall see, the whole business was more overtly political and more contentious from the start.

As the School Board set to work in late 1870 and early 1871 Edwin Foster continued with his duties at the Industrial School. His brief appearance as a candidate seems to have confirmed his position as one of the town's leading teachers and in the summer of 1871 the School Board called him in for a series of weekly meetings with some Board school headmasters and several clergy, to advise them on school organization. With most of the committee, Foster favoured the 'triple classification', that is, in place of an infant school plus boys and girls, there would be infants, juniors and seniors. Within these groups, infants and sometimes juniors would be mixed but the older boys and girls were usually kept separate at this time.[17] When it came to the question of numbers it was clear that the Board schools were going to be large. Foster spoke of his experience with 500 at Kirkdale but he recommended departments of no more than 400.[18] In the event there were several Board schools with over 1000 pupils but only one, Arnot Street, exceeded 2000.[19]

It was during this period of consultation with the Board that Foster and his wife received their notice to quit from the Kirkdale Industrial School.[20] What were they to do, with five children to support and no home to live in? Foster should have had no trouble in finding himself a school vacancy somewhere though less easy, perhaps, to find one quickly and as well paid as the couple's joint post at Kirkdale. He must have turned his thoughts at once to the School Board but the problem here was that schools for the Board would not be seeking staff for another couple of years. Those few at present under the Board's control had been handed over by voluntary managers as going concerns. There were, however, posts in administration and Foster was offered one of these in January 1872.[21]

It looks as though someone on behalf of the Board had made him a promise of employment because we find an 'Edwin Foster, book-keeper' sharing a house in Huskisson Street about this time. Though poorly paid, this is work that Foster could have done while waiting for something better. However, when the Board's offer came it was a conditional one, the General Purposes Committee resolving in January 1872 that 'Mr Foster should be appointed as an officer of the Board...for a probationary period of six months'. No other appointments of the large number made at this time were probationary. Was opinion divided, perhaps, on Foster's worth and reliability? The salary, though, was good; at £200 it was equal to that of the best-paid schoolmasters in the town.[22]

His immediate problems were solved, within six months his appointment was confirmed[23] and, on the strength of this, the family moved, some time that year, into a house in Newstead Road, off Smithdown Road, in south Liverpool (Fig. 12). The location was just outside the town boundary, a sensible choice for a man who was to have administrative duties relating to all children and schools within the School Board area. The house itself was one of the new-style semi-detached 'villas', not one of the largest and with only a small backyard but dating from the late 1860s when the patch of ground on the rise above the Toxteth workhouse was first developed.

Because of the slope the back windows of 7 Newstead Road looked out to an open expanse, part grave-yard, part brickfield, with the workhouse in the distance. Not an attractive or rural aspect but the location was fresh and airy. The Board's headquarters were then in the Municipal Buildings in Dale Street and to take Foster to work, horse buses ran from the top of Parliament Street to the town centre, a distance of some three

Figure 12. *Number 7 Newstead Road, south Liverpool, the Fosters' home from about 1872. (Sketch from a recent photograph)*

miles. Into their new family home moved Edwin and his wife Sarah, her sister Elizabeth Flockton, and five children: sons eleven, nine and seven and daughters five and a few months. Four years later their last child Ethel Elizabeth was born in this house.

Edwin Foster's acceptance by the Board as a senior and responsible employee was further confirmed in July 1872 when he was called upon to join a small committee judging architectural plans for new schools. A number of these had been submitted in a public competition announced by the School Board in May that year and three local firms of architects were rewarded with contracts once the plans had been scrutinized.[24] Foster and several headmasters examined the entries with the help of Mr Robson, architect to the London School Board. It was Foster's friend Thomas Mellard Reade (earlier from Melling) who won the Chatsworth Street contract for a site a stone's throw from Foster's home address (illustrated on cover) and Reade went on to build several more Board schools later.[25] The friendship between the two men continued as Reade was appointed architect to the Board, responsible for repairs and alterations.[26] From that time on it was natural that the two men should be moving round the city together on many occasions in their daily work.

In these early months Foster was mainly concerned with the employment of teachers and school organization but in March 1873 the Board created the new post of inspector.[27] In this new role he was subservient to Her Majesty's Inspector who still exercised a great deal of authority over the grant-assisted schools in the town, both Board and voluntary. However, in January 1874 his salary was increased from £200 to £250[28] so that he was now earning rather more than the best-paid schoolmasters but, even then, less than the Superintendent of Visitors (who ran the compulsory attendance machinery) and much less than the Clerk to the Board, an ex-barrister on £400. But this, for Edwin Foster, was at last work commensurate with his abilities; he now had security of tenure and a reasonably good salary. What was expected of him day by day, week by week, in this new post?

Here we have to look carefully at the Board's minutes, for the Liverpool School Board like all the others was trying to devise methods and machinery as it went along, showered with instructions from Whitehall and beleaguered by local controversy over how it should spend the tax-payers' money and run the schools. In the new Act it seemed there were no final answers to any of the deep-rooted problems of financing public education. To the sectarian rivalries so characteristic of this town were added the practical difficulties of enforcing attendance and collecting fees. Then there were the schools' maintenance and running expenses to be carefully watched and the procedures for the selection of teachers and setting rates of pay to be monitored. All these were dealt with as matters of policy by the Board at its monthly meetings but it was the officers and teachers who had to make sense of the flow of directives that came down to them.

When Foster was first taken on in January 1872 it was said that his duty would be 'to act as direct medium of communication between the School Board and the school managers'.[29] Now, many of these managers were either professionals—clergy lawyers or doctors—or small tradesmen and shopkeepers[30] and Edwin Foster should have mixed on easy terms with at least the latter group; this, after all, was the milieu he was brought up in, but the managers, formally appointed as representatives of the Board, held aloof from the teachers and this man who was similar to them in background, the local inspector. So while Foster spent many of his working hours in the company of school managers he did not emerge as their spokesman with the Board. Either the chairman or secretary would communicate direct, a simple process where Board members doubled as managers or where, as so often, they shared business or professional concerns with them. And if there were serious problems the Clerk was called in.

At this stage there was really no-one else at Foster's precise level in the organization and, placed as he was, it was unlikely he could please everyone. Quite early on he was criticized publicly in a Board meeting and though there seems to have been a personal element and little real substance in the complaint the incident was irksome and a warning to him to watch his step. A report appeared in the new journal of the National Union of Elementary Teachers, *The Schoolmaster*, in May 1873, thus:

> The Board has appointed Mr Foster as an inspector to make visits of surprise to the schools and report the results. The Board teachers are far from pleased at this and having conferred with each other have expressed their dissatisfaction. Everything depends, of course, on how these 'surprises' are conducted and reported. There is a wonderful difference between a spy and an inspector—or at least there ought to be.[31]

The London journal went on to quote the *Liverpool Courier* on the subject:

> The official system seems a great deal more likely to annoy the teachers than to benefit the scholars: we do not wonder at the declaration of some of the aggrieved that they will not stand the sort of interference with their work. The Board should be careful not to do anything to lower the teachers in the eyes of the children for such a course could not be otherwise than inimical to the efficiency of the schools.

It was on 12 May that the matter was raised, somewhat obliquely, at a School Board meeting. A tactful member of the Board rose to say that Mr Foster's reports were proving useful but this was quickly countered by Thomas Pritchard who declared that he had heard a great deal of objection to them and that the managers he served with 'looked on Mr Foster rather as a spy'.

The source of the trouble lay within one school and, as it turned out, with one schoolmaster, Foster's earlier colleague, Edward Jones. A whole year before, Foster had resigned as President of the local teachers' association handing over to Jones. Now, as inspector, Foster was on record for reporting Jones to the Board for a misdemeanour—leaving school for a couple of days without permission. The Pleasant Street log book did indeed show the master absent on 16 and 17 April with no excuse given; Jones, though, claimed he had leave from the managers. At the Board meeting it was Pritchard, a manager of the school, who defended Jones and attacked Foster for what he clearly saw as petty interference.[32]

Was this more than a personal squabble? Perhaps so, for the inspector may have been resented as a staunch churchman by the staff and managers of Pleasant Street school which had a long and honourable record in the non-sectarian education of mixed groups of children. In the early 1870s less than half of them were Church of England and the chairman of managers was the influential Unitarian businessman, William Rathbone. Then Pritchard himself was something of an outsider. Brought in to the first School Board as one of two 'token' artisans he, too, was a nonconformist.[33]

Perhaps this kind of reaction against Foster was inevitable but the inspector was warmly defended on this occasion by other members of the Board. The old and saintly chairman, Christopher Bushell, said that Foster was 'a gentleman in whom they had every confidence' and, going on to defend the system, he explained that managers 'were not as a rule practical teachers' and it was essential the schools were looked at more often than once a year on the government inspector's visit, Mr Foster's inspections, he concluded

> would be carried out with every delicacy to the teachers and nothing would be made public save in very exceptional circumstances.

Foster was clearly suffering from his sudden promotion to a level just above that of his previous friends and colleagues and to an office of unproved status—and all this just as the teachers themselves were beginning to flex their muscles in response to the demands of their new employers.

Meanwhile he continued with his duties now firmly centred on the need to monitor the daily work of the schools so that when Her Majesty's Inspector called once a year to examine the children they would perform well and earn the maximum grant. By the end of 1874 there were 16 schools under the Board's control and Foster was required to report on all of them, monthly. Extracts of these reports were regularly sent to the managers.[34]

In this first decade of the School Board's existence there was constant change and expansion. An Organization and Management Committee was set up in 1872[35] and it was to this committee that Foster was answerable in the first place, attending all their weekly meetings from early in 1874.[36] If this were not enough to fill out a heavy programme of work for one man, he was also asked to take on a range of incidental duties. For example, in February 1874 he was set to draw up a list of books for use in the Board's schools[37] and then to design a timetable. In that year, too, he started his important work with the pupil-teachers, checking the capabilities of each candidate before the managers made their appointments.[38] That autumn he was even asked to report on the managers themselves, how often they met and how often they visited their schools. As a result, in August 1874, Pleasant Street school's committee was rebuked for holding no meetings at all for three months.[39]

Before long it became apparent that the work of inspection was too much for one person and the Board resolved to appoint a female 'inspectress'. After widespread enquiries to the various training colleges for women (conducted not by Foster but by the Clerk to the Board) a Miss M.E. Bailey was chosen, at first to keep an eye on the infant schools and the girls' sewing[40] but later to share some of the general duties as well.

Miss Bailey was not typical of the women who, in small numbers, were beginning to take important roles in public elementary education. Her background was London's middle-class intelligentsia and she had acquired her expertise through her work for the Froebel Society. Later she published a small book on Froebel method which was put on the Board's official list in March 1876.[41] By this time, though, the Board had set up a (female) Pupil Teachers College[42] and Miss Bailey left to become Principal, staying in post only a year before returning to London. Her successor was out of the more usual mould for School Board employees. Born to a tailor and his wife in Windsor in 1842, Sarah Yelf had trained as a pupil-teacher and went on to the college at Salisbury. After a spell in charge of a school she returned as vice-principal there.[43] Miss Yelf was Foster's colleague until the summer of 1884.

So, by the mid-seventies Edwin Foster was part of a complex system of management and one very different—as we shall see—from that adopted by the Leeds School Board. That he was by now established as a senior official is shown by an important task allotted to him in 1876.[44] He and Miss Yelf were asked to prepare a booklet on managers' duties to be published as 'Suggestions to the Managers of Public Elementary Schools' based on Liverpool's General Rules but giving advice in line with the best current thinking for all kinds of school manager.[45] A first draft was submitted to Her Majesty's Inspector, locally, for comment in December 1877. Two hundred copies were ordered from a publisher in London and were ready for distribution by September 1879.

Half of this book was taken up with a print-out of the Board's Rules, tables of salary scales and so on, the other half with advice to managers on how to conduct their ordinary duties and their visits to the schools. In these latter pages we find a vivid description of the ideal elementary school, from the best methods of control—'with a look, a gesture or a quiet word' to 'the condition of the atmosphere' and, in teaching, the avoidance of 'leading questions' and impatience with 'slow scholars'. However, much of the expertise is taken wholesale from Fearon's 'Inspection of Schools' published in 1876[46] lending this handbook a certain weight but telling us proportionately less about Foster and Yelf. A new edition appeared in 1880 but few copies were sold elsewhere in the country.

Towards the end of 1879 Edwin Foster and Miss Yelf were asked to draw up a full report on their duties.[47] There were now eighteen day schools (plus two day industrial schools, a truant school and three evening schools) most of them larger and all more closely regulated than the National schools of the past or present. The inspectors were run off their feet.

They told the Board they considered their annual examination of all the schools had 'a salutary influence upon the scholars and upon the teachers'. The inspectors believed this occasion should remain formal but if only some of the children were examined orally and not in all subjects the work could be got through in a half day in all but the larger schools. This, they estimated, would take up six to seven working weeks, summer and winter, using mornings only. Equally formal was the regular examination of the pupil-teachers in a complex pattern fitted around the visit of Her Majesty's Inspector and the timetable of the Pupil Teacher College. But Foster wanted to set weekly tests in the College and to examine exercise books to make sure these youngsters were 'carefully supervised by the headteachers' and were completing the syllabus.

Then there were the 'occasional visits' to schools so much disliked in Foster's early days. He hoped every school could be seen about fifteen times a year and he was confident they could raise the general standard

> by causing the inferior schools to emulate the better ones and by moving the better ones to improved work in order that they might have it exhibited.

This fearsome programme of work was thus designed to put further pressure on the teachers, already apprehensive about the government inspection and the risk of losing status and their personal share of the annual grant—or even 'a year of service' if their school performed badly.

To one side of all this but equally a focus of effort and concern was the teaching of religion in the schools. No longer part of the grant-earning schedules, religious instruction was still close to the hearts of those who administered and those who paid for the Board schools. What were the policies of the Liverpool School Board and how were the inspectors involved? If we look at the 'Suggestions to Managers' we simply find the basic rules starting with the law of the land

> the provisions of the Elementary Education Act of 1870 shall be strictly observed both in letter and spirit viz. that no attempt be made to attach children to, or detach them from, any particular denomination.[48]

With this proviso the Board decreed that prayers and hymns should be used and the Bible read daily

> and there shall be given from the latter, by the responsible teacher...such explanations and instruction in the principles of religion as are suited to the capacities of the children.[49]

As already mentioned the law imposed a double safeguard, no 'creeds or formularies' and the timetable conscience clause, but in Liverpool if there were numerous Roman Catholic children in a Board school they were allowed to use the Douai version of the Bible, as a further concession to religious freedom.[50] It is all the more surprising that school managers were not directed to monitor these lessons, only to see that the main rules were obeyed. So who, if anyone, policed this most sensitive area of the curriculum?

Under the Act the HMIs no longer dealt with religious instruction. The Board was wary of asking clergy—of any denomination—to work regularly in the schools and perhaps because they, too, were a mixed lot the managers were not thought suitable, either. The Board, though, did use their own inspectors trusting them to be both capable and impartial. Was their trust justified?

Before the middle of 1875 there was no formal plan and the schools seemed reasonably content with the prayers and hymns recommended for their use. One headmaster, Edward Jones of Pleasant Street school, had spoken up in 1873 about a hymn book the Management Committee wished to introduce, 'Gems of Song'; it was, Jones said, 'strongly tinted with dogma'.[51] But the question of what was 'doctrinal' or 'dogmatic' was never easily defined and this teacher's objections were ignored.

It was in April 1875 that the Board decided on new plans for a six-monthly examination of each school in both secular and religious subjects,[52] these to be conducted alternately by an inspector of the Board and 'some other person who does not belong to the regular staff' and it was shortly after this that the idea of a syllabus for religious instruction arose. In November that year Miss Bailey was asked to prepare one for the infant schools and to recommend prayers for infants and juniors.[53] In October 1876 she and Foster produced schemes of Scripture references for the pupil-teacher course and for different Standards in the junior and senior schools.[54] There were a few grumbles about this system from time to time but no changes were made.

Foster, though, was personally in trouble with a group of managers several years later. The Granby Street committee under their (Anglican) chairman Revd R. Irving and secretary J. Harrison Jones (a Welsh Calvinist) complained to the Board that the inspector had not only given a lesson instead of examining the pupils but had introduced doctrinal matters.[55] The pattern of Foster's own, mature, beliefs could be relevant here and we should pause for a moment to look at evidence of his churchmanship at this time.

He had clearly strayed some way from the evangelicalism of his boyhood for in the mid-1870s he and his family were attending St Philip's, Hardman Street then under a high church vicar. Very likely they were attracted to this church by the quality of the music for Foster himself was a talented singer and the three boys took various music examinations and were choristers there.[56] The same feature, perhaps, took them later to the ultra-high church St Agnes in Ullet Road after it was built in 1885. How much of this doctrine Foster absorbed we shall never know but the slightest hint of this kind of 'churchiness' in his approach to the children would have been enough to bring down the wrath of most school managers upon him.

On this occasion the School Board took his side. Unsympathetic to the Granby complaint they refused the managers a personal interview and, later, a request that they should be allowed to examine the pupils themselves.[57] So the Board having put Foster in this position of trust were prepared to back him up; to their enemies this was just one more example of Church of England bias and all along the churchmen on this Board seemed unassailable. Not so the Anglicans in Leeds where, as we shall see later, Revd William Barnes had a difficult few years representing the church on the Board for this town.

There were no more important changes in the pattern of Edwin Foster's work but with the government ready to support an ever-widening curriculum and with more pupils and more schools each year the strain upon him increased all the time. In February 1884 he was granted an extra £50 a year 'in consideration of the increasingly difficult work now devolving upon him'.[58] His salary, which had been £250 a year since January 1874[59] was now £300 and by 1884 the two inspectors had two full-time assistants. One, Elizabeth Frater, a joiner's daughter from the north-east, was a pupil-teacher in Liverpool for some years but trained at Durham.[60] The other was Duncan Ferguson, son of Neil a prison officer, who had spent a couple of years as a Poor Law official while Foster was at Kirkdale. Duncan would have come to Foster's attention as an exceptionally bright pupil-teacher by the mid-seventies (if not already known to him through his father), and he emerged, after his apprenticeship, at the top of the nation-wide order of merit list for college entrants in 1879. From this lofty position he chose to spend his two years training at Cheltenham from where he passed out, again, first class. By 1891 he was Duncan Ferguson MA (Trinity College,

Dublin) but it is worth noting that he was given a responsible role under the School Board without ever being in charge of a school.

In 1884, too, there was a change of female inspector. Miss Yelf became mistress of the new Liverpool undenominational training college for women in Durning Road and Miss Shirley (from the college at Derby) was appointed to her place as inspectress and Principal of the Pupil Teacher College.[61]

While Foster's little empire expanded in this way in the 1880s strains upon him were compounded by a series of family tragedies. Since the death of their fourth son as an infant in Melling the family with six children lived uneventfully in their south Liverpool home, the three boys attending the Liverpool Institute School. But in December 1882, Edwin Flockton, the eldest, working then as a bank clerk, died at home of scarlet fever. His younger brother, Arthur Edward, shortly after leaving Cambridge, died of consumption in Mentone, France in March 1887. A few months later Ethel Elizabeth, aged twelve, died at Ramsey, Isle of Man, of a similar affliction. And sometime in the intervening years the Fosters lost their eldest daughter Florence Mary. Perhaps she went abroad for there seems to be no record of her death (or marriage) in the British Isles.

By the spring of 1888 Edwin and his wife had one remaining daughter at home, eighteen year old Gertrude Eliza, their second son Herbert was in India and Elizabeth Flockton was still with them. About this time Foster's health began to fail. On 5 April the School Management Committee decided to grant him six months leave of absence.[62] Some time before Ethel's death in 1887 the Fosters had moved home, leaving Newstead Road for a more substantial house nearby in Arundel Avenue (Fig. 13). Here at number 41 there were more and larger rooms and they now had use of a small garden at the back (but they were still, in 1891 without a living-in servant). A narrow path and a small gateway led through to the Toxteth Park cemetery behind the house; from their upper back windows the Fosters could, if they wished, look out to where Edwin and Ethel were buried. Much later in 1921 when Sarah Foster died, Gertrude arranged for a new headstone to be erected and it now stands bearing the

Figure 13. *Number 41 Arundel Avenue, south Liverpool, the Fosters' home from the mid-1880s. (Sketch from a recent photograph)*

names of her parents and the other six children of the family all of whom predeceased her.

Returning to the late 1880s we find Edwin Foster back from his leave, still frail but under the same pressures as before. There were now more than twenty Board schools and though Foster was helped by two assistants and his female colleague he was constantly on the move round the city and on call for official meetings. By the end of 1889 he had found it necessary to resign as librarian to the Liverpool Geological Society, a post he had held for thirteen years.[63] Though he never wrote any papers for them he worked assiduously behind the scenes and in the Society met some of the town's leading citizens including members of the School Board and their clerk, Edward Hance. On a more personal level, he shared this hobby with Thomas Mellard Reade, the architect who had been his friend since Melling days.[64]

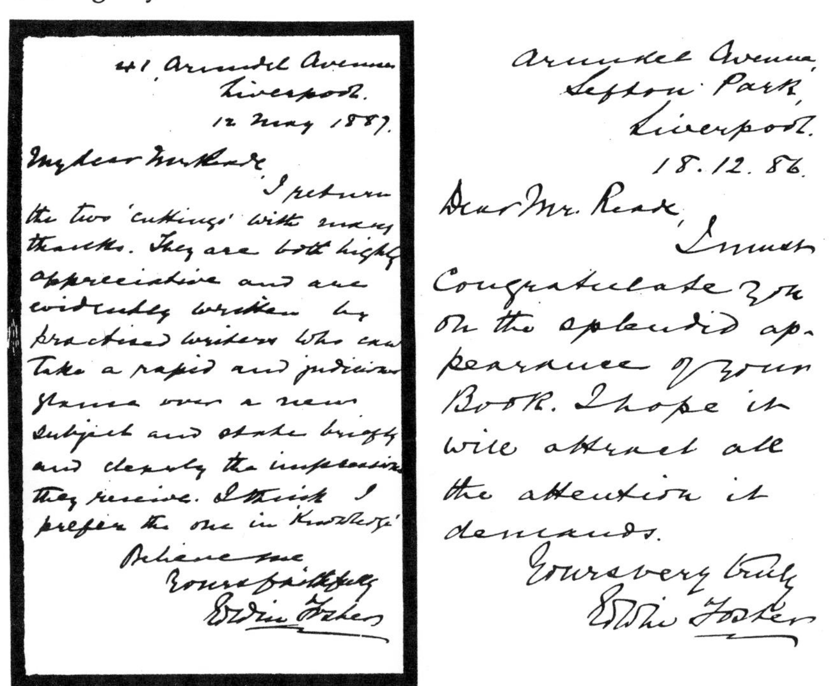

41, Arundel Avenue
Liverpool.
12 May 1887.

My dear Mr Reade,
I return the two 'cuttings' with many thanks. They are both highly appreciative and are evidently written by practised writers who can take a rapid and judicious glance over a new subject and state briefly and clearly the impressions they receive. I think I prefer the one in 'Knowledge'.

Believe me
Yours faithfully
Edwin Foster

Arundel Avenue,
Sefton Park,
Liverpool.
18.12.86.

Dear Mr. Reade,
I must congratulate you on the splendid appearance of your Book. I hope it will attract all the attention it demands.

Yours very truly
Edwin Foster

Figure 14. *Two letters written by Edwin Foster to his friend Thomas Mellard Reade. The black border around the first marks the death of his son Arthur; the book somewhat obliquely praised in the second was Reade's 'The Origins of Mountain Ranges', 1887*

Then, early in 1890, while Ferguson was studying for his degree—and in deference to Foster's needs—the Board resolved to appoint a second male inspector. They chose Arthur Thomas Bott from Bede's College, Durham,[65] a few years older than Ferguson and much more experienced. As master of the Model School, there, Bott was lecturer, demonstrator and organizer of teaching practice for all the students. Son of a humble gas-lighter in London, his early training was at St Mark's Chelsea, the high church college mentioned earlier (Chapter IV). By the time he came to Liverpool he had an Oxford BA (non-collegiate) and, like Foster, he was an accomplished musician.[66] The two men became good friends in the last few years of Foster's life.

For both these inspectors and their colleagues life in the early 1890s world of elementary education in Liverpool was complicated by an administrative crisis in the town's schools, the result of some misguided decisions on the part of the Liverpool School Board in response to new government provisions for free education. The essence of the problem lay in the Board's plan to run free and fee-paying schools side by side—an administrative nightmare. On one occasion the Clerk to the Board was called out early in the morning to deal with a crowd of angry parents but it was Foster and his team who coped with the daily chaos in the schools.[67]

The strain was too much for his weakened condition and Foster, now aged fifty-nine, took to his bed in the summer of 1893 and he died on 9 July of the same kind of consumptive illness that had claimed two of his children. He was buried in Toxteth cemetery in the family grave on 13 July and the local papers reported an impressive turn-out of teachers and officials; the chairman and vice-chairman of the Board were there, Foster's old friend Reade, and his sister Mary from Wakefield with her second husband, Joe Haslegrave. As the *Mercury* said, 'The gathering was indicative of the feeling towards Mr Foster with those with whom he was brought most closely in contact'.

The final ceremony was preceded by a choral service at St Agnes church in a display of ritualism which must have been repugnant to the many evangelical clergy and laymen in the assembled company, not least the chairman of the Board, Revd Major Lester. But whatever their feelings about his churchmanship, latterly, Board members spoke well of Edwin Foster's 'experience and knowledge of his work, his mastery of detail and his knowledge of teachers'. He was, they said,

> always a friend to (teachers) and took pleasure in promoting their interests. His work was quiet and unobtrusive but he was indefatigable in its prosecution and he brought to it geniality, kindness and tact.[68]

One of the clergy members of the Board, Revd F.B. Tyrer, said later that Foster's work had contributed to the success of both the voluntary and the Board schools[69]—a remark wholly in keeping with the attitudes of this very church-oriented Board and fitting for this man whose religion was so obviously central to his life as a public official.

Edwin Foster's widow, Sarah, her sister and her daughter settled into quiet obscurity. The only remaining son, Herbert, whose work in India will be described later, was granted special leave and came home for three months at the start of 1894. However, as he died not long after and Gertrude remained a spinster, unless Florence had given birth to a child in some foreign place, there would be no direct descendants to give personal witness to the life and achievements of this particular Victorian schoolmaster.

XI

William Barnes and John Crosfield in Leeds

1870–1872

In Leeds, as we have seen in Liverpool, the passing of the Education Act in 1870 opened up a new arena for local politics, laid down a challenge for civic leaders, churchmen and rate-payers and promised new scope for hundreds of teachers in the elementary schools. The particular duties and the strains which came with Edwin Foster's promotion at this time have already been described. William Barnes, on his arrival at Leeds, was soon caught up in School Board affairs and his brother-in-law John Crosfield who followed him a couple of years later as a Board school headmaster, was at once drawn into the machinery of this new and powerful administration. With another twenty years or so ahead for these men let us look first at the settling-in period for Barnes who arrived first.

After two peaceful years in Westmoreland with the new status of a clergy family the Barnes were now back among city streets. They were here at the invitation of the Marshall brothers, flaxspinners of Holbeck, a family with roots in the eighteenth century merchant community. John Marshall (1765–1845) had been a Unitarian but, like the Armitage descendants in Farnley the next generation were firmly Anglican. It was the younger sons James Garth and Henry Cowper Marshall who, at their own personal expense, built the church of St John the Evangelist, Little Holbeck in the late 1840s.[1]

If Barnes hoped for something grander by way of a parish he must have realized that such were not on offer to clergy of his kind of background, however able. As an ordinand his status had been of the lowest, a 'literate' without formal training in a university or theological college.[2] But there was no doubt that he was needed in Holbeck. Up to the mid-1840s the parish of Leeds had a population of more than 150,000. There were 21 churches then but 18 were without 'cure of souls';[3] if pastoral work was done at all it was by private arrangement between the incumbent of the chapelry and the vicar—and only a third of the churches had a residence for the clergyman. All the working-class areas were poorly served, but Holbeck and Little Holbeck were both independent parishes by 1850 and this area, though drab, was not as poverty-stricken as nearby Hunslet.

The new parishes owed their existence to the self-sacrificing zeal of Revd Walter Farquhar Hook, vicar of Leeds from 1837 to 1859. Though Hook disliked the extremes of the Tractarian movement,[4] he was a high-churchman at heart and he had a rough passage, at first, with the townspeople. Within a few years, however, he had won the respect of his colleagues and of many nonconformists, too. But greatly distressed by the spiritual state of the vast and growing population he foresaw 'large and festering masses of heathenish ignorance and vice' if the church failed to reach out to the working population of the town.[5]

By the end of 1843 Hook conceived a plan to divide the living and give to each church its own parish while he would retract much of his own personal influence—and income—from this huge area and continue simply as vicar of the old parish church of St Peter.[6] He retained the patronage of most of the churches but when St John's was built it was kept in the hands of the Marshall family. Though these wealthy men had moved their residence from near their old premises in Meadow Lane to New Grange (now Beckett Park) in 1805 they continued to oversee the flax manufactury, school and church for most of the nineteenth century.[7]

The church which was to become Barnes's care in 1870 had been consecrated on 2 November 1850 by the Lord Bishop of Ripon. As appropriate to the industrial neighbourhood it had been designed with a plain exterior but the interior was decorative with polished marble columns and stained glass in all the windows. Serving a population of 4000–5000 the church could seat 565, most on the floor area, some in small gallery[8] and, under Hook's Act of 1844, all the seating was free; no-one, not even the incumbent, could draw money from pew-rents.

Even more important for the Barnes family was the parsonage house, purchased and rebuilt by the Marshalls in 1863.[9] Though in a low-lying, industrialized corner of the city near to the railway, the house was substantial; with its own grounds, by far the most spacious accommodation the family had yet enjoyed, while church and school were a minute's walk away. When the census was taken in 1871, Revd William Barnes and his wife Margaret were at the parsonage with Horace William (aged nine) and William Arnold, now two years old. There were two living-in servants (aged 15 and 25) but the elder girls were away, possibly at school. Another daughter, Sarah Ellen, was born later that year and a son, Richard Hibbert, in 1876, bringing the family to six. When Barnes came to Leeds the living was worth £250 a year, soon raised by the Marshalls to £300.[10] With a clergyman's incidental earnings the new vicar was able to pay out some fees for school and university in due course but he accepted financial help from his wealthy friends at least once more in future years.

We should pause now to consider if Revd William Barnes was chosen for more than his obvious capabilities and his experience with working-class people. Were the Marshalls looking for a distinctive style of churchmanship, for example? Barnes was their fourth vicar but there is nothing on record to suggest an established tradition for this church, either high or low. However, Barnes later described himself as Broad Church and there are good reasons for supposing that someone of this particular orientation would have been acceptable to his patrons.

The term Broad Church seems to have been used first in 1853 and it embraced those in the Church of England

> who were interested in science, in Biblical criticism, in a rational approach to religion and were leaders in the attempt to relate the Church's teaching to the new thought and conditions of the nineteenth century.[11]

With this set of intellectual attitudes went a certain tolerance, a dislike of party labels, social conscience and a wish to see churchmen of all kinds working together for the common good. These were all characteristics of families like the Marshalls who came into the Anglican church from Unitarianism and whose stance was somewhat different from that of the Armitage family, for instance, who came to it from Baptist nonconformity and who were strongly evangelical.

Important in this context was a family connection, Revd Frederick Myers, whom John Marshall chose for a church he built in Keswick. Myers became a prolific writer and spokesman for the Broad Church; his 'Catholic Thoughts on the Bible and Theology' were reprinted over several decades.[12] Myers died in 1851 but an edition of this essay in 1879 still carried the 1841 Preface. In it he set out the underlying question

> whether the Idea of the Christian Church includes as essential a mediatorial priesthood...or exclusive caste of any kind through which alone the blessings of Christianity can be conveyed and received.[13]

Myers addressed himself earnestly over the years to those who felt that, on the contrary, spiritual responsibility should rest with individuals, the belief, as he saw it, at the centre of Protestantism.[14] But he parted company with some of the narrower evangelicals (like Revd Francis Close, Dean of Carlisle[15]) in his attitude to human learning. This activity was not—as some would have it—opposed to spiritual insight, nor was revelation imperilled by 'honest and reverent criticism'.[16]

It is not known, of course, whether the two Marshall brothers who built the Holbeck church had accepted this as a kind of family orthodoxy nor what exactly they saw in the young William Barnes in 1870. Much of his intellectual development was yet to come but it seems likely he was moving away from the more rigid evangelicalism of his mentors before that date into a churchmanship which sympathizers would call liberal or progressive and its detractors 'latitudinarian' or 'indifferent'.[17]

If this was indeed Barnes's caste of mind as a new vicar in 1870 how would he fare with his new colleagues in the town? What he found was a very diverse group of clergy, both major parties represented but with many who were ready to set aside their differences. And, they were fortunate in leaders who, through strong individual men, did not encourage the rank and file to take up divisive attitudes.

Overlooking them all was their father in God, Robert Bickersteth, the Bishop of Ripon. Diligent and devout, he was viewed by the evangelicals as one of their sort but he tried nonetheless to be bishop of a diocese rather than bishop of a party.[18] It was, however, the successive vicars of Leeds whose influence was most directly felt in the town. Though losing some of their power under Hook's Act they gained from their status as rural deans, the town, under its vicar, almost a sub-diocese.[19] And following Hook there were three more high church vicars; in Barnes's time, James Woodford (appointed in 1868) and John Gott who took over from 1873.[20]

It was Hook who first set the tone for the acceptance of a high church minority in the town and though he and his successor met opposition from leading evangelicals at St George's, these antagonisms had died down by the time of Barnes's arrival In any case, it seems there was no focus, here, for the kind of militant Protestantism that was so strong in Liverpool.[21] Vicar Woodford strove for 'union of life and teaching' among his clergy insisting that once a year in Lent they should preach in one another's pulpits.[22] Then, to bring the community together he set up a Conference of Clergy and Laity in 1870 soon after Barnes's arrival.[23] John Gott, who 'loved Leeds even to its smuts' also wanted to encourage good relations between the churchmen in his area[24] so it was not difficult for a newcomer like Barnes to work his way towards acceptance. He seems to have been on good terms with his nearest colleague, for instance, Revd Nicholas Greenwell at St Barnabas Holbeck, one of the town's leading ritualists,[25] and we shall see as the years went by how he was drawn into co-operation with numerous other clergy in his work for the School Board. Two of them should be introduced at this point.

One of these men was Revd Samuel Flood, vicar of St Matthew's, Camp Road. He had trained first as a surgeon but took Holy Orders in 1846–47 and was appointed to the parish where he stayed until 1880. Looking ahead to that year, his departure from the town was marked by a display of admiration and respect from men and women of all persuasions. Revd Barnes was one of the subscribers to 'testimonials' which, with a large public meeting, was organized by a Presentation Committee; among its members was John Crosfield, then resident in his parish. Flood seems to have been a genuine non-party man and, according to Revd Gott, 'The church has few parish priests...who have devoted their lives more fervently to lead the working classes godward'.[26]

Another cleric who was important to Barnes and a key figure in Leeds education for even longer, was Revd Edward Jackson, vicar of St James. As a young adult Jackson travelled for his father's tobacco firm but in 1837 he became a Sunday School teacher. In 1845 he was ordained as a curate under Hook at the parish church and three years later, still without formal academic training, he was granted a 'Lambeth degree'. Jackson at first seemed inclined towards the high church—he even joined a community for celibate clergy created by Dr Hook for St Saviour's—but later he could be seen regularly on evangelical platforms. By the mid-fifties he had purchased the proprietary rights for St James and, in this central area 'strewn with social wreckage' he set up elementary schools and taught classes of young men, 'turning mill-hands into gentlemen' and sending out from Leeds a stream of clergy, teachers and missionaries.[27] Jackson said later that he had known Barnes as a young man at York[28] and this cleric was certainly in the background when Barnes came to Farnley for he was connected to the Armitage family as a devoted god-father to William James (the son of James and manager of the Iron Works school in the late 1860s).

So Revd William Barnes when he came to Leeds in 1870 must have felt both welcomed and challenged. However, though Leeds that autumn was astir with preparations for its first School Board it was too early for Barnes to push forward with his broader views on education and he applied himself straightaway to the needs of the children in his own parish. By the middle of October he had stepped into his role as manager and official correspondent for Marshall's factory school,[29] a remarkable institution which had served the work-force and the parish since early in the nineteenth century.

John Marshall the elder had been a pioneer in this field, setting up a school near his factory in the 1820s. A stream of children from the youngest to those in their teens, some his employees, some not, passed through the day, evening and Sunday schools in the succeeding decades. By the 1870s, Marshall's was generally regarded as a church school and all Barnes's predecessors at

St John the Evangelist took an active interest in its well-being.[30] From 1854 Her Majesty's Inspectors confirmed that it was in the upper ranks of elementary schools at this time; by 1871, Marshall's took in more than a thousand day pupils and 750 part-timers.[31]

Revd Barnes made his first official visit to the school on 18 October and he was back again with James Garth Marshall on 21 October. Thereafter he was in the school several days a week and, as might be expected, taking a strong managerial role. Early the next year there were visits from the School Board[32] and ten years after that, when Barnes himself had moved into public life as a member of the Board, the school was taken under their jurisdiction. In the meantime it worked with considerable success under government inspection and Barnes's capable management. However, as early as the end of 1871 Barnes's own role had begun to widen to that of spokesman for the needs of elementary school children throughout this area of south Leeds.

We must now retrace our steps briefly to explain the origins of the Leeds School Board, William Barnes's involvement with it and John Crosfield's arrival in the town. In 1869 when it seemed as if legislation was inevitable, politicians at Westminster and local activists were trying to find reliable measures for the obvious inadequacies in school provision for the working-classes. Liverpool had been surveyed for this purpose by D.R. Fearon HMI; he also covered Manchester while J.G. Fitch HMI was dealing with Birmingham and Leeds. By March 1869 Leeds MPs and townsfolk had the benefit of a detailed report.[33]

Fearon had produced an estimate of the shortage of places for children of the 'poor' in Liverpool as somewhere between 13,000 and 30,000 and the data that Fitch collected suggest that the situation for Leeds was no better. At one point he speaks of a morning's walk through some of the worst streets in the town where he counted, between the hours of ten and twelve, no fewer than 900 children (apparently under twelve), unoccupied and uncared-for. He concluded as follows:

> ...it has become impossible for me to resist the conviction that a large field remains yet unoccupied and that of the portion already enclosed much of it is most unskilfully and imperfectly tilled.[34]

By the start of the Education Act debate in February 1870, members of Parliament for Leeds were thus well-briefed on the needs of their constituency. Edward Baines the Liberal MP, now a man of seventy, and William Wheelhouse, Conservative, were both in favour of the Bill, Baines declaring it would 'raise the character, intelligence, morals and prosperity of the people at large'.[35] As a one-time voluntaryist, Baines was ready to concede the justice of allowing a denominational sector to continue teaching its own precepts but he was prepared, now, to support rate-aided schools with religion in them provided it was like the 'Bible Christianity' taught with such success in the nation's British schools over the years.[36] With his fellow nonconformists he was, however, suspicious of the local clergy should they achieve significant influence in the new administration and his paper, the *Leeds Mercury*, was ready to do battle against them.

At this stage, however, the church was offering no threats. The Bishop of Ripon told his clergy in October 1870 that they should be deeply thankful for the Education Act. Attempts to destroy the denominational system had 'signally failed' while the idea of religious education 'was firmly rooted in the public mind'. Speaking at the Conference of Clergy and Laity that month in Leeds,[37] the vicar, Canon Woodford, was again, conciliatory—the church should set itself to work the new legislation 'thoroughly and honestly'—but he urged his colleagues to mobilize their resources to take advantage of the final six months in which building grants would be available. There was no suggestion that churchmen should try to undermine the work of the School Board but all could see the prospect of conflicting interests. Nonetheless, Revd Barnes's patron, James Garth Marshall, looked forward to a School Board where men would set aside 'the old bitter feeling that had so long existed between the two great sections of Christianity in England'. He was, of course, referring to orthodoxy and dissent; no-one in Leeds saw the Catholics as serious opponents in this field.

It is therefore not surprising that when in November the Town Council received the go-ahead from London to form a School Board, local churchmen were poised to offer names and support for candidates, but at some point it seems they agreed—in line with colleagues in Liverpool and elsewhere—that the clergy themselves would hold back. A date was set for the election and the various parties planned their campaigns and booked halls for meetings. In mid-November a group of prominent citizens called a 'town meeting' to try and agree a set of fifteen names to go forward as the first School Board without election. As in Liverpool, where this tactic succeeded—the once—there was much high-minded talk about non-party action for the common good. But old habits asserted themselves, it was clear there was no consensus and soon a Conservative/Church faction was facing a stronger group of Liberals, mainly nonconformist. A final list of 38 was made up of five official church candidates, eight Liberals, two Roman Catholics and a variety of others including some 'working men' and two ladies.[38]

The town's elementary schoolmasters were, of course, awake to the implications of this new rate-setting authority and one of their number wrote to the *Yorkshire Post* complaining that they had not been approached when the Yorkshire Board of Education (a voluntary body) were considering candidates. However, at a meeting a few days later, certificated schoolmasters of all denominations declared themselves satisfied with the 'gentlemen of influence, Christian principle and practical acquaintance with popular education'[39] who were coming forward and they declined to take independent action. A more deferential group than their colleagues in Liverpool they simply agreed to support those candidates who declared in favour of religious education. In spite of the 'general feeling' noted by the Bishop there was a faction among the nonconformists who wanted to see religion kept out of the rate-aided schools altogether.

On the Friday before the School Board election a 'magnificent meeting' for the church candidates took place in the Victoria Hall.[40] Vicar Woodford was in the chair; one of the five selected for this role was William James Armitage, ironmaster of Farnley. William Barnes, his employee two years earlier, was in the hall with Revd Edward Jackson and about twenty other clergy. They were there, said the vicar, because upon the religious education of the children depended

> the social order, the good government, the domestic peace and security of every family in the realm.

At this point, Woodford, the high churchman, went on to commend the kind of plain Bible teaching in the schools which many clergy (and some laymen) had declared would be spineless and inadequate. But with the church staking a claim to places on the Board it was no more than good sense to follow the Bishop's lead and declare public support for the exclusion of 'creeds and formularies' as set out in the new regulations. How the policy would work in practice no-one yet knew.

On Monday 28 November the *Yorkshire Post* reported less excitement than was usual for a council election but the polling booths were busy, some 20,000 burgesses coming forward out of a possible 45,000. Those in Barnes's section of the Holbeck Ward went to the Mechanics Institute in Sweet Street where

> almost all the voters seemed to be aware of the gravity of the (occasion) and to discharge their suffrages with perfect intelligence.

Some women brought papers signed by their husbands but were told the men must return, themselves, after work. There were a few cases of 'personation' but 'the utmost quiet and order' prevailed. The voting papers were collected up in carpet bags and conveyed to the Town Hall where 64 clerks counted the votes between 6.30 p.m. and 7.00 a.m. the next morning.[41]

All five church candidates were returned and all were near the top of the the list according to votes received, W.J. Armitage second only to John Jowitt, wool merchant and respected superintendent of a Congregational Sunday School.[42] But neither main party had grasped the complexities of the plural voting system; Jowitt was not one of the eight official Liberal candidates; only two of these carefully-chosen men were returned and they appeared at the bottom of the list of fifteen with a solitary church outsider. So while the church party made a good showing at this first important election their final strength of six still left them in a minority and the Liberals swept into action at the start of 1871 for the first of three triennial periods of office in which they shaped the town's new education system.

Influential on the Board, however, was the single church outsider, Revd J.H.F. Kendall, vicar of Holbeck and Revd Barnes's close neighbour. As the Leeds clergy had decided to hold back from representation he had received no support from them—nor from the Conservative party—but he was popular with a group of Conservative working-men in his parish. Once elected he took on the challenge of the new compulsory attendance system, a godsend to the managers of church schools who always had trouble filling the places so expensively provided, and his diligence impressed everyone.[43] The siting of new schools, a related problem, was from the first a highly contentious matter between the Board and the church and it seems that at an early stage Kendall turned to Barnes to act as spokesman for the needs of their particular locality.

In fact, Barnes's first appearance as an education expert for the church was on 13 December 1871 in a deputation to the School Board organized by the vicar of Leeds. With him were just four men; Revd Henry Temple, vicar of St John's, Revd Kelk of St Stephen's Burmantofts, Revd Samuel Flood of St Matthew's Camp Road.[44] Temple, an Oxford man, had spent some years as headmaster of Worcester Grammar School and he had taken a turn as Diocesan Inspector for the area but compared with Barnes's experience of elementary schools, his was remote and second-hand.

Wishing to co-operate with the Board without provoking rivalry, the town's churchmen were nonetheless unhappy with some of the Board's early plans. Clergy at a Deanery meeting had drawn up a list of points to be raised, starting with an urgent plea that new schools should be placed at some distance from the old. Having studied the Board's new schemes they judged the staff 'establishment' too high and the pay too generous. On religious instruction their demands were modest, simply that all teachers, right down to the apprentices, should be free to take part. All these points and some others were presented in the form of a memorial bearing 57 signatures. William Beckwith, a free Methodist, at once declared that the clergy had come in a 'meddlesome and dictatorial spirit', their viewpoint 'sectarian and narrow', but he was persuaded to calm down; the matter was deferred for further discussion, then quietly dropped.[45]

It was in this same month, in the run-up to his second Christmas in Leeds that William Barnes stepped into the controversy over school provision in Holbeck, Hunslet and Beeston. By then, the School Board had embarked on plans for 25 schools, with a detailed scheme for salaries, instruction and so on, placing children meanwhile in a scatter of temporary schoolrooms hired from churches and chapels. Using the official Fitch report the Board was trying to estimate local need with enough accuracy to justify the large expenditure soon to be made from the rates. Sub-committees were set up for different areas and they designated as one 'locality' the 'Potter Street site', a little to the east of Barnes's church and partly in Hunslet. Here, the Board planned to set down a school for 700 children. Working locally to promote the scheme was Board member, Jabez Woolley, a Wesleyan builder with a house in Hunslet.[46]

The argument over population data—numbers of children, where they lived, age and class—and capacity in existing schools, went on for several months within the Board, between the Board and the Education Department in London, involving Revd Pickard HMI, the local inspector of returns, Board members and Revd Barnes. In a letter to the *Leeds Mercury* of 23 December, Barnes questioned some figures given by Woolley at a Board meeting the day before. The matter was a small one—a miscalculation for half-timers at Marshall's school—but the thrust of Barnes's argument was that the area did not need a new school at all, a view shared at that time by all the officials, local and central. Barnes set out his own calculations adding a PS:

> I do not call into question the goodness of Mr Woolley's intentions; no-one has more sincere respect for his uprightness of purpose than I have.

Woolley replied just after Christmas with a return of courtesy to Revd Barnes: 'Above all, let us not fall out by the way lest we hinder the good work...', and he gave a set of corrected figures which, he maintained, still showed a deficit of more than a thousand places. Barnes must have spent much of the Christmas period, when not in church, in his study for in a long letter of 28 December he dissected the argument further, taking the position not of a churchman but of an ordinary ratepayer:

> The building of schoolrooms for 400...to say nothing of their maintenance cannot cost much less than £1,500 and the ratepayers of Leeds...have a right to demand the utmost economy...

Nearly all the public opposition to the Board's plans from church sources over the years was phrased like this. Among themselves, though, churchmen deplored the weakening of their sectarian hold over the masses as children of the lower classes flooded into the Board schools. As Revd Cookson of St Matthew's, Holbeck, put it several years later:

> We are fighting the Church's battle at great odds (against) Board schools close to us with grand buildings, good teaching staff and an unlimited purse.[47]

This was to be the reality for churchmen in the large towns and it is greatly to their credit that so many of them worked so hard for the dual system. As for the Potter Street site, a school was built there eventually but in the meantime the Board pressed ahead with the opening of thirteen temporary schools. A first few hundred children were thus taken off the streets and into the schoolrooms—the Board's first visible achievement.[48]

These schools were to open in January 1872 and before Christmas the Board placed advertisements for male and female teachers. From 136 schoolmaster applications twenty were selected, ten were called for interview and eight were appointed. Most were from church schools in the midlands and north but in this final group were two Londoners and teachers from two Wesleyan schools and one British. In spite of objections from the clergy, the men were taken on at £150 per annum; the women, however, were offered only £75—an unusually wide differential.[49]

One of these schools was in Sheepscar Street, a mile north-east of the town centre and the new schoolmaster here was John Daniel Crosfield from Knutsford, now with a first-class certificate, division two. Like so many of his peers who came into the towns to work for the new School Boards at this early stage, Crosfield found conditions worse, not better, than he was used to. His school for four whole years was a Congregational chapel built in 1858 on the corner of Sheepscar Street and Barrack Street; behind it was a metal works and for a quarter of a mile south there were gas and chemical works, a foundry, a tannery and a shoe factory. For several hundred yards round the school there was only back-to-back housing or small terraces.

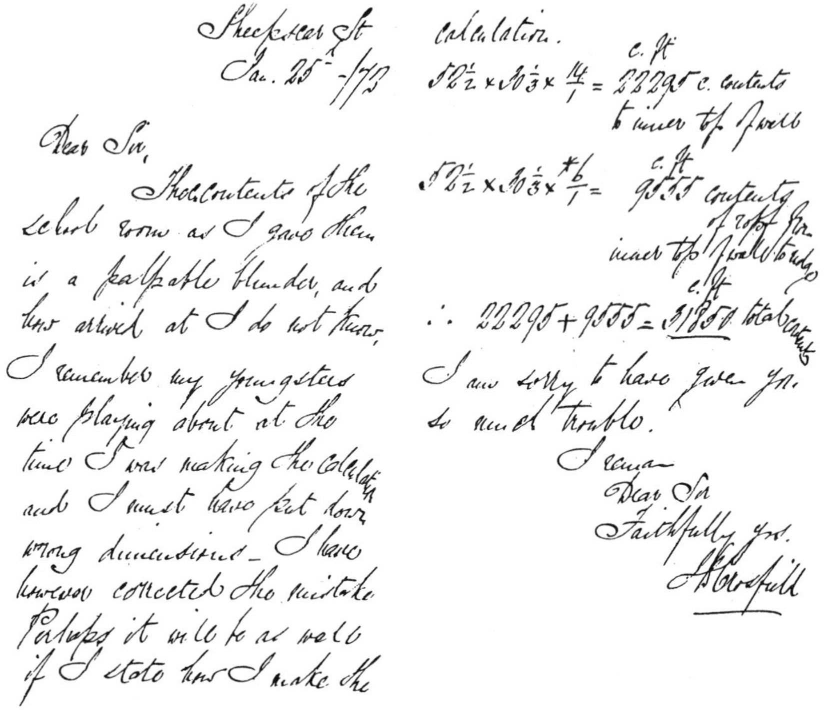

Sheepscar St
Jan. 25 – /73

Dear Sir,
The contents of the school room as I gave them is a palpable blunder, and how arrived at I do not know. I remember my youngsters were playing about at the time I was making the calculation and I must have put down wrong dimensions – I have however corrected the mistake. Perhaps it will be as well if I state how I make the calculation.

$52\frac{1}{2} \times 30\frac{1}{3} \times \frac{14}{1} = 22295$ c. ft contents to inner top of walls

$52\frac{1}{2} \times 30\frac{1}{3} \times \frac{6}{1} = 9555$ c. ft contents of roof from inner top of walls to ridge

$\therefore 22295 + 9555 = 31850$ c. ft total contents

I am sorry to have given you so much trouble.
I remain
Dear Sir
Faithfully yrs.
J Crosfield

Figure 15. *Letter written by John Crosfield to the Education Department in London explaining some errors in his 'return' on the dimensions of his school in Sheepscar Street, Leeds in 1873*

The chapel had doubled as a school under a board of trustees and was not, apparently, inspected; now unoccupied weekdays, it was offered to the Board in late 1871 for a rent of £30 per annum, while retained for use by the Sheepscar Independent Society evenings and Sundays. The schoolroom desks were made 'convertible into forms with backs' for the Sunday school, the reconversion to be completed each week by 9.00 a.m. on Monday.[50]

With the pulpit looming over it, this average-sized schoolroom took, at first, some 80 boys and 80 girls, but there were two classrooms for them to overflow into. All the same, the Inspector noted in November 1872 that although the school had begun well, it was really too small for the numbers of children.

Nonetheless, by late 1875, at the end of Crosfield's stint here, he had won this accolade from the Inspector:

> The greatest credit is due to the Master for the work that he has done here under such disadvantageous circumstances. The scholars have passed an excellent examination...and the teaching is most thorough and intelligent.[51]

During this lengthy settling-in period the Crosfield family lived in a small street tucked away between Roundhay Road and Tramway Street to the north, a few minutes walk from the school. Though less than ten years old Artillery Terrace was no more than a double row of two-up, two-down cottages. There were no porches or bay windows at the front but the ten houses at the Roundhay Road end of the street were somewhat larger with small back extensions. Number seven, the Crosfield's house, was one of these (Fig. 16). At the back of each house was a small yard; at the front a small square of garden, the front gates facing each other across a narrow path. The occupants of this road (in 1881) were small tradesmen or skilled artisans and not one house had a living-in servant. In number seven were John Crosfield and his wife Caroline and their four children, Louisa Augusta (now fourteen), Helen Maud (ten), Harry Arthur (seven) and Walter Harold (four). (Note the reference to these 'youngsters' in Crosfield's letter in Fig. 15).

It seems that John Crosfield attached himself to the local Teachers' Association very soon after his arrival in Leeds and in January 1874 he was one of a group of schoolmasters who wrote to the Board asking for an increase of salary. The men stated that the cost of the 'necessaries of life' had risen by 20 per cent to 25 per cent since their appointment on £150 per annum and they also claimed recognition for working hard and efficiently with 'ill-adapted buildings' and inexperienced teachers. A month later the Board approved increases to £175 for most who had applied, including Crosfield.[52] Two of the churchmen on the Board voted against the move; there would be many occasions thereafter for this party to resist what they saw as 'extravagance'.

Thus it is clear from the mid-seventies that with William Barnes associated with the church faction on the Board and Crosfield a humble employee, the ties of affection between the two families could be under some strain. Apart from anything else, they were now living a couple of miles from each other across the city centre in houses very different in style and comfort. The social and economic gap between them was to widen even more as John's wife Caroline and the young Crosfields, in turn, were caught up in the work of the town's Board schools and yet again as Revd William Barnes himself was elected publicly to the Board.

Figure 16. *The southern end of Artillery Terrace, north Leeds. The Crosfield family were here from 1872 to about 1875. (Sketch from a photograph of 1966)*

1872–1879

Though William Barnes had taken a great step forward socially in moving to Leeds as vicar of Little Holbeck, we find him in the mid-1870s somewhat less in the public eye. The reason is not far to seek. Some time in 1872 he signed on as a student of Trinity College Dublin to work for the university degree that was so clearly within his powers. Trinity was an obvious choice; for years this Irish university had made provision for non-resident students from England, many of Barnes's colleagues among them.[1] But for the new vicar there was still the cost to be considered—fees, travel, books and so on—and, more seriously, Barnes would need a curate to take over some of the parish work while he was closeted with his books. Once more, we are told, he was beholden to his friends for assistance.

Between 1872 and 1878 Barnes employed two young men as curates, both of them the beneficiaries of the same kind of patronage that he had received. John Harper, who came to him in February 1872, was the son of a wool-sorter in Halifax; he went to Hatfield College Durham between 1869 and 1871 and Barnes took him on after his ordination at a salary of £110. In February 1875 he engaged the services of Francis Ratcliffe Harpham, son of a local farmer, who was trained at St Alban's Hall, Oxford. Harpham, who was brought up a dissenter, was a protégé of Revd Edward Jackson by whom he was re-baptized in the Leeds parish church at the age of twenty-four.[2]

Whatever these arrangements precisely, the records at Dublin show that William Barnes was able to graduate as Bachelor of Arts in 1876. But his ambitions went further than this; opting for one of the 'professional' courses he went on qualify, that year, LL D (Doctor of Laws), and was known thereafter in Leeds as Revd Dr Barnes.[3] It is strange that he did not simply choose theology and he may have intended this at one stage for he won the Elrington essay prize in 1877 writing on 'The Literary Contest of the Early Church with Paganism'. But it seems he had wider intellectual interests and perhaps he already saw for himself a secular, political role in the town where he was vicar, one to which 'law' would bring a useful set of skills.

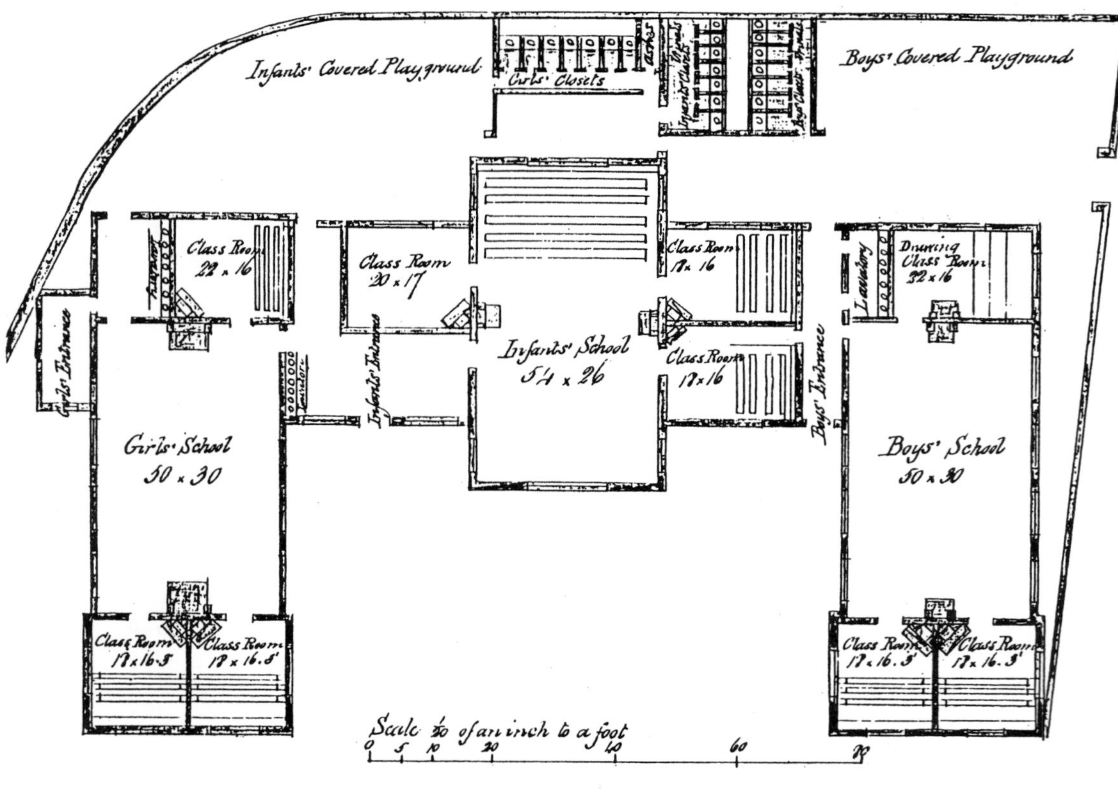

Figure 17. *Plan of the new Sheepscar Board School, Chapeltown Road, Leeds c. 1875 as drawn by Crosfield himself in his 'return' to the Education Department in London that year.*

If we now retrace our steps to pick up the threads for John Crosfield we can see that his life was also on the up-turn. Back in 1871, just before he arrived in Leeds, a Sheepscar church, St Clement's, had set out plans for a new school for 500 children as part of the strenuous efforts by local clergy to pre-empt School Board building. By 1873, though, these plans had foundered and the Board was free to press ahead for a new school in Roundhay Road to replace the one in Sheepscar Street. It took the Board a little while to convince the authorities in London that Sheepscar, though on the outskirts of the town, was an area of growing population,[4] but permission was given at last, building started, and Crosfield took up his duties in the new school on 15 November 1875[5] (Fig. 17).

For John Crosfield, now forty-one years old, here was a new challenge to his professionalism. Three-department schools had been common enough—Christchurch, Liverpool was one such—but the lay-out of this new Board school was conspicuously more generous compared with the cramped and overshadowed building where Crosfield and Barnes had their early schooling. With a frontage of about 170 ft, the one-storey structure favoured by the Board at this time, contained three large schoolrooms, each with three small classrooms attached. The Board was, naturally, criticized for extravagance for this and other schools of the period. Revd Kendall wanted all the roof heights lowered[6] and the Department had tried to forbid the use of 30 ft wide schoolrooms, considering 20 ft quite sufficient.[7] But the Leeds School Board went ahead with what they hoped would be pleasanter, more airy rooms. They even gave the infants ten square feet of space, each, when the regulations permitted eight for these smaller children. When completed, the new Sheepscar school was a handsome brick building faced with stone; the roof of dark Westmoreland slate had a bright red edging. In place of the old schoolroom stoves there was a central heating boiler in the basement giving welcome warmth in the winter.

In May 1876 members of the School Board made a visit of inspection. There were, by then, about 800 scholars on roll (in three departments—boys, girls and infants) rather less in average attendance; discipline was excellent and some of the adults present confessed themselves outclassed by the older boys solving problems in Euclid.[8] Later that year the Inspector commented that although there had been a large influx of children 'who had received little instruction'—the school was obviously needed—examination results were good. The headmaster, it was said, 'displays great zeal and his efforts are well-seconded by the teachers'.[9]

By the mid-seventies Crosfield was at the peak of his powers, an accomplished teacher and, to use the old phrase, 'schoolkeeper'.[10] Moreover, he was now drawing his family into the profession with him and the process started with his two daughters. Louisa had been a pupil-teacher at the Board's temporary Nether Green school since 1873 while Helen Maud was apparently receiving private tuition somewhere. With the opening of the girls department in their father's school both girls entered as pupil-teachers under Miss Coxe in 1876.[11]

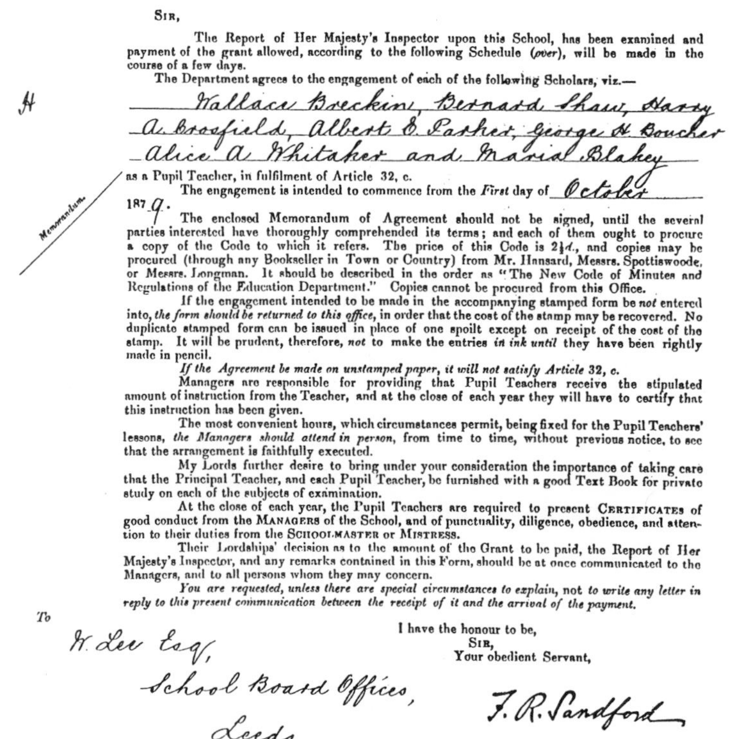

SIR,

The Report of Her Majesty's Inspector upon this School, has been examined and payment of the grant allowed, according to the following Schedule (*over*), will be made in the course of a few days.

The Department agrees to the engagement of each of the following Scholars, viz.—

H Wallace Breckin, Bernard Shaw, Harry A. Crosfield, Albert E. Parker, George H. Boucher Alice A Whitaker and Maria Blakey

as a Pupil Teacher, in fulfilment of Article 32, c.

The engagement is intended to commence from the *First* day of October 1879.

Memorandum.

The enclosed Memorandum of Agreement should not be signed, until the several parties interested have thoroughly comprehended its terms; and each of them ought to procure a copy of the Code to which it refers. The price of this Code is 2½*d.*, and copies may be procured (through any Bookseller in Town or Country) from Mr. Hansard, Messrs. Spottiswoode, or Messrs. Longman. It should be described in the order as "The New Code of Minutes and Regulations of the Education Department." Copies cannot be procured from this Office.

If the engagement intended to be made in the accompanying stamped form be *not* entered into, *the form should be returned to this office*, in order that the cost of the stamp may be recovered. No duplicate stamped form can be issued in place of one spoilt except on receipt of the cost of the stamp. It will be prudent, therefore, *not* to make the entries *in ink until* they have been rightly made in pencil.

If the Agreement be made on unstamped paper, it will not satisfy Article 32, c.

Managers are responsible for providing that Pupil Teachers receive the stipulated amount of instruction from the Teacher, and at the close of each year they will have to certify that this instruction has been given.

The most convenient hours, which circumstances permit, being fixed for the Pupil Teachers' lessons, *the Managers should attend in person*, from time to time, without previous notice, to see that the arrangement is faithfully executed.

My Lords further desire to bring under your consideration the importance of taking care that the Principal Teacher, and each Pupil Teacher, be furnished with a good Text Book for private study on each of the subjects of examination.

At the close of each year, the Pupil Teachers are required to present CERTIFICATES of good conduct from the MANAGERS of the School, and of punctuality, diligence, obedience, and attention to their duties from the SCHOOLMASTER or MISTRESS.

Their Lordships' decision as to the amount of the Grant to be paid, the Report of Her Majesty's Inspector, and any remarks contained in this Form, should be at once communicated to the Managers, and to all persons whom they may concern.

You are requested, unless there are special circumstances to explain, not *to write any letter in reply to this present communication between the receipt of it and the arrival of the payment.*

To

W. Lee Esq,
School Board Offices,
Leeds

I have the honour to be,
SIR,
Your obedient Servant,

F. R. Sandford

Figure 18. A Section of Her Majesty's Inspector approves the engagement of Harry Crosfield as a Pupil Teacher at the Sheepscar Board Shool in 1879

The life of an apprentice in a Board school in the 1870s was remarkably little changed from that of a pupil-teacher in the first decade after 1846 when Crosfield and his friends were boys. But the Crosfield girls were presented with a somewhat wider curriculum. Letter-writing was now included under 'Composition' and history was started earlier. Candidates for the college entrance examination (the old Queen's scholarship) could now offer one of four languages and a science while drawing and music were optional. Examinations, though, still tested a mixture of the abstruse and academic with the relevant and practical and, as from the start, less was expected of female candidates.[12] Then, shortly after the two girls were appointed, the regulations were changed to allow a shortened course (of not less than two years) for young people coming in with a good education[13] and in 1878 the minimum age of entry was raised to fourteen.[14] Harry Crosfield—as will be recounted later in Chapter XII—came in under this new rule.

As for ordinary classroom life it seems this, too, was much like it had been since the 1860s, with payment-by-results still firmly entrenched. However, post-1870 Codes had made the tests for each Standard a little more demanding.[15] What is more, while schools had earned grant money for passes in a range of 'specific' subjects since 1867—geography, history, science, languages and branches of mathematics for example[16]—the Code of 1875 took this process further with the introduction of 'class subjects' individually examined and rewarded.[17] For teachers like Crosfield (and Barnes in his day) a syllabus going well beyond the 'three Rs' was nothing new but for the post-1870 generation of teachers these changes were all part of a long, slow, move to raise academic standards in the elementary schools and, in due course, to replace individual testing by general assessment of the school.

In this period of renaissance for elementary education, with John Crosfield in a substantial post and his daughters in training, the family's situation was looking brighter in every way. By the spring of 1876 the girls were earning around £15 to £20 a year. Their father's salary was put up to £200 in February 1876;[18] a month earlier his wife Caroline had been appointed examiner in needlework for the Board's infant and girls' schools. For a salary of £50 a year she was required to work five afternoons a week, or more at the discretion of the Clerk.[19]

Mrs Crosfield had apparently been visiting the nearby Alfred Cross Wesleyan school as sewing teacher up to the end of 1875. This school fed into the new Sheepscar school in 1876 and her duties as examiner brought her into the department where her two daughters were employed. It seems she had no great influence over her elder daughter for on 29 November (the headmistress's log book tells us) Louisa Crosfield and two other girls

> spent the entire sewing hour this evening in playing and laughing. For the future they will sew in the main room...[20]

The mature careers of the two Crosfield girls will be described later (Chapter XII). Returning to the family, we find them moving house about this time, choosing Studley Terrace, about a quarter of a mile north of their old home but still within easy walking distance of the school in Roundhay Road. Here the Crosfields were among a superior clientele listed in a Directory of 1877 as 'Court' rather than 'Trade'; several of the households—another schoolmaster, two Professors, a commercial traveller, a coal agent and a linen-draper—had living-in servants. The Crosfields' help was a young woman of twenty-one.

It is clear, though, that Studley Terrace had quite recently come up in the world and it was hardly on a par with the area of superior villas and terraces immediately to the north across Leopold Street. All the Studley Terrace houses and those in the parallel streets were built after 1862 when a large tract of land was sold off by Lord Cowper to developers. The odd-shaped area to the south of Leopold Street and backing on to the Cavalry Barracks, was not considered suitable for high class development. It was sold off rapidly and cheaply and on individual plots as small as 268 sq. yds were built a curious mixture of through-houses and back-to-backs.[21] On the east side of Studley Terrace, the Crosfield's house, number nine, was one of the larger ones. On a frontage of about 20 ft the plot went back about 28 yds giving room for a small square front garden and a backyard. The ground plan of this house was only slightly larger than that of their previous one but with a bay window, steps up to the front and back doors and a commodious cellar it was obviously a superior dwelling.[22]

Meanwhile, as the decade drew to its close, the Leeds School Board and its employees could look with pride on all that they had achieved. There were now some 17,000 children in daily attendance in voluntary schools (two-thirds of them in church schools) but a further 18,000 or so were in the 45 Board schools erected and run at public expense. Admittedly the best efforts of Revd Kendall and the school attendance staff had not been able to fill the schools every day, but nonetheless vast inroads had been made into the problems of an expanding, illiterate and uncultured working class. John Crosfield himself was one of a team of 106 qualified headteachers in the Board schools; along with 56 certificated assistants and 76 uncertificated the Board employed no less than 504 pupil-teachers and candidates. It was to be some years before the balance in the profession, anywhere, swung to the adult, qualified teacher but the Leeds School Board could, in 1879, claim a pupil-teacher ratio in the low twenties as compared with a national average of more than thirty.[23]

The autumn of 1879 thus saw the Crosfields secure in the new, advancing profession of elementary school teaching. Edwin Foster was now at full stretch working as inspector for the Liverpool Board, both men greatly indebted to those who had laboured to set up these new local authorities and keep the machinery in good order. But all the School Boards in the large towns had been set up in late 1870 and a fourth election was imminent. Constitutionally, the Liverpool Board was the more stable with a denominational majority for the whole 33 years of its existence.[24] In 1879 and 1880, as we have seen, this Board was conducting an important review of practice and re-writing their rules. In Leeds, though, churchmen continued to fight a rear-guard action and the 1879 election was as contentious as any. William Barnes had just emerged from his long spell of academic study and was ready to offer his services to the Board should there be church—and public—support for his election.

Going back for a moment to the end of the Leeds School Board's first triennial period of office, it was already clear, then, that all pretensions to a non-sectarian, non-party system had been shed. If there were to be religious factions controlling the town's elementary schools then, the church party decided, there was no further need to keep the clergy under wraps. In 1873, two more clergy came forward to join Revd Kendall[25] and all three served again from 1876.

So we find that in November 1879 when Revd Dr Barnes, resplendent with his new degrees, was proposed as a candidate for the Leeds School Board the old battle-lines were clearly drawn between the church and unsectarian parties.[26] The campaign arguments fell into a predictable pattern. On one side, facts and principles were used to build up a picture of a successful, orthodox Board, after nine years adhering scrupulously to the Act and giving a generous, unsectarian education to half the town's poor. On the other side, different facts and principles were invoked to show that the Board was hostile and harmful to the schools which educated the rest of the children, that religion as taught in the Board schools was sketchy and ineffective and that the Board was extravagant, unfair to ratepayers in general and to church ratepayers more than any.

But if certain arguments recurred in a predictable way, the personal alignments were far from clear. Determined to keep control, the official Liberal party fielded eight candidates but one of them was a churchman. The Conservatives backed five Church of England men, including William Barnes[27] whose politics had always been on this side of the great divide (unlike those of his employers, the Marshall brothers, who were churchmen but also prominent Liberals). Meanwhile, to confuse the picture further, both Revd Edward Jackson and Revd Flood chose to stand as independents—and they were not acting in unison. (Kendall, one of the churchmen from the previous Board, had died earlier that year). The only constant feature was the pair of Roman Catholics who, each election, could rely on plumped votes to get them in.

What can we find in the ensuing formalities of the election campaign to reveal the character of Barnes himself or of the men who were his allies? Public meetings for candidates were not usually occasions for debate but important claims were made. The campaign for the Church of England team was launched in the Mechanics Institute, Holbeck on November 11th[28] and Revd Barnes spoke first. He took up his stand against those who saw the churchmen as 'interfering' in the work of the Board—members of the controlling Liberal group who were accusing the church party of plans to indoctrinate the pupils with their own, sectarian views. Barnes was indeed concerned about the state of religious education in the schools; it was not what it ought to be, he declared, and could not result in much good to the moral character of the children—but he and his colleagues protested they had no wish to bend the rules on the use of 'formularies' in the classroom. On the theme of economy, Barnes challenged the Board's expenditure on its new offices and on the salary of the Clerk, recently raised to £700 per annum. Hundreds of men, he said, could be found to do the work as well for half as much.

Revd Barnes returned to the religious question at a later meeting in the Victoria Hall chaired by the vicar of Leeds Revd John Gott.[29] He pointed out that the Leeds Board, unlike some others (Manchester and Liverpool) had no scheme for checking on the religious teaching in the schools since this aspect of the curriculum had been taken out of the hands of the Inspectorate. Barnes was intent on improving the system and without breaking the rules; no-one had the right, he said, to 'impugn their integrity and truthfulness' on this question.

Later in this meeting an issue was raised that would cause trouble for Barnes and his colleagues in the coming months. It was already well known that some School Boards were designating 'higher' schools for the better class of pupil, and the church party in Leeds were united, for the moment, in opposing this trend. Revd Wood declared it would deflect resources while crowds of poor children still roamed the streets; underneath was a lurking suspicion that the brighter and more tractable pupils would be enticed out of the voluntary schools.

Meanwhile, Revd Jackson, now in his sixties, conducted a lone campaign. He reminded his supporters of his long experience in the town. He and a friend had set up a school for poor children in 1838 and he praised the Leeds Board for carrying the work forward in the interests of the nation as a whole.[30] All the expense was justified, he felt, even the Clerk's salary. And Jackson thought it was quite fair that the managers of church, Wesleyan or Roman Catholic schools should pay something to make these distinctive schools their own—a view uncommon among churchmen. He also found himself aligned with the Liberals over religious education; unlike his friend Barnes, he was quite happy with the way the Bible was read in the schools according to the old, British school principles. Another day he even spoke up for the policy of 'higher' Board schools; if education for the masses were not extended how could the nation compete in the world's markets? Revd Jackson, commanding massive support in the community was, nonetheless, a genuine independent.

As usual the newspapers sent their men round to the polling stations for the voting on 23 November. At Holbeck, where Revd Barnes was suddenly an important public figure, it was observed that 'a crisp covering of fresh snow' gave the neighbourhood 'a more wholesome aspect than it usually presents'. The report in the *Yorkshire Post* went on: into this community of 'honest and prudent industry and robust family life' had come a candidate whose educational experience and qualifications would make him a valuable addition to any School Board.[31] The turn-out in Holbeck was 2,988 voters, just under 50 per cent of the householders qualified to vote and slightly fewer than the percentage city-wide. But the polls had closed at 4.30 p.m. and though many working people took the afternoon off it was not easy for those with the strongest direct interest to record their votes.

On 25 November, the Conservative-owned *Yorkshire Post* was glad to report 'a splendid and complete victory for the friends of fair play'. Leeds, they said, 'has spoken with a voice of thunder'.[32] All but three of the Liberal candidates were defeated. The five churchmen were all returned with the two Roman Catholics, two Wesleyans, Revd Flood and Revd Jackson. Perhaps overconfident, the Liberals failed that year and now a Liberal majority had given way to a denominational one of nine to six. Here was a chance for the church party and their new colleague, Revd Dr William Barnes, to put their ideas into practice.

1879–1882

The December of 1879 ushered in a new era in School Board administration in Leeds. At the first meeting of the newly constituted Board[1] Revd Samuel Flood was voted chairman and one of the church laymen, William Rothery, his vice-chairman. More contentious was the question of who should lead the all-important Education and Management Committee. The Liberal minority group stepped in first with the name of Revd Edward Jackson but Revd Wood put down an amendment that Barnes should be chairman and the Liberals were outvoted. Barnes may have been uneasy displacing his old friend but he knew his capabilities and the expectations he had aroused. At the next meeting on 8 January 1880[2] he was on his feet at once with arguments and proposals emanating from this committee.

This new work for William Barnes, the parson and experienced schoolmaster, was so intensive and his diligence so marked we can hardly do him justice with the small selection of events that can be mentioned here. Let us start with a financial matter and a chain of decisions that he would be called upon to defend later. While payment-by-results still dominated the schools, the Board's work was judged most publicly by the examination results achieved and the grant earned; local ratepayers much preferred to see the money coming from general taxation, for what could not be earned in this way or from the children's pence, came out of their own pockets. As always, staff were the most important element and Barnes was not happy that previous Boards had exercised the right kind of selection or control.

At his first Board meeting as spokesman for the Committee, he moved to tidy up an anomaly; seven young teachers straight from college had been appointed en bloc, not even their names minuted. There were no obvious vacancies but places in schools were found for them. Told they were needed as a 'reserve' Barnes pointed out there were now plenty of applicants for every post and by the end of that year he had drawn up a tight new schedule for the staffing of the schools (Fig. 19)—efficient, as he saw it, and economic. His aim, he said, was to advance 'the thoroughly competent and deserving' taking into account for each master or mistress qualifications, length of service and size of school.[3] Unfortunately the scheme led to a slight increase in the overall pupil/teacher ratio and this brought trouble for Barnes in a few years time.

Meanwhile, this old hand in school management also knew that teachers would benefit from close supervision. Back in 1873 Revd Kendall had pointed out the Board would need an inspector 'if the work were to be properly done'. At the end of 1874 they made an appointment, choosing from 200 applicants Alfred Murray, headmaster of the endowed school at Wentworth, South Yorkshire. For £200 a year he would work under the Clerk, take in applications for relief from fees, direct the attendance officers and visit the Board schools, leaving his comments in a special book.[4]

It can be seen at once that Murray's 'inspection' was much less thorough than Edwin Foster's in Liverpool. Not only was Foster spared all the fees and attendance duties, he also spent much time in the classroom, with the Education Committee and with the committees of managers based in the schools. Moreover, it was exactly at this time that the Liverpool School Board took on a second, female inspector. It was two whole years before Caroline Crosfield was appointed to supervise needlework and she was not replaced by a qualified 'inspectress' for the Leeds schools until 1884.

The difference in managerial style is interesting. William Barnes who, in the old days would probably have favoured professional oversight was now, as a clergyman, trying to strengthen the lay element. Earlier, we find W.J. Armitage, who had used Barnes as 'manager' for the Farnley schools, briefly, after his ordination, advocating 'schools managed by persons appointed by the School Board' (on the Liverpool pattern) and he also favoured 'enlisting the co-operation of ladies'. Though greeted by cheers in 1870[5] this suggestion was set aside and two years later teams of 'managers' were assembled, two or three Board members for a group of schools.[6] This half-hearted scheme was doomed to failure and in May 1880, in Barnes's first year of office, he put forward a new proposal that Board members should visit the schools in a regular and systematic way. Had he studied Edwin Foster's book on management, newly published in Liverpool? It seems likely, but even with a new schedule for 'visitors' the scheme was never really effective.[7]

Using his expertise more directly Barnes tried to improve the elementary teaching in the schools. In the summer of 1881 he decided to encourage the use of the new phonic system for teaching children to read considering that it 'abridged the time of acquiring the mechanical and intellectual art of reading by about one year' while helping to eradicate 'provincialisms' in the speech of the pupils. Barnes arranged that any teacher using this system effectively should receive a prize of £5. At the same time he offered a prize of £4 to infant teachers adopting the Froebel or Kindergarten system, an innovation also being promoted by the Liverpool Board at this time.[8]

He was even more concerned to extend the academic range and depth of the curriculum, generally, in the schools. Towards the end of 1881 he persuaded his colleagues to employ a new, graduate inspector's assistant cum science demonstrator[9] and he offered to teach a Latin class himself in what had been Marshall's and was now Little Holbeck Board school.[10] It was about this time, too, that Barnes turned his attention to what we should now call 'in-service training'. Yorkshire College (later Leeds University) already made provision for 'occasional students' in various ways. Reporting for 1881 the College welcomed

> efforts in this new session by the College staff in conjunction with Revd Dr Barnes...and other members of the Board to interest certificated teachers in the means of instruction here.

Saturday and evening classes for teachers were now well-supported and for the next session there was to be

> a complete curriculum of classes preparing for London University Matriculation on Saturday mornings for a moderate fee.[11]

Through schemes like this, Barnes and others were offering new rewards to the ordinary elementary school teacher and, of course, new benefits to their pupils. But the task of raising the aspirations and the practical and intellectual competence of the mass of the first-generation educated was a more complex one.

At the lowest level in the schools were those children about to leave for work; for them it was agreed that only the barest minimum need be provided but what should that minimum be? In May of Barnes's first year on the Board they were debating which Standard to insist on before pupils could be released for part-time work at the age of ten. Some Boards asked for Standard II or III; Barnes found himself opposing—unsuccessfully—a proposal for Standard IV. He would have settled, in fact, for Standard I, having seen (in his parish, presumably),

> many cases of extreme distress where it would have been simple cruelty to have pressed full-time attendance and a pass at Standard IV.[12]

With little support from the Board he nonetheless forced a concession for the children of families in the direst need, provided that all such cases were brought before the Board.

Though reluctant to force schooling on the poorest families Barnes fought hard to widen opportunities for the rest as his arguments were to show when, in due course, he lent his weight to the promotion of higher grade Board schools for the town in 1882. Offering specialized subjects beyond Standard VII, several of these schools already existed elsewhere[13] and some discussion about them had already taken place, publicly, and within this School Board.

For instance, back in 1874, the designation of three Board schools as 'higher' had provoked a rather silly argument about fees. Revd Flood had raised objections; two of the schools were in his area and at Wintoun Street the Board had a placard offering 'a thorough English education' for 6d a week—twice the average Board school fee. Flood, with his own St Matthew's school to run, was sensitive to this competition for the most promising children of the district. He claimed 'a mischievous principle' was at work, these schools not only costing the ratepayer more but serving just those families that the Education Act was designed to exclude. The nonconformist leaders of the Board simply retorted that it was up to them to charge the highest fee the locality could bear—and all the placard meant was 'higher fees'. Faced with this rejoinder, Flood switched his tactics to demand they set the highest possible fee of 9d and cover thereby the schools' real costs.[14]

In fact, though irritating to local clergy like Revd Flood, these 'higher' schools did not go far enough in extending the curriculum to satisfy those—William Barnes among them—who wished to see real benefits for the town's poorer children and it was Barnes who raised the issue again just before the demise of the 1879 Board. Let us see what he had in mind and how his proposals were received. It is worth quoting his speech as reported for it represents the considered views of one whose experience in public education was unique for a man of his social position. He started by making a clear distinction between the majority of children and the rest. There were those, he said,

> who would come hereafter to manual labour...they should start life as fully equipped for their work as possible, by a knowledge of reading, writing and arithmetic and by the ability to take an interest in the affairs of the State. For the great mass of people a perfect education of a limited kind was the only one suited to them.

Then, he went on:

> Over and above that large class there was another large and important sector the children of shopkeepers, foremen, clerks and skilled artisans who desired for their children a higher education, not more thorough but more extensive. These people formed a very large and important class: they were highly respectable. Many would be prepared to make the sacrifice of a higher fee.

And then, most significantly, from the depths of his own experience, he commended to the Board

> a third class of children whose circumstances were comparatively straitened but who had been gifted by nature above the average intelligence of ordinary children. These were the boys and girls who under adverse circumstances had worked their way to the front. Lest the noble seed which was planted in these children should perish a free opportunity should be given to them of cultivating their gifts to the highest point...poverty should be no bar.

Barnes concluded with the bones of a practical scheme:

> A School Board might take part in a system of links which enabled a boy to pass on from the poorest schools to the highest places of education in the country.[15]

Note how positively Barnes defines the lower middle class, that sector of society that he at first aspired to, then passed beyond, as schoolmaster and cleric, to reach a position where he could now pronounce upon their worth, their attitudes and their needs. In fact, by 1882 (as Chapter XII will show) when this speech was given there was already some extra provision for the children of this social group in Leeds and tenuous links were in place for a small number of poor but gifted pupils. Returning to the meeting, we can see that Barnes report was adopted, though Mrs Buckton, the Board's only woman and a strong-minded Unitarian, produced the standard arguments against such an elitist plan—that it would be socially divisive and the money would be better spent at the lower levels. However, with a new Board imminent, no further action was taken.

Before moving on to the next and final phase of William Barnes's life as a School Board member, we must review in some detail his actions on a matter even closer to his heart—religious education. First, the background to his accusation in 1879 that the teaching was 'unsatisfactory'. At the end of 1871, just before the first batch of temporary schools was opened, the Board issued some rules for the religious teaching which the law now declared should take place at the start or the end of the school day. Prayers and hymns would be selected by the Board; explanations of Bible readings should be 'suited to the capacities of the children' and given by headteachers only. Teachers were expected to include 'the principles of morality and religion' but on no account should they try to 'attach the children to or detach them from any denomination'.[16]

Even this plan, based on that of the London School Board, was beset with difficulties. The secularists still insisted that religion should be left entirely to ministers and clergy. The Roman Catholics were unhappy about the doctrinal content in hymns (like Edward Jones in Liverpool, from another point of view). There were arguments about the use of the Lord's Prayer and churchmen were still vainly asking for the instruction to be shared with assistants and pupil-teachers. By March 1872 they were struggling with the question of supplying Bibles;[17] were children to have copies or only the staff? Eventually it was agreed that pupils from the third Standard upwards should have their own Bibles to read and the Lord's Prayer was admitted that April.[18] But the whole issue came to the surface again in 1875.

In spite of the negative pull from the secularists there seemed to be a constant need to define and redefine the religious element in the Board's curriculum, the churchmen always hoping to extend its range, the nonconformists to set up further safeguards. The plan in late 1875 was as follows: nine o'clock hymns and prayers, a Bible lesson according to an approved course, pupil-teachers to attend with scholars and to receive at least half-an-hour of Bible instruction a week, out of school hours. These apparently innocuous proposals led to weeks of bickering, sometimes good-natured, more often not.[19] When someone protested that argument was untimely and would lead to strife, Revd Flood retorted that 'nearly every good law in the country was brought about...after discord, discussion, variance and ill-will'.

The idea of Board-approved prayers seemed to have fallen into disuse and now a Methodist, Harrison, objected to teachers free to offer up prayers of their own devising when some of them, he said, were 'unacquainted with experimental religion'. Supporting him, Legg, a Wesleyan, agreed there were teachers 'who never prayed for themselves'. 'Really Mr Legg', the chairman interposed, 'we can't assume we have only a lot of heathens under the School Board'.

Meanwhile, Revd Jackson was prepared to trust the teachers; in forty years, he said, he had never met a more conscientious body of men and women. He persuaded the Board to allow them to use the Lord's Prayer, by itself, if they wished. Revd Flood, though, who could not leave well alone, tried to forge ahead with a scheme like that of the Manchester Board with a complete list of texts and set forms of morning and evening prayer. Nearly two years later, Jackson again declared his confidence in the teachers; at a prize-giving he said 'the reading of God's Holy Word was done reverently and with great intelligence and impartiality'.[20]

During the 1876–79 triennial passions seem to have cooled and shortly before the 1879 election which brought William Barnes on to the Board, Revd Flood was able to persuade them to accept 'a graduated system of Bible instruction' as used by London and the church-led Boards of Manchester and Liverpool.[21] In spite of mutterings about 'denominational influence' only Mrs Buckton voted against the motion. A scheme was drawn up and presented to the Board on the 6 November but like so many end-of-term proposals it was set aside for the next Board to consider.

Thus the scene was set for Revd Dr Barnes to take on this important matter in his new capacity as chairman of the Education Committee in 1880. After another deferral on 15 December, members were asked for their views at a meeting in April. Mrs Buckton came in first with a long series of objections; she wished to scrutinize all the examination questions set, while John de Morgan asked to check through all the hymns. Barnes protested that they had tried 'honestly and sincerely to avoid the slightest appearance of violating the rights of one sect or another' and wisely he suggested that discussion be deferred once more.[22]

When the scheme came back to the Board in May 1881 the main elements were these: headteachers would instruct the older pupils, assistants and pupil-teachers the rest; pupils, according to age, would learn by heart hymns and moral songs, the Lord's Prayer, the Ten Commandments, passages of Scripture and several psalms. All the children and the pupil-teachers would be examined by the Superintendent, Alfred Murray, and prizes awarded if funds could be obtained from voluntary sources. The model here could well have been Liverpool where Foster was involved as inspector and where the Liverpool Council of Education gave prizes for Scripture.[23]

William Barnes said, at the start, that he hoped for consensus—a matter such as this could not properly be governed by a simple majority. He argued at length, referring back to the House of Commons debate of 1870,[24] that no feature of the present scheme could possibly be held to contravene the law. If any such clause were found,

> he himself would be the first to move that it be removed from the scheme.

Mrs Buckton came back at once; the scheme was 'full of dogmas'. As a Unitarian she could not accept the phrase 'through Jesus Christ our Lord' as it occurred in so many prayers, with the idea of mediation and propitiation. She claimed it was a 'formulary', to be excluded by the Cowper–Temple clause in the 1870 Act. Revd Barnes pointed out, quite reasonably, that the phrase was in common use among Anglicans, Catholics, Wesleyans, Baptists and Independents and that it was accepted by some of the abler Unitarian divines (he named two). John de Morgan, who was also concerned about doctrinal content, formally proposed that

> the scheme of religious instruction is a distinct and clear violation of the Education Act of 1870 and is calculated to give false and erroneous ideas to the children.

but no-one seconded his motion, not even Mrs Buckton.

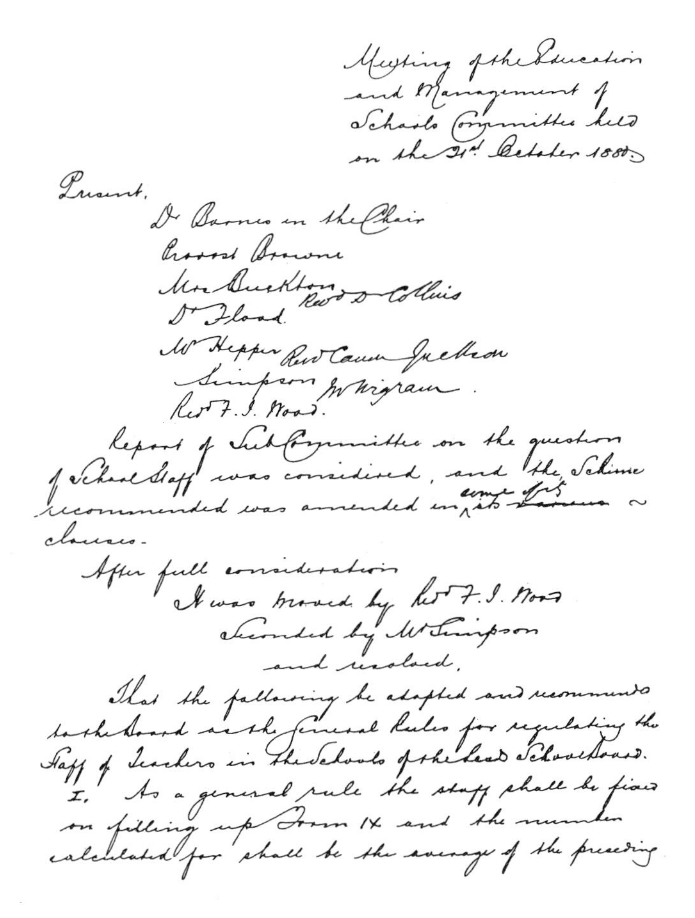

Meeting of the Education and Management of Schools Committee held on the 21st October 1880

Present.
Dr Barnes in the Chair
Provost Browne
Mrs Buckton Revd Dr Collins
Dr Flood.
Mr Hepper Revd Canon Jackson
Simpson Mr Wigram.
Revd F. J. Wood.

Report of Sub Committee on the question of School Staff was considered, and the Scheme recommended was amended in some of its clauses.

After full consideration
It was moved by Revd F. J. Wood
Seconded by Mr Simpson
and resolved.

That the following be adopted and recommended to the Board as the General Rules for regulating the Staff of Teachers in the Schools of the Leeds School Board.

I. As a general rule the staff shall be fixed on filling up Form IX and the number calculated for shall be the average of the preceding

Figure 19. Revd William Barnes chairs a meeting of the Education and Management Committee of the Leeds School Board in October 1880

Morgan then produced a long catalogue of alleged difficulties—geological, astronomical and historical—with regard to the Bible account of the Fall of Man, the Flood, etc. He insisted that it was unwise to leave teachers free to give their own interpretations of these controversial matters and here he was on firmer ground. It is likely, for instance, that pupils here and there were still being taught that the world began in 4004 BC when educated opinion in the church had already moved away from such crude and literal interpretations of Scripture. We know that Barnes was among those with modern or liberal views but all he could say to Morgan on this occasion was that the pupils would be examined on 'facts not dogmas'.

Now that the teachers were under the spotlight, someone asked if they, like the pupils, could opt out of this section of the curriculum on grounds of conscience. Barnes replied that if a School Board had settled, publicly, for a scheme of religious education they could surely select teachers who were Christians but he promised that he would deal sympathetically with any headteacher who came to him in person. Revd Wood rather cynically assured the meeting that disaffected teachers could find posts in those areas where School Boards had no religion in their schools (these were confined to Wales) or which had simple Bible reading only (there were few of these anywhere). Catholic objections to the scheme, that there was much scope for Protestant claims and assumptions to pass unnoticed, though reasonable, were surprisingly low-key. Perhaps there were relatively few of their children in Board schools by 1880; no figures were quoted. Revd Jackson supported the scheme, conceding that the Board's nine-year experience had shown that religious teaching without tests or checks was open to abuse.

Throughout this long discussion Barnes had done his best to find common ground between the disputants but the matter was eventually forced to a vote and carried by the church party, eight to four. There was a notable lack of uniformity on the nonconformist side[25] and it is not surprising that when they later came back into power no attempt was made to dismantle the scheme that had caused so much dissension.

1882–1889

While in Liverpool Edwin Foster laboured on, burdened and unwell, the decade following the eventful years of the 1879–82 School Board in Leeds saw the two lives which had run parallel in this town since the early seventies come to a natural close. For John Crosfield, though he lived longer, there were no more important challenges or changes in life-style but for William Barnes, now a figure of power and influence, the election of 1882 was to plunge him into one of the most stressful periods of his career.

By the summer of 1882, Revd Barnes and his colleagues knew they had a precarious position to maintain. For three years the church party had reigned supreme, but knowledgeable observers, looking back, considered their victory of 1879 was something of a fluke, due to a failure of Liberal organization and to wasteful conflict within the nonconformist community.[1] Now it was clear they were determined to stage a return. Unfortunately they had a new and powerful weapon to hand—a set of official figures which seemed to show that standards in the Board schools had slipped badly in the three years of church control.

This was not all. By way of explaining to an excited public why this particular Board had let them down, Liberal spokesmen dug out some more figures to demonstrate that since the end of 1880 (after one year in office) the Board had cut back on teachers in the interests of economy. And, to add insult to injury, it was alleged that in making the more senior appointments this church-oriented Board had been favouring candidates of its own persuasion.

Some of the facts were incontestable, others were explained or denied; it is difficult to be sure, now, where the truth lay but the Board's triennial report for 1879–82 dealt fairly and openly with the question of examination results, school attendance and staffing. The percentage of passes in reading, writing and arithmetic had indeed fallen from 85 per cent in 1877–79 to an average of 82.8 per cent for the triennial after 1879. Barnes, for the Education Committee, declared that the pass-rate was not the only factor, nor the most important. He pointed out that grant money could now be earned by good results in the class or specific subjects and by the school's tone and discipline and that overall grants had undoubtedly risen year by year. He went on to explain that the tests of the 'three Rs' were becoming more exacting and there were more entries each year from the upper Standards where the risk of failure was greatest. At the same time, Barnes said, the attendance machinery was bringing in more neglected children than ever before; 'the class of child whom nothing but continued pressure...can keep at school'.[2]

Supporting the leaders of the Board in this crucial period, A.G. Legard HMI did not even hint, in his report of 1883, that this Board had shown failure or neglect. He did point out that Leeds had more Board schools than the larger towns of Liverpool, Manchester and Birmingham and that in any case they should not take

> too commercial a view of their schools...and should exercise a judicious reticence about that most insane of modern prejudices, high percentages.[3]

Sadly, this vote of confidence came too late to help the churchmen at the 1882 election and they still had the problem of staffing to deal with. The triennial report stated that with five new Board schools bringing the total to 51, the numbers of head and assistant teachers had increased to about 350 while pupil-teachers had stayed more-or-less constant at around 500. Challenged about the resulting increase in the pupil-teacher ratio, Barnes, in a speech before the election, pointed out that teachers were not equal as to quality—and there was no need, as some were asserting, to increase them in direct ratio to the number of pupils.[4]

The question of religious bias was a deal more troublesome. Barnes said that of 54 appointments of headteachers, 24 had been churchmen or women, the rest nonconformist. This was not denied but J.W. Crawford, a Wesleyan from the 1879 Board, insisted that only the ten external candidates over those years were important and of these, nine were church-trained. Furthermore, Crawford went on to say that of 31 ex-students taken on, 14 were from the town's own Board schools but of the other 17, 13 were from Church of England colleges. Everyone agreed—and most regretted—that there was an imbalance in the provision of training but this fact gave one reasonable explanation for the pattern of Leeds appointments. Beyond that, Barnes could only deny, yet again, that there had been any such bias.[5]

If all this were not enough, Barnes found himself in trouble with his own side over the question of higher Board schools. It was embarrassing to him that prominent Liberals welcomed his stand on this issue and warned of danger to 'existing plans' should the church party be returned.[6] And, at the same time, the vicar of Leeds, Revd John Gott, was insisting that to pay for a school devoted to the 'higher subjects' would be 'an abuse on the rates' and 'a fraudulent use of the Education Act'. The vicar of Bramley went further; he wanted Revd Barnes 'thrown out' and his plans with him. It seems, however, that the church party were willing to overlook this transgression on Barnes's part for at a final meeting on the 16 November he was put forward as the first and most prominent speaker: he took a lofty view of the Board schools as 'a great national institution' not, as his opponents liked to think, as 'schools for dissenters' and he repudiated all charges of bias or double-dealing. Revd Wood of Headingley and all three laymen each addressed the meeting briefly and there was a summing-up from the (Conservative) MP William Jackson. No-one mentioned higher Board schools.[7]

In spite of these threats to his credibility as a loyal supporter of the church, Barnes's real qualities were recognized by the community and he was returned fourth in the list of new Board members when the results were announced on 20 November. However, both the Wesleyans were defeated and even with the two Roman Catholics returned, power swung back to the Liberal/unsectarian party. The reign of the churchmen was over.

The *Leeds Mercury* was, of course, triumphant. This 'great victory' was seen to prove the justice of the Liberals' claim to a majority of seats on the Board—'after all, Leeds is a Liberal constituency'—and the effectiveness of their new electoral strategy.[8] Meanwhile, the *Yorkshire Post*, disappointed with the result, accused the Liberals of misrepresentation, dishonourable motives and election trickery.[9] When all the shouting had died down Revd William Barnes found himself a target of hostility within the Board, his influence there severely curtailed.

On the 7 November Barnes had been warmly thanked for his leadership of the Education Committee. Now, a month later, at the first meeting of the new Board the eight Liberals put their nominee Edward Butler into the chair with J.M. Fawcett as vice-chairman. The controlling party then put down a complete list of members for all the committees; Revd Wood and two church laymen were placed on the Education Committee but Barnes was not. The churchmen moved, without success, that the committees be dealt with in turn, then again, unavailingly, that Barnes should substitute for one of the laymen on Education. Clearly this would not have affected the balance of votes; Barnes's exclusion was deliberate and personal.[10]

Early the next year an obviously disgruntled Barnes rose in a Board meeting to comment on a couple of teacher appointments. Though he 'had not the privilege of being on the Education Committee' he hoped that in the selection of teachers

> no regard would be paid to what political party or what religious sect they belonged to. The late Board adopted that course and he trusted the same would be followed by the present one.[11]

A few months later he tried, without success, to amend some salary proposals. Currently, teachers were paid a bonus on their yearly examination results if, in boys schools, they could achieve 85 per cent passes, in girls schools, 80 per cent. Barnes sought to base the calculations on the estimates of 'fair, good or excellent' made by the Inspector on his yearly visit, for this took into account the location of the school and the type of children in it. The Board school at Little Holbeck, for instance, scored consistently lower than Crosfield's school on the other side of town, but the Board was almost unanimous against him, wishing to keep the allocation of bonuses in their own hands.[12]

Relations between the parties were still strained when, in June, a church layman tried to question the briefing for a School Board deputation to London. In reply, Cockburn (one of the Liberal newcomers) said,

> he sympathized from the bottom of his heart with the painful position in which the minority now found themselves. A few months ago he hoped they would be able to sink their feelings and recognize that although they were on a Board where they had

> had years of rule and power they must now recognize they were in a minority and must pay the penalty...[13]

In the face of attitudes like this, Barnes and his fellow churchmen continued to oppose those motions they disagreed with, allowing others to pass, but in due course when the committee structure was reviewed at the beginning of 1884, Barnes was quietly put back on the Education Committee. After this change of heart by his opponents he could again be active on this committee and though without his early influence he could at least spend the last few months of his life and service to the Board in a more cordial atmosphere.[14]

In this short period, Barnes was involved with a sub-committee looking into over-pressure in the schools, with plans to appoint a female Superintendent[15] and with new arrangements for teacher training under the Yorkshire College. At his last meeting on 4 November he approved the appointment of his niece, Louisa Crosfield, as headmistress of Sweet Street infant school in Holbeck.

Up to the last minute Barnes was engaged in all his multifarious duties for School Board and church and it was after a very short illness—a heart condition complicated by pneumonia—that he died at the Parsonage on 3 December aged 47. The chairman of the Board delivered this generous tribute on 11 December:

> The Board record their deep sense of the loss sustained by them in common with all educationalists of Leeds in the removal by death of their esteemed colleague Revd Dr Barnes MA, LL D. He brought to the service of the Board great natural ability, long and special culture, the experience of a life devoted to education, unswerving diligence and unfailing conscientiousness and the Board desire to convey to his widow and family their deep sympathy with them in a sorrow which is in this world irreparable.[16]

The response from town and church was also warm and immediate. The *Leeds Mercury*, no friend of the Establishment, came out with a long obituary on 4 December. The editor referred to Barnes as a 'self-made man', to his remarkable talents and to the help he had received from James Armitage and others in furthering his career. In his great contribution to the life of the town, Revd Barnes, it was said, 'was distinguished alike by a capacity and an indomitable resolution for work'.[17]

On Monday 8 December, this paper carried an even longer report of William Barnes's funeral and his interment in Holbeck cemetery. In the presence of numerous friends and colleagues—fifty clergy were named and the church was quite full—his old friend Canon Jackson delivered 'a touching address'. William Barnes, he said, was no 'ordinary man' and his talents 'he willingly placed at the call of all to whom he could be of service'. Jackson went on to speak of Barnes's

> great kindness of heart, of his deep sensibility, of his almost womanly tenderness and of his warm, active, sympathy with sorrow and distress wherever it might exist.

With these personal qualities went an 'earnest devotion to his pastoral duties' while 'his great preaching powers made him welcome in the pulpit of many a church in Leeds and round about'. Finally, we have a glimpse from Jackson of Barnes's churchmanship:

> Few men I have met have been so largely read in all modern subjects and modern science. Yet in spite of all the wide and varied knowledge, some of it so highly calculated to excite doubt and misgiving, I can say of my departed brother that no-one could be more perfectly convinced of the truth of our most holy religion.[18]

In due course, the congregation of the church of St John the Evangelist with 'schoolchildren and friends' erected a handsome gravestone in Holbeck cemetery 'as a token of affection and respect'. But, strangely, there was no further memorial—no personal 'memoir' or 'life' would appear in print at a time when such were commonly produced for clergy and men in public life. And the knowledge of William Barnes's long, slow climb out of obscurity, though hinted at in public comments after his death, seems to have been lost within a generation or two in his own family. Thus clean was the break he had made with his own humble origins.

For John Crosfield present, naturally, at the funeral, Barnes's death marked the end of a relationship going back for both of them to early boyhood. The sisterly bond between the wives could have remained of course, but even this seems to have been forgotten by William Barnes's twentieth-century descendants—and by the Crosfields—suggesting that it was already weakened by the 1880s. John Crosfield lacked the special talents, or perhaps the ambition, to raise him out of the milieu of the elementary schoolmaster and he was to spend the last five years of his life working, as he had done since 1872, for the Leeds School Board in charge of Sheepscar school.

Since 1875, when Crosfield took over the new school in Roundhay Road, his performance seems to have impressed Her Majesty's Inspectors. For example, the mathematics results were commended in 1879 and 1881 and through to 1887 the boys' school was said to be 'very efficient' with the boys usually passing 'a good exam'. The Inspector's schedule for grants earned on 30 September 1886 shows the boys' pass rate to have been over 90 per cent and the maximum 'merit grant' was awarded that year for good organization and discipline and intelligent instruction.[19]

But now and then the Inspector noted that the boys were under less then perfect control. In 1882 he wrote:

> The discipline is not so good as I would wish...the boys' behaviour is by no means what it should be in a well-ordered school but I trust that undue severity will not be employed in the place of judicious firmness on the part of all the teachers.[20]

There was an improvement the next year—'order firmly maintained'[21]—but it seems that Crosfield was in some difficulty, neither heeding the Inspector's warning nor the local rules for he was reported 'on a charge of corporal punishment'[22] to the School Board that December. How he had infringed the rules is not clear, but the Board members who had been chosen as 'visitors' for Sheepscar were told to reprimand him.

As with Edwin Foster's troubles at Kirkdale, it is difficult to know how serious a matter this really was. By the 1880s, though caning and other physical punishment was commonplace, all public authorities, led by the Inspectorate, had been preaching caution and moderation for several decades. Had John Crosfield been given to using harsh measures, earlier incidents would surely have come to light. And the oddly personal letter he wrote to the Education Department in 1873 (Fig. 15) suggests that he was, then at least, a relaxed and kindly man. Nor was he alone in facing this kind of charge though most of the culprits, here and in Liverpool, were the younger staff, mostly pupil-teachers, who found themselves overwhelmed.[23]

Could it have been this year that Crosfield's health began to fail? In 1886 and 1887 the Inspector noted a slight falling-off in the results from the boys' school and his report of October 1888 was somewhat mixed.[24] By this time it was plain that Crosfield could not be blamed; he was 55 years old and he had fallen prey to consumption. In March 1889 he decided to retire and after a few months in the healthier climate of the Isle of Man he died at Port Erin on the 30 July. John Crosfield received a brief tribute from the chairman of the School Board at their next meeting[25] but his funeral at Rushen church was quiet and unreported. The Board appointed a successor and for most of his family there followed a long period of residence in Leeds with continued service to the School Board and later the Education Committee of the City Council.

Thus, with Edwin Foster's death in 1893, already described, we come to the close of the three life-histories portrayed in this book. Each of these men was overcome by illness while still at the height of his powers but not before reaching a kind of plateau of social acceptance, financial security and material comfort. Two questions remain; how far, in the end, had each man risen from his own roots—and can we view the achievements of these three elementary schoolmasters as typical of their particular generation? Or were these lives, each with its slow climb of the social ladder, in some way distinctive or unusual? In the last two chapters we look first at the family context and then at the professional scene for answers to these questions.

XII

A Place in Society

We have seen how, year by year, three men born in humble obscurity were able to gather to themselves the fruits of academic study, hard work and submission to the authority of church and state. It was their good fortune that in these middle years of the nineteenth century elementary schoolmastering first began to offer the rewards of a formal career and the promise of entry into a profession and by the 1880s, all three men, who had been put forward, as boys, for the new pupil-teacher scheme of 1846, had earned for themselves a secure place within the middle-class communities of their respective towns.

But then, as now, the term middle class was used somewhat widely; at the lower end of the scale it could be applied to those who had only just escaped the stigma of working class—with its image of manual labour, a small weekly wage and limited culture—but it stretched right up to the base of the older, landed (or the newer, industrial) aristocracies. With clerks, shopkeepers, petty officials and now schoolmasters occupying the centre of this large amorphous group, there were, nonetheless, many fine gradations of status; of these the most important was the point in the ascending hierarchy at which a 'man' became a 'gentleman'.

Here, though, was another elusive category, the title adopted or bestowed for a variety of reasons, sometimes through courtesy, sometimes personal pride. But among the overt criteria for admission to the locally-recognized gentry would, of course, be a certain level of income with the appropriate demonstrations of life-style. For instance, Mrs Beeton prescribed her rules of 'Household Management' for a home where £400 to £600 could support the employment of four living-in servants.[1] Now, on this basis, even Revd William Barnes would hardly have qualified but he had the quite separate advantage of his professional standing. As the vicar of a parish—and with his circle of School Board colleagues—he could surely have counted on acceptance, at least from the time of his graduation and doctorate.

So where on this scale might Crosfield and Foster be placed? We know that Edwin Foster had been promoted above his erstwhile colleagues and that his social life included membership of the Liverpool Geological Society where he consorted with his friend Reade, the architect, the School Board clerk, Edward Hance and other gentry. What is more, it seems that he designated himself 'gentleman' when applying to Balliol College, Oxford for his son Herbert in 1881. Later, though, for Arthur's entry to Cambridge, he fell back on 'Board School Inspector'; he was apparently pleading poverty at this time and his son was entered as a 'sizar'.[2] Crosfield's position was even more ambiguous but it seems likely that he could expect to be looked up to as a 'gentleman' by those inferior to him, that is, most of his pupils and their parents.[3]

There is no final arbiter to be sought in such matters but for Barnes, Crosfield and Foster we can turn our attention to another set of clues to their social standing among friends and colleagues—the plans and aspirations they had for their children and how they were realized.

We cannot deduce very much from the rather meagre facts available to us about the education of the children when young. We do know that the two Crosfield girls attended 'Mrs Drinkwater's' and 'Miss Pennington's' in Knutsford in the 1860s (and possibly the two boys, being younger, were with them) but neither Barnes nor Foster were in places where such private schooling was available and we must assume that all these children attended their fathers' schools. It is at the next, secondary, stage that the three families, now in busy towns, were presented with real choice. However, we should bear in mind as we compare the opportunities for these young people in the 1870s and 1880s with those of their parents' generation—and as we compare the families with each other—that the teenagers of Leeds and Liverpool were sharing the benefits of a noticeable expansion in this field, everywhere. It would be another 70 years or so before everyone had a right to secondary schooling but already access to all kinds of extended education was becoming easier for those on limited incomes. In this context, a review of the aims and achievements of the Barnes, Crosfield and Foster children is particularly interesting.

Here we have three men whose own education had swept them way beyond the expectations set for them by fathers who were artisans, or at best, shopkeepers, and who may have had no formal schooling of any kind, themselves. Now, as parents, what kinds of institution were available to them given what we know of their standing and income at this time?

We can surmise that Revd Barnes, with a vicar's income £300 a year or more was looking towards local fee-paying establishments rather than boarding schools, though this possibility cannot be ruled out. Edwin Foster, earning £200 a year in 1872 (when his eldest son was eleven) and elevated to a position superior to the ordinary schoolmaster's, no doubt had plans like William Barnes's. John Crosfield, though his salary rose to £200 in 1876 when his eldest son was ten, had already taken the boys into Sheepscar school with him while the two girls were employed locally as pupil-teachers. Of the three men he is the only one who might at some stage have been in two minds about the virtues of conventional secondary education when there was this vocational alternative which had already served him well. Let us now follow through what actually happened.

Concentrating first on the boys, whose needs even in enlightened households would present as more urgent, we find that seven of the sons of these three families took much the same course. For Revd Barnes's family, Leeds Grammar School was tailor-made. An old foundation, its status had dropped somewhat since the wealthier men of the town (like the Marshalls) had started to move their homes into the country and their sons into public schools, but it was still highly regarded as a school for the gentry and professional classes. Both Horace, who entered in 1872 and William Arnold in 1882, were fee-payers most of the time but Horace won an internal scholarship in 1877.

Notwithstanding its position in the town this school was inexpensive enough for some of the better-off tradesmen and officials and the governors set out to widen access further in the late

1870s by means of a new batch of scholarships. There were no more than a couple of dozen of these each year and most went to boys of limited means from middle-class homes. But a handful were set aside for pupils from the public elementary schools and it was, perhaps, this concession that persuaded John Crosfield to enter Harry in 1877 and Walter Harold in 1880. Both were 'School Board scholars'.[4]

In fact, when Crosfield steered his sons towards the Grammar School he must have known there were cheaper options had they failed to win scholarships. Both the Mechanics Institute schools and the Parish Church Middle Class schools were used by the shopkeeper/tradesman class but there was a substantial gulf in popular esteem between these and the Grammar School. Appearing in due course was another challenger to all three—the Higher Grade Board school, argued for so passionately by William Barnes but coming on the scene too late for him to appreciate or for the Crosfield family to use.

The situation for Edwin Foster in Liverpool was rather different. Though there was an 'organized science school' under the School Board much later on, there was nothing equivalent to the Higher Board school or the two lesser secondary schools in Leeds. There were, however, three grammar schools to all of which there was some limited access by way of scholarships.[5] One of these, the Liverpool Institute, had a large lower or Commercial school and judging by the register, boys came here from quite modest homes; there was clearly an overlap with the clientele of the better-placed Board and voluntary schools. It is unlikely that any of Foster's children attended the public elementary schools, however (since their time at Melling) but he was prepared for the boys to join this rather mixed group at the Institute to begin their secondary education. Edwin Flockton and Herbert started there in 1872, Arthur in 1875. At this stage all of them paid fees but when they moved up to the High School the two younger boys were assisted by scholarships.[6] So it came about that whatever the divergences in the life-styles of their parents, all these boys were on much the same footing for a few years at least.

At these two city schools the boys had access to the same kind of academic curriculum and from both pupils were sent forward to the major universities though Leeds Grammar had the edge in terms of academic success.[7] Assuming that all three parents would have backed their sons through this next stage we find, in fact, that only three of the seven went on to university, presumably those who were able to meet the demands of this particular kind of study.

Horace Barnes and Herbert Foster were together at Oxford between 1881 and 1883 but following very different courses. Barnes won a Hastings scholarship to Queen's College to read classics and he went on to become a master at Bedford School and finally, ordained like his father, a housemaster there.[8] Herbert Foster was at Balliol training for the Indian Civil Service; this was a two-year course which did not lead to a degree[9] but he made his way up through the grades in India and was appointed Registrar to the High Court in Madras in the early nineties.[10] The other graduate was Herbert's younger brother Arthur. He was a talented mathematician who was classed as 'Eighth Wrangler' after three years at St John's College, Cambridge. Sadly though, he was consumptive and this young man whose 'intellectual power was joined to an affectionate and gentle disposition' died, after months of illness, at the House of Rest in Mentone in the south of France, in 1887.[11]

Meanwhile, the other four boys went their various ways. William Arnold Barnes became an engineer and went to America. The oldest Foster boy, Edwin Flockton, worked as a bank clerk but died in 1882 at the age of twenty-one. Walter Harold Crosfield was something of a rolling stone. He went as a tutor to Mexico and then, in the early 1900s he was employed as a clerk to the Vancouver Gas Company. Harry Crosfield left Leeds Grammar School to become a solicitor's clerk but soon turned back to join his father and sisters in the teaching profession. After a shortened pupil-teacher course he spent two years at Culham College, Oxford and was employed by the School Board and the Leeds City Council until his retirement in 1927.

Turning now to the girls in these families we find some interesting contrasts. Unfortunately the records in Liverpool are too scanty to enable us to track the school careers of the Foster girls—if, indeed, they had such; only one of them, Gertrude, the youngest, lived beyond the age of twenty-one and she seems to have died a spinster without occupation in 1940. But William Barnes and John Crosfield both had aspirations for their daughters and the pairs of cousins followed paths appropriate to their fathers' station in life. Thus, as we have seen, the Crosfield girls worked their way as pupil-teachers in Leeds Board schools, Louisa from 1873 and Helen from 1876. In due course both girls passed their 'Queen's scholarship' examinations and went on to college.

At this point John Crosfield, who apparently retained no special loyalty to his alma mater in York, chose for them the new college at Darlington set up by the British and Foreign School Society. Here, they were enabled 'at small cost to themselves to enter an honourable profession and earn a comfortable livelihood'.[12] Though the framework of expectations set up by this institution seems to embrace at least an echo of the old 'lofty aims and lowly duties'—religion, if undenominational, was still absolutely central—an element of material self-interest was allowed in, too. But while these young women knew that they could look forward to a position of modest influence in working-class circles, their own social standing was unlikely to be much higher than that of their pupils.

In fact it was in this sphere above all others, perhaps, that the lower middle class were most sharply divided from those with aspirations to be considered as gentry. For instance, an experiment in the south of England to train 'young ladies' for work in public elementary schools was not a success. Once qualified at Bishop Otter College (so it was reported) the 'ladies' were not welcomed by the 'ordinary teachers', no School Board sought their services and even the clergy who took them in for their parish schools would not allow them to mix with their own daughters.[13] But within this circumscribed world the Crosfield girls were successful, achieving a series of promotions under the Leeds School Board and before they retired, together, in 1917 as headmistresses of Council schools.

Prospects for the daughters of William Barnes were very different. Educated privately after the Farnley period—we must assume this, we do not know where—Helen Barnes achieved a couple of passes, in English and Logic, in the Cambridge Higher Locals, one of several sets of examinations taken by boys and girls in secondary schools nation-wide at this time. With this behind her, Helen, at eighteen, offered her services to the new Leeds Girls High School in August 1876 and she was taken on as the headmistress, Miss Kennedy's, first (junior) assistant at £40 a year. In December another young woman was appointed. In July the next year Helen's salary was raised to £50. Then in July 1879 Eva Barnes joined her (on £50) and in July 1881 Helen's salary went up again to from £60 to £70 (and Eva's from £50 to £55). These sums are significant for it was only at this later stage that Helen's pay reached the level earned by her two cousins, trained and certificated, in the town's Board schools.

But the question of status for these educated women was far from straightforward. Whereas qualifications and responsible work would automatically grant status to a man in employment, it was by no means the case for women. And this could pose problems for employers and employed in a school of this kind. Leeds Girls High School, opened in 1876, was advertised as a

> high class day school (to provide) under well-trained teachers a sound, systematic and liberal education for girls between seven and nineteen.[14]

What kind of girls had they in mind? Miss Kennedy with her assistant Miss Ludlow had come from Cheltenham Ladies College, then highly selective, socially. The founding committee were all 'ladies' and preference for entry was given to the daughters of shareholders. But the strongest clue to this school's place in the community comes from a statement made by Miss Kennedy some twenty years later. Conscious of comparisons being made, over the years, with Leeds Grammar School (whose policies for recruitment have already been mentioned), Miss Kennedy said:

> I have found in this and other schools for girls no desire to encourage the introduction of girls from elementary schools by means of scholarships, the headmistresses in most cases being evidently unwilling that such scholarships should be created.

She went on,

> The Class feeling which does not seem to affect the boys' schools is very strong in the girls' schools and the same parents who

> are...willing...to allow their boys to mix with boys of all classes are not willing to do so in the case of their girls.[15]

This set of attitudes, justified or not, does at least confirm for us the social status of Revd Barnes's daughters as sufficiently ladylike to be in charge of the sheltered youngsters who were not allowed to 'mix'. But this is where the problems could arise. Not all parents of girls who were suitably equipped, socially and scholastically, to act as teachers in such schools were happy to see their daughters leave home each day for paid work. A 'good education' was fine if it only led to passive accomplishments. One such parent caught up in this situation has left us a record of his doubts and eventual disapproval.

Helen Barnes's first young colleague was Lucy Heaton, a daughter of Dr J.D. Heaton, well-known Leeds physician and member of the first School Board. His wife was one of the campaigners for and organizers of the High School. Lucy, she felt, would profit by a 'useful occupation' rather then spend her time in 'desultory and indifferent' pursuits. 'However', Heaton confided to his diary in late 1876,

> it is so contrary to custom for young ladies not necessarily dependent on their own exertions to undertake any kind of remunerative occupation that this innovation occasioned considerable comment and I had some doubt of its expediency.

While Revd Barnes was apparently untroubled by such concerns, Heaton's disquiet increased. By 1878 his mood was set against his daughter's employment and he withdrew her from the school.

> I did not think it consistent with our position...that she should continue to give up the whole of her life to drudgery for a small pittance, depriving herself of all recreation and the customary pursuits of a young lady living at home.[16]

So much for Lucy Heaton's aspirations; Helen Barnes, though, was encouraged to take her career a step further. In 1883 she left the High School for Cambridge where she spent a year at Newnham College, not, it seems, reading for a degree (which would have required three years) but for one more Higher Locals pass, this time in Latin. Here, in this ancient seat of learning was a new and still unusual experience for a clever, well brought-up young woman. It is true that advanced education for women still aroused scorn and hostility in some quarters but the two colleges, Girton and Newnham, were well-established by the mid-eighties and degree examinations were open to their students even if, at the end, they received only a grading and a certificate. And Helen was with a group of thirty or so in her year from all over the country, with no less than four students from America, including two daughters of the poet Longfellow—a stimulating set of companions.[17]

Most of the women, about half of them with degrees, left to teach in girls' day or boarding schools, a few to pupil-teacher colleges and the like and Helen took up a post in another of the newer High Schools, in Worcester. Here, the headmistress, Alice Ottley, remembered her as 'brilliant and attractive', but she did not stay with them long, leaving after only a year to get married—only to die soon after at the birth of her first child.[18] Her sister, Eva, meanwhile, had left the Leeds High School after their father's death in 1884 and it seems she never went back to teaching. Their young sister Sarah Ellen was also a stay-at-home spinster.

This sketch, locating the younger generation socially among their contemporaries, would not be complete without reference to all the four marriages which were entered into in the 1880s and 1890s; a new partner could consolidate or shift the pattern of social expectations that each individual had formed by early maturity. Thus we find that in Helen Barnes's marriage, her chosen partner was Samuel Wilkes Waud, an engineer, descended from a line of professional men (of that name) going back to a great-grandfather who was an 'attorney' in York. This kind of pedigree was something new for the younger Barnes who were only second generation middle class, but the Wauds were not rich and Helen's domestic life would have been much like that of the Holbeck parsonage. There was a chance of continuity for this line in the life of their son, another Samuel Wilkes Waud, but eventually both father and son disappeared in South America, the father soon after Helen's death, the son, brought up by grandmother and aunt, in early adulthood.

In 1889 Helen's brother Horace married the daughter of a naval man connected with wealthy quarry owners in Wales and, from a position of material comfort and security at Bedford School this couple were succeeded by a line of public-school educated professional men. Harry Crosfield, meanwhile, had married a Wesleyan girl, the daughter of a Leeds newspaper manager, the relationship starting, perhaps, when Harry took up his first teaching post after college at the Holbeck Wesleyan school. This couple had four daughters and a son; one of the girls, Marjory, followed her father into the teaching profession; the son was a commercial traveller.

Finally, we come to another short-lived marriage but one of great interest and significance in this set of family histories. Herbert Foster, who by then had a good post with the High Court in Madras set off home in March 1895 on only his second furlough since 1882 and in October that year he married Mary Horsfall, niece of one of his senior colleagues in the Indian Civil Service, Jeremiah Garnett Horsfall, by then retired.[19]

It seems likely the couple met in Scotland where J.G. Horsfall and his brother Alfred—Mary's father—had a country house on long lease near Dalbeattie. Though never the owners, they designated themselves, officially, 'of Auchendolly, Kirkudbright shire' until they retired to Exmouth some time before 1900. The marriage, however, took place near Clitheroe where an uncle of the bride, James Garnett, had lived for many years as a wealthy and influential cotton-spinner. Garnett wrote in his diary on 11 October: 'the Great Event of the day has been Mary Horsfall's marriage to Mr Foster of the Indian Civil Service'.[20]

Herbert Foster impressed Garnett as an 'affable, clever and well-informed gentleman' but it was known his health was poor and Mary had been advised to put off such a serious commitment. But she was then 35 and Foster 33 and he was due back in India before the end of the year—neither wished to delay. Foster, prudently, had a new will in favour of 'his beloved wife' witnessed by members of the wedding party before they left. The couple arrived in Bombay on the 23 November but on the way across India Herbert Foster was suddenly taken ill and died at Gooty on 25 November.

Had Herbert lived he would have made the greatest social leap of all his generation in the three families for not only was his final posting prestigious and well-paid—he was earning about four times his father's salary in 1890—but Mary Horsfall was a well-connected young woman. Earlier Garnetts and Horsfalls were north of England textile manufacturers; her father Alfred had taken an independent line by going to sea. Having captained some ships for the Moss shipping line in Liverpool he was later employed as a dock superintendent.[21] By the time of his death in 1917 he had accumulated some £100,000. If Mary had been endowed at the time of her marriage at a level remotely commensurate with this the couple could have lived very comfortably indeed.

This record of success and professional advancement confirms that the Barnes, Crosfield and Foster households were among those able to encourage and support their children in the disciplines of academic study. Now, this was not an exclusively middle-class virtue; in these more open times small numbers of boys (and a very few girls) were making their way up from homes much poorer in both material and cultural terms. But while the actual numbers coming through in this way remained small, the institutions of secondary and higher education retained a strong middle-class tone and to have young people set on this particular ladder was bound to reflect well on the social status of the parents concerned.

Then, as one opportunity led to another, the process was naturally continuous. For example, the two young men from these three families who did best (in these worldly terms) Herbert Foster and Horace Barnes, rose to positions where they had access to a whole new range of material and less tangible benefits. They found themselves working with gentry and the sons of gentry and they both married into this upper section of the middle class, facts, which when generally known must have cast a further, strong and favourable light on their parents' own standing in the community. By way of contrast, John Crosfield's apparent satisfaction with the rewards of ordinary school teaching led to three useful careers in the service of the School Board but no particular advancement of his own or his children's status beyond his own.

While these professional histories show a sequence of doors opening for Barnes, Crosfield and Foster from boyhood onwards—and then for their children—there was nothing inevitable about their steady progress in social and material terms. For these men and their colleagues a step sideways off the career ladder was quite possible or even a step downwards into some manual or petty commercial occupation. Perhaps this record of effort, opportunity and success gives an unbalanced picture of the potential in elementary schoolmastering in this period of expansion and change. Were these three men unusually able or specially fortunate? Only with a retrospective glance at what is known of their contemporaries in this field can we attempt to answer this final question.

Conclusion

As we embark upon a final review of the biographies set out in this book let us remind ourselves, first, of the nature of the world of training and practice for elementary school teachers in the mid-nineteenth century and of Barnes's, Crosfield's and Foster's place within it. To start with, teaching under government supervision was an exclusive vocation; though open to many thousands of boys and girls the tests for intending pupil-teachers were strict and as late as 1853, when William Barnes, John Crosfield and Edwin Foster had completed their five-year apprenticeships, the young men were in a group of only 700 or so nation-wide;[1] in 1856 they were among only 521 male teachers to emerge successfully from college.[2] But such was the demand for this new breed of qualified teacher—and the improvement in schooling generally—there were some 5,000 of them in the schools by the mid-sixties.[3] John Crosfield, the only one still at work in the classroom, was one of about 17,000 certificated schoolmasters at the time of his death in 1889.[4]

There is no way, of course, that even Crosfield could be said to be typical of this vast number but, tracing these events from their origins in the Minutes of the Committee of Council on Education, 1846, we can see how each one of these men could be claimed as representative of some limited category within the expanding profession. In their formative years, for instance, all three shared the majority experience of an upbringing in church schools. Numerically, these schools and their pupils far exceeded all the other categories put together, despite the efforts of non-conformists, Roman Catholics and others to provide for their own. And while the whole vast network of church schools was swallowed up within the parish system, the lives of its teachers were supported—and confined—in their quasi-spiritual role by the local clergy who managed the schools. This was the old order in the field of elementary education; parish schoolmasters as 'workers in Christ's vineyard', the Parochial Minister's 'right arm and assistant'.[5]

It was in 1854, when Barnes, Crosfield and Foster were at York that the senior cleric who coined these phrases went on to insist that teachers, though by then enjoying Treasury 'augmentations', should reject the claims of the state to be 'a separate and distinct agent for the education of the poor'. But the rewards the church was offering, by this stage, were too intangible for these hard-working men and women and too remote. Revd Watkins HMI, a few years later, took up a more realistic stance:

> It is most unreasonable to expect in a schoolmaster higher or less selfish motives than those which influence the lawyer, the physician, the literary man or the clergyman. Open to them an honourable career and they will rightly and speedily avail themselves of it.[6]

And so, in due course, as he had predicted, schoolteachers who had been checked in through the narrow gates of religious faith and institutional loyalty felt free to admit to worldly aims alongside the 'lofty' ones they were still expected to profess and, when service to the state became an option after 1870 many of these teachers changed their allegiance to be joined, in due course by large numbers of the newly church-trained.[7]

Thus it came about that, in the latter years of School Board rule, qualified teachers were located roughly half in the state and half in the voluntary sector of the elementary education system but the proportion of the older, experienced church-trained masters who, like Crosfield had made the change soon after 1870, was relatively small. This fact can be gleaned from a list of the alumni of St John's College, York (the old 'training school') made in 1894;[8] though incomplete for these early years it shows that among the 200 or so graduating before 1862 (and the upheavals of the Revised Code) only a small group went on, later, to teach in Board schools. Many more were listed as masters of parish schools, mostly in the north. If this impression is correct, Crosfield's later career—for a man of his experience—was an unusual one.

The York list also helps us place the careers of the other two men in some kind of perspective. As academic achievers, Barnes and Foster were both in the running for promotions and, while this made them to some extent untypical, the life-pattern for neither was unique. To start with, most of the larger School Boards appointed inspectors or superintendents picked from the ranks of experienced schoolmasters so that Edwin Foster's promotion, if among few made, was a routine feature of this new administration. A fellow student was later promoted to work as a small-town School Board clerk, but a couple more described themselves (in 1894, for this list) as 'Her Majesty's Inspector'. At a glance this would take them way beyond Foster's level, but in fact both started as Assistant Inspector and only one rose to Sub-Inspector. The Assistants, all schoolmasters, were chosen by HMIs after 1863 to help with the routine work of examination under the Revised Code; commonly addressed as 'Mr' while HMIs were 'Esq.' these men were rarely promoted beyond Sub-Inspector rank.[9] Though subordinate in the hierarchy a Board Inspector's life was probably just as rewarding; he was likely to be a great deal more influential, locally, than a junior HMI.

William Barnes, meanwhile, had joined a small but steady stream of teachers who came to the attention of the clergy as potential ordinands during their training or later. These were men who might earlier have been picked up by wealthy patrons and steered through University to ordination or who, as the century progressed, were more likely to find their way into the new theological colleges. As we have seen, Barnes's training at York stood him in good stead but courses of this kind were not generally regarded as adequate preparation for the ministry. It is therefore interesting to note that, of the fifteen clergy in the York lists trained before 1862, only one other, like Barnes was ordained as a 'literate' without formal training[10]—and unlike Barnes he did not enter on further studies later. Of the others, two graduated from Trinity College Dublin, two were at Cambridge, two at Durham and one was at Oxford. In the end, though, Barnes was the only one in this small group who earned himself a doctorate.

For the church authorities the progression of a trained schoolmaster to cleric—particularly with academic honours—was wholly welcome and they seemed to find acceptable promotions of elementary schoolmasters to grammar school posts (eight in this list), to 'higher grade' or 'middle class' schools or to other reputable occupations such as solicitor, customs officer or borough analyst—all to be found among York alumni of this period. They were, perhaps, less happy with defections to trade; five (listed here) became shopkeepers and a few took up work with family businesses.

This brief look at some of the alternatives to a life in schoolmastering for those selected and trained for the work confirms that the careers of Barnes, Crosfield and Foster, though in the end different from each other, were all set in conventional moulds. But this spread into other avocations also reminds us that many of these teachers and potential teachers stayed close, socially to the world of small tradesman, artisans and clerks from which most had been drawn. And even those who climbed out of their class were likely to have been single individuals leaving behind a cluster of relatives in the process.

In this respect at least Crosfield and Foster were entirely typical. The family trees (in the Appendix) researched and drawn up for all three men and their wives, show, for example, that long after Crosfield and Foster were established in the scholastic profession each still had an artisan brother, one in Liverpool, one in Wakefield. Both were joiners and married with children in the 1880s and 1890s; a son of Thomas Crosfield's was a coppersmith. Meanwhile, two of Edwin's younger sisters were in domestic service, another was a milliner and Foster's mother, widowed in 1861, worked as a school and office cleaner until her death in 1884. The same kind of pattern can be seen on the female side of the combined families. In the end it was Foster's sister, Mary, who perhaps came nearest to following her brother into the middle-class when her second husband (who had himself been a teacher) was promoted to assistant town clerk in Wakefield.

This said, we must not forget the long-established avenues to social advance through trade and manufacture and there are comparisons to be made, sometimes within families, between those who took the slower but more reliable route through book-learning and those who risked their livelihoods in commerce. It so happens that the Fosters, so many of whom stayed on the borders of the working and middle classes had a line which achieved gentrification through success in the family business of brass-founding; a cousin Edward Foster died in 1884 worth some £10,000 having just married off a daughter to a scion of Louvine, shipbuilders of West Hartlepool.

So in various ways the lives depicted here have a claim to general significance. Moreover, to have concentrated the focus of research on just three men has made it possible to uncover a very full sequence of events for each of them, yielding some sharp and accurate impressions of family life and personal problems while displaying the nature of the daily routine in a variety of ordinary schools. More broadly, such biographies reveal something of how elementary schoolmasters of this period took up the opportunities laid before them and how they responded to the demands of managers, employers and inspectors at each stage of their careers. In fact the narrative shows that while the aims of these public servants continued 'lofty', the status of their duties became, in time, less 'lowly'.

Then, finally, the tracking of such lives opens a window on to a wider and far more complex scene with schools of many kinds, their proprietors and teachers in unique relationships with each other and with the communities whose needs they served. And behind all that we can glimpse something of the shifting pattern of public and private motivations and the drive—balanced by economic and religious constraints—to bring about the expansion of popular education in Victorian times. John Crosfield, William Barnes and Edwin Foster were just three among thousands who gained some personal advantage while devoting their lives to this important and civilizing venture.

Appendix

The Family Trees

Notes for possible descendants of these families

All the trees are likely to be incomplete especially in the earlier generations. However, the author holds a fair amount of detail, places of birth and so on, relating to the others and would be happy to pass this material on to anyone with a direct interest.

Abbreviations

b.	born
bp.	baptized
c.	circa
d.	died
dtr	daughter
m.	married
s.	son

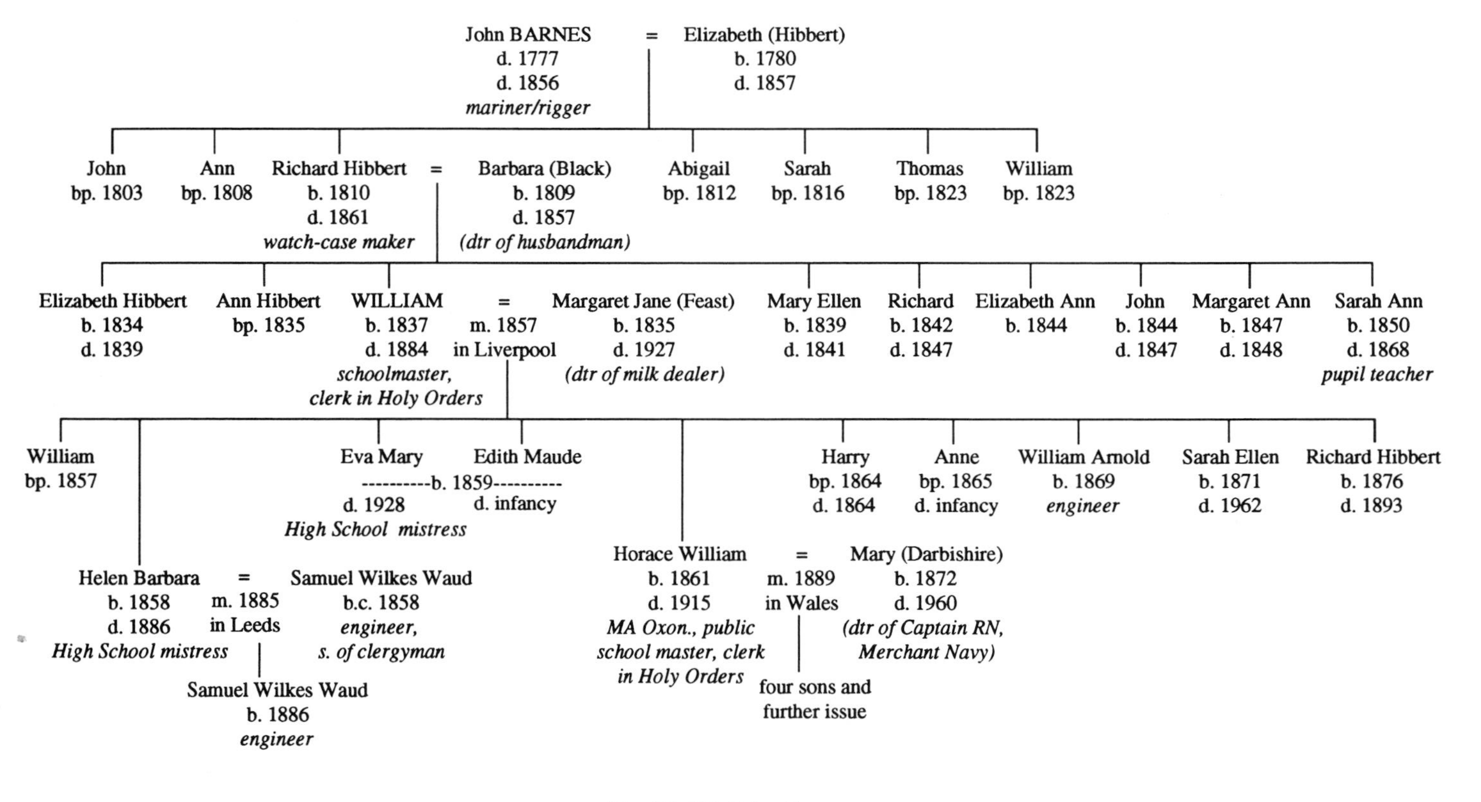

The BARNES family tree

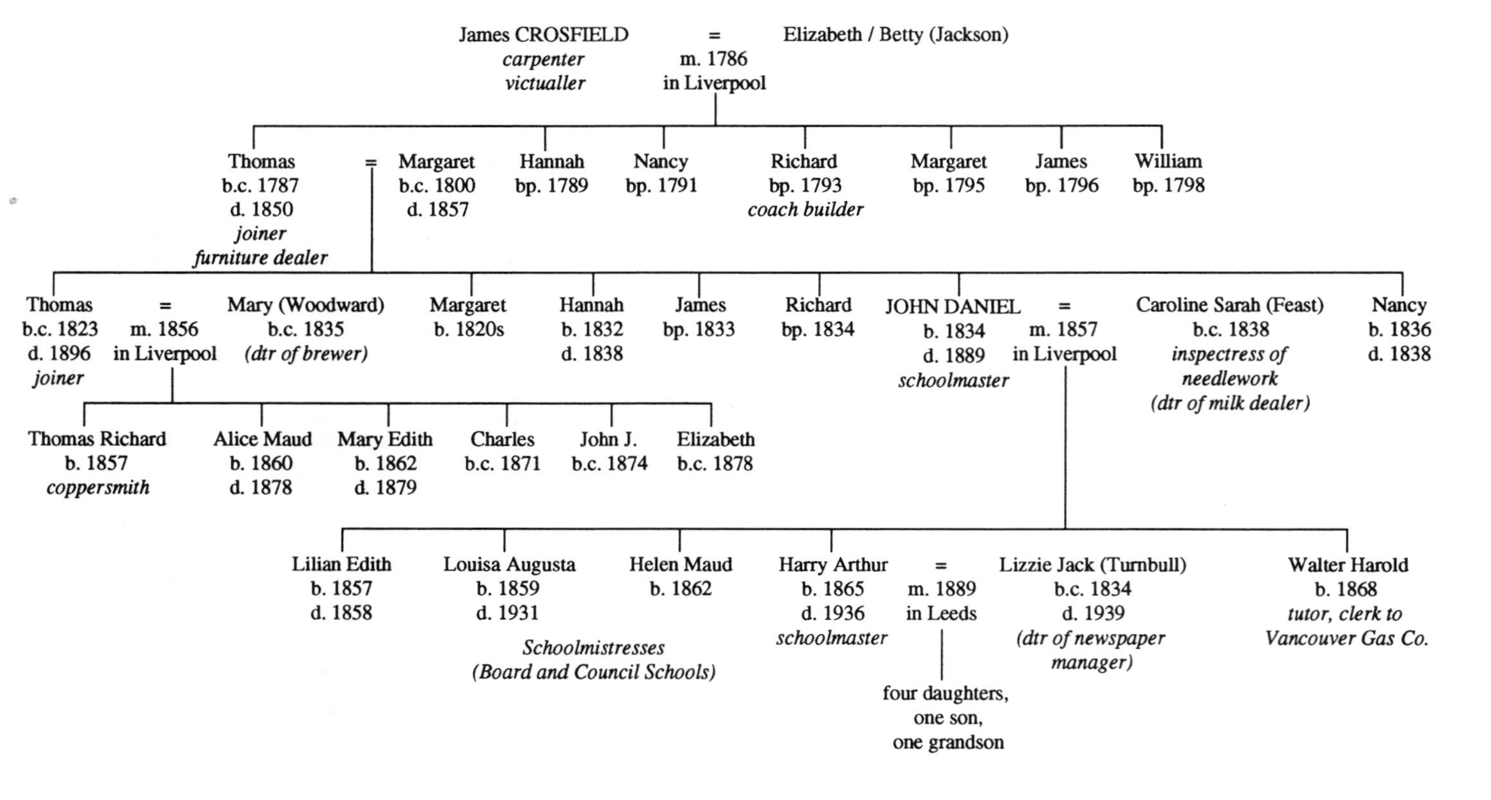

The CROSFIELD family tree

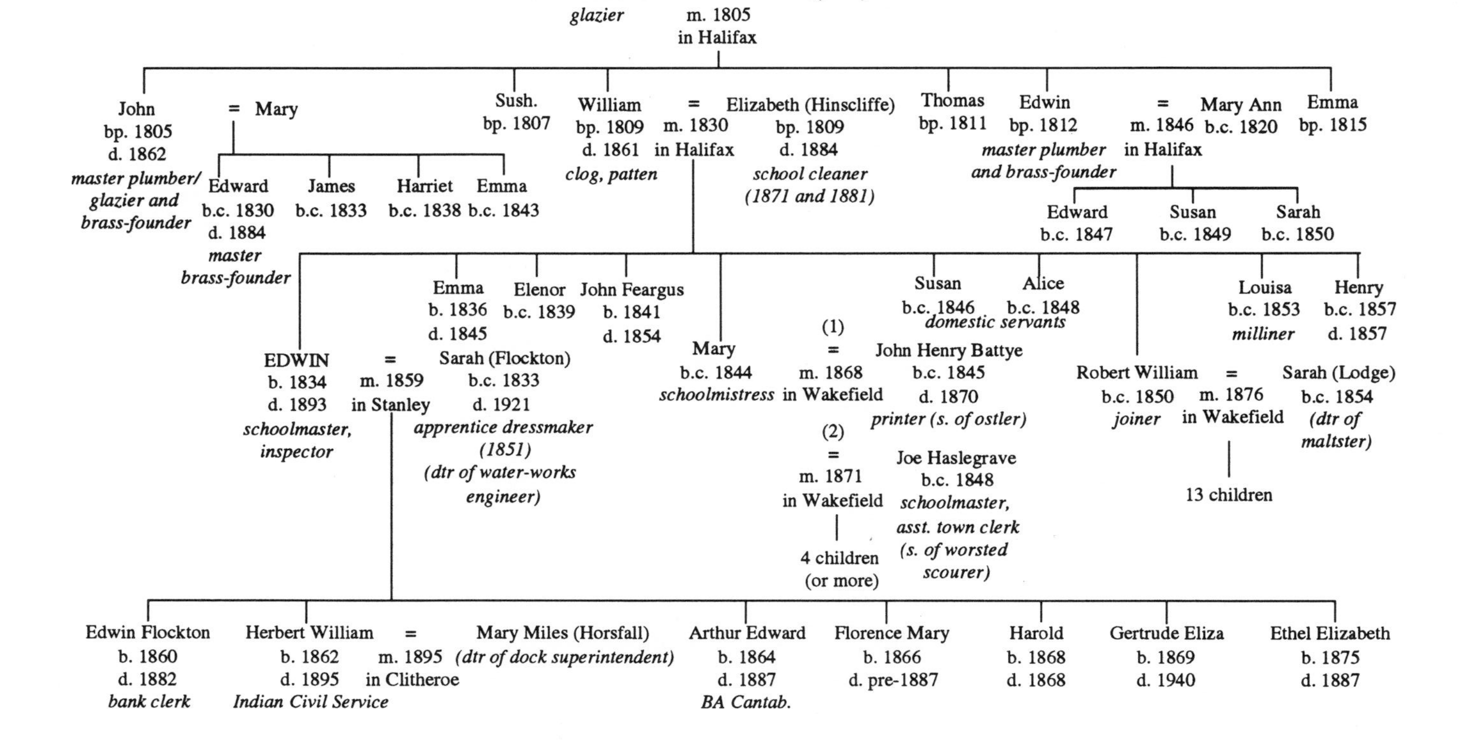

The FOSTER family tree

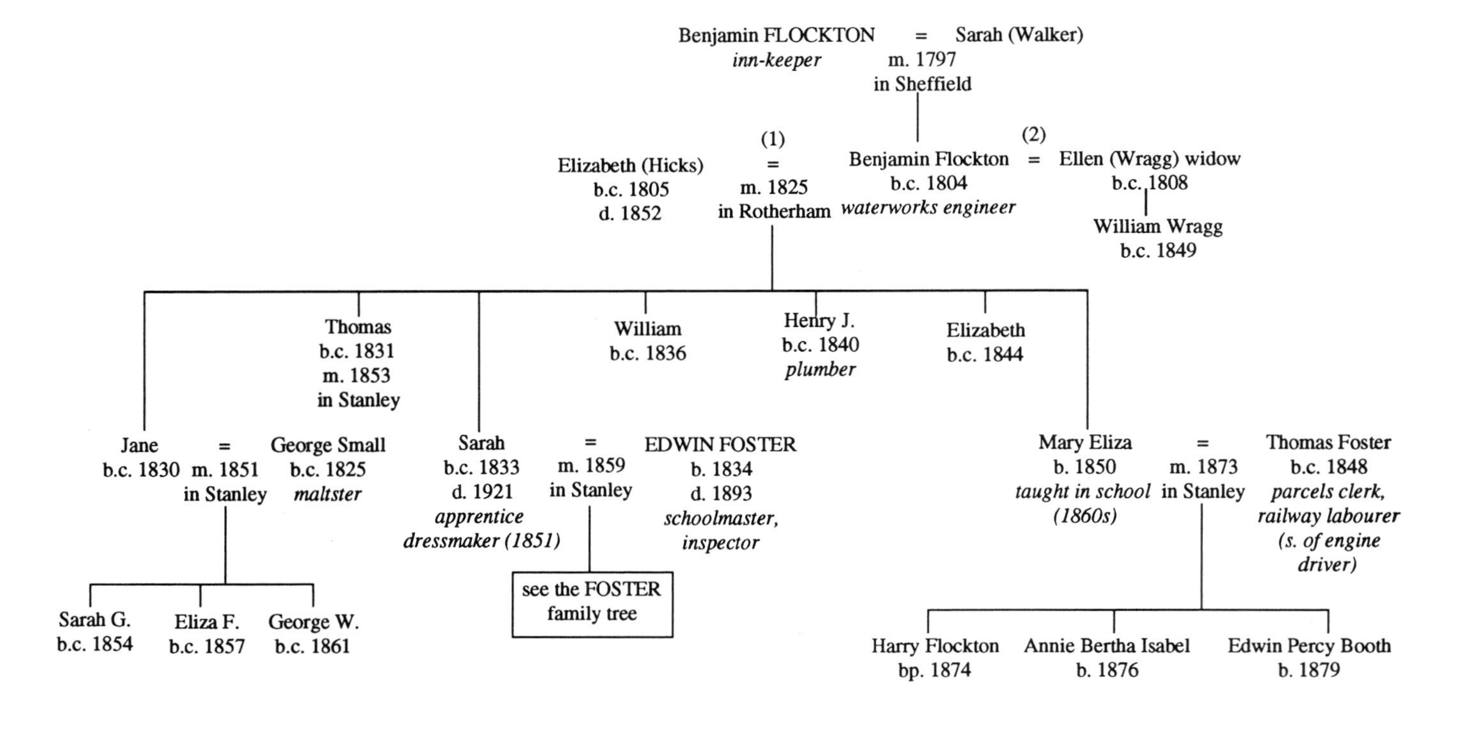

The FLOCKTON family tree

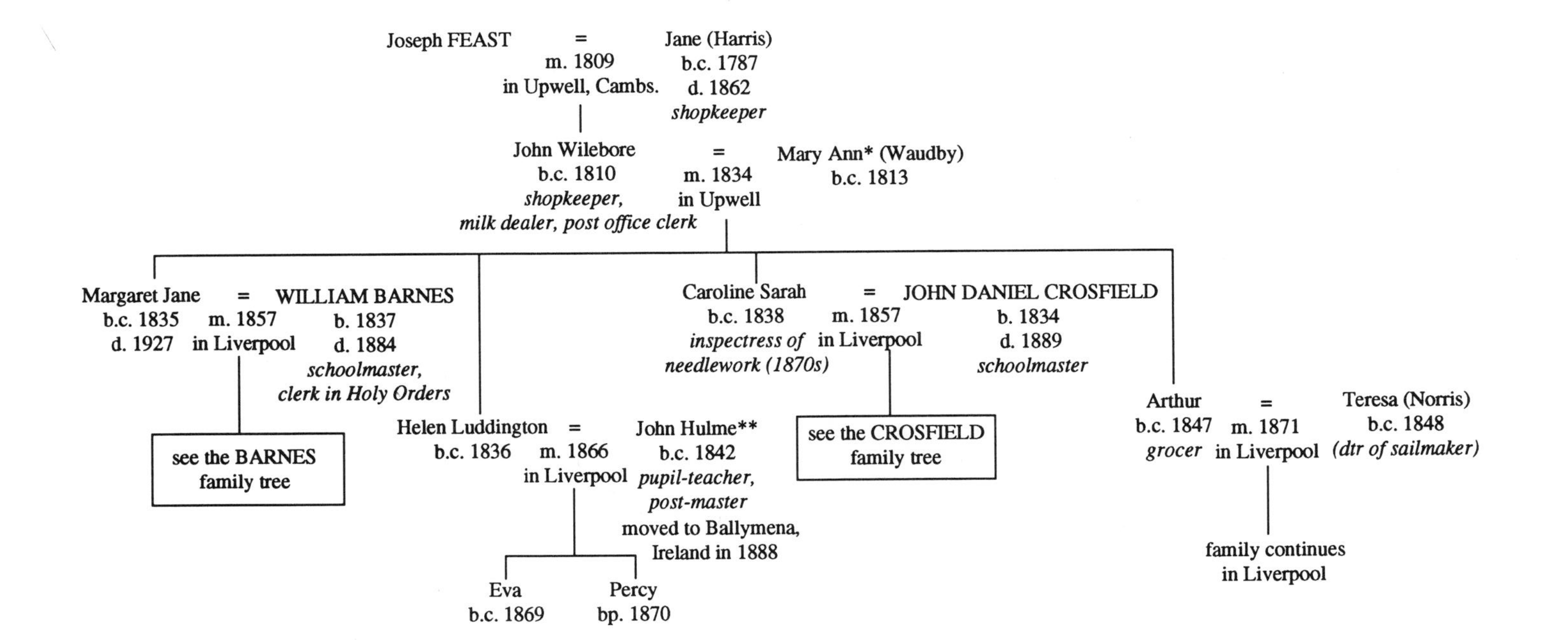

The FEAST family tree

References

A Note on Sources

Elementary education in the nineteenth century is a well-researched and well-documented field of study. The non-specialist reader who would like to know more about the curriculum, school fees and attendance, the building of schools, the role of the Inspectorate, the contribution of the various religious denominations or the broad political changes underlying the movement described in this book, would do better with access to a good library—and the advice of a knowledgeable librarian—than with a simple reading list. Meanwhile, there are two useful publications which review the available sources for anyone who wishes to pursue an interest in these topics at a personal or local level.

C. Chapman, *The Growth of British Education and its Records* (Stroud: Lochin Publishing, 1991) available from Family Tree Magazine, 15–16 Highlode Industrial Estate, Stocking Fen Road, Ramsey, Huntingdon, Cambs., PE17 1RB . £5.39 (inc. p. and p.)

W.B. Stephens and R. Unwin, *Materials for the Local and Regional Study of Schooling 1700–1900* (Archives and the User, no. 7; London: British Records Association, 1987), available from BRA, 18 Padbury Court, London E2 7EH. £6.75 (inc. p. and p.) or £4.50 to members.

The first of these books, Chapman, ranges more widely but the second, Stephens and Unwin, covers the field of elementary education a great deal more thoroughly.

Family historians who are seeking to trace individuals rather than pursue themes will need to make use of purely local school records and the archives of the National Society and the British and Foreign School Society (addresses below), but they may like to know that, for a limited period of years, names of teachers were printed in the official Minutes (later Reports) of the

Committee of Council on Education. This run of yearly volumes contains:

1. Lists of pupil-teachers by county, place and school (1847–1855/56)
2. Lists of certificated and registered teachers (1848–1855/56)

College examination successes are also included for 1853/54–1855/56 and they appear, too, in the National Society's Monthly Papers, along with lists of Queen's scholars and their schools, from the start of the formal training system in 1847 until 1875. The journal of the National Union of Teachers, *The Schoolmaster*, began to publish the, by then, extremely long lists of college and certificate examination results as they were announced each year from 1872.

Finally, the school by school Inspectors' reports in the official 'Minutes' occasionally mention teachers by name but these detailed reports cease to appear after 1860 and for the last three years they were published separately in a pair of volumes called 'Inspectors' Tabulated Reports 1858–60'. All the 'Minutes' should be available in major libraries on microfiche but it is worth enquiring around for the printed volumes which are a great deal easier to use.

National Society
Church of England Record Centre
15 Galleywall Road
Bermondsey
London
SE 16 3PB.
Tel. 071 222 7010

British and Foreign School Society
West London Institute of Higher Education
Lancaster House
Borough Road
Isleworth
Middlesex
TW 7 5 DU
Tel. 081 568 8741 Ext. 2615.

Notes to Chapter 1

1. H.J. Burgess, *Enterprise in Education* (London: SPCK, 1958).
H.J. Burgess and P.A. Welsby, *A Short History of the National Society* (London: National Society, 1961).
2. National Society School Files: St James, Halifax.
3. NS School Files: Christchurch, Christian Street, Liverpool.
4. R. Muir, *A History of Liverpool* (Liverpool: Liverpool University Press, 1907).
5. White's *Directory of the Clothing Districts of Yorkshire* (1858), p. 645.
6. J. Crabtree, *A Concise History of Halifax* (London: Simpkin & Marshall, 1836).
T.W. Hanson, *The Story of Old Halifax* (Halifax: F. King & Sons, 1920).
J.W. Houseman, 'The Growth and Development of the Parish of Halifax 1760–1848' (MA Thesis, Liverpool University, 1928).
A. Dingsdale, 'Yorkshire Mill Town: A Study of the Spatial Patterns and Processes of Urban-industrial Growth and the Evolution of the Spatial Structure of Halifax 1801–1901' (PhD Dissertation, Leeds University, 1974).
7. I.C. Taylor, *The Court and Cellar-dwelling: The Eighteenth Century Origin of the Liverpool Slum* (Liverpool: Transactions of the Historic Society of Lancashire and Cheshire, 1970), 122, p. 70.
8. J.A. Picton, *Memorials of Liverpool* (Liverpool: Longman's Green & Co., 1875), v.ii p. 367.
9. See n. 6.
10. White's *Directory of the Clothing Districts of Yorkshire* (1853), p. 350.
11. K. Cowlard, 'The Urban Development of Wakefield 1801–1901' (PhD Dissertation, Leeds University, 1974), p. 105.
12. T. Cann Hughes (ed.), *The Rolls of the Freemen of the Borough of Lancaster 1688–1840* (Record Society of Lancashire and Cheshire, 1935), I.
13. J. Ainsworth, *The Boot and Shoemaker's Assistant* (London: Groombridge & Sons, 1853).
K. Brooker, 'The Transformation of the Small Master Economy in the Boot and Shoe Industry 1887–1914 with Special Reference to Northampton' (PhD Dissertation, Hull University, 1986) and letter to author.
14. *Liverpool Review*, 24 September 1892, p. 14.
15. Minutes of the Committee of Council on Education, 1863/64, p. xxix.
16. Minutes of the CCE, 1867/68 p. lxxxv.

Notes to Chapter 2

1. Report of a Committee of the Manchester Statistical Society on the State of Education in the Borough of Liverpool in 1835–36 (London, 1836), pp. 7, 28.

2. National Society Annual Report, 1837, p. 54.

3. For a fuller account see J. Murphy, *The Religious Problem in English Education: the Crucial Experiment* (Liverpool: Liverpool University Press, 1959).

4. National Society School Files: Christchurch, Christian Street, Liverpool.

5. NS School Files: Christchurch, quoted by Revd Ould in correspondence.

6. NS School Files: Christchurch; Trust Deed, Christchurch, Liverpool, 1838

7. Revd C. Bullock, *Hugh M'Neile and Reformation Truth* (London: Home Words, n.d.), p. 66.

8. These were published as one item in a series of textbooks for the Irish schools which catered for Protestant and Catholic children together at this time. See D.H. Akenson, *The Irish Education Experiment* (London: Routledge & Kegan Paul, 1970).

9. Murphy, *The Religious Problem in English Education*, p. 120.

10. Authentic Report of a Great Public Meeting, 29 October 1835 (Liverpool: 1835) and see Murphy, *The Religious Problem in English Education*, Chapters 3 and 4.

11. Murphy, *The Religious Problem in English Education*, p. 93. This society was still active several decades later; see *Liverpool Daily Post*, 15 September 1868 for a report of 'three schools and fourteen more...'

12. NS Annual Report, 1837, p. 174.

13. NS School Files: Christchurch.

14. NS Annual Report, 1837, p. 54.

15. H.M. Walmsley, *The Life of Joshua Walmsley* (London, 1979), p. 89.

16. Religious Census 1851, P.P. 1852/53 xxxix pp. 92, 101.

17. E. Baines, *The Social, Educational and Religious State of the Manufacturing Districts* (London: Woburn Press facsimile, 1969 [1843]), tables between pp. 31 and 53.

18. F.W. Cornish, *The English Church in the Nineteenth Century* (London: Macmillan, 1933), I, pp. 6, 77, 83.

19. NS School Files: St James school, Halifax.

20. NS School Files: St James.

21. Baines, *The Social, Educational and Religious State.*

22. The Factory Act of 1833. See A.H. Robson, *The Education of Children Engaged in Industry in England 1833–1876* (London: Kegan Paul, 1931).

23. NS School Files: St James.

24. NS, Committee of Correspondence Minute Book, III, p. 10, 19 July 1839.

25. NS, General Committee Minutes, 29 April 1840.
26. K.M. Lyell, *Memoir of Leonard Horner* (London: Women's Printing Society, 1890), LXV, p. 13.
27. NS, General Committee Minutes, 23 May 1840.
28. St James, Victoria school, Halifax, Trust Deed (C 54 PRO).
29. Minutes of the Committee of Council on Education, 1839/40, p. 21.
30. *Northern Star*, 12 December 1840.
31. British and Foreign School Society, Annual Report, 1834, p. 56.
32. British and Foreign School Society, Annual Report, 1837, p. 8.
33. Baines, *The Social, Educational and Religious State.*
34. Minutes of the CCE, 1846, p. 400.
35. Holy Trinity School, Wakefield, Trust Deed (C 54 PRO).

Notes to Chapter 3

1. M. Arnold, 'The Twice-Revised Code 1962', *Fraser's Magazine*, March 1862, p. 360 and reproduced in G. Sutherland (ed.), *Arnold on Education* (Harmondsworth: Penguin Education, 1973).
2. N. Ball, *Her Majesty's Inspectorate 1839–1844* (Edinburgh and London: Oliver and Boyd, 1963), Appendix II, pp. 252-55.
3. Minutes of the Committee of Council on Education, 1845, II, pp. 78-181.
4. Minutes of the CCE, 1846, I, pp. I-II (Minute of 25 August 1846).
5. *Edinburgh Review*, April 1835, LXI, p. 475.
6. Minutes of the CCE, 1846, I, p. 3.
7. Minutes of the CCE, 1852/53, I, p. 68. Pupil Teacher Broadsheet.
8. Minutes of the CCE, 1847/48, p. clxxiii-clxxv.
9. Minutes of the CCE, 1852/53, I, p. 68.
10. D.R. Fearon, *School Inspection* (London: Macmillan, 1889), p. 32.
11. Minutes of the CCE, 1847/48, p. clxix and p. clxvii.
    Minutes of the CCE, 1848/49, p. 110. Circular to Her Majesty's Inspectors.
12. Minutes of the CCE, 1856/57, pp. 295-303.
13. Minutes of the CCE, 1850/51, p. xvii.
14. Minutes of the CCE, 1852/53, I, p. 9.
15. Minutes of the CCE, 1847/48, I , p. 205 and p. cclxxxvi.
16. or 'Kitchingham'.
17. Minutes of the CCE, 1847/48 to 1851–52 Lists of schools receiving grants.
    Minutes of the CCE, 1851/52, p. 501, St Andrew's school.
18. Minutes of the CCE, 1845/46, p. xix.
19. Minutes of the CCE, 1850/51, p. 188.

20. Minutes of the CCE, 1848/49, 1849/50, I, pp. 174, 175.

21. Ripon Diocesan Board of Education. Minutes, Leeds District 28 December 1843.

22. Minutes of the CCE, 1847–48, pp. 532-37.

23. Minutes of the CCE, 1847–48, pp. 210-12.

24. Ball, *Her Majesty's Inspectorate*, p. 224 and Minutes of the CCE, 1852/53, I, p. 68. Augmentation Broadsheet.

25. Minutes of the CCE, 1850/51, II, p. 193.

Minutes of the CCE, 1851/52, p. 542. The Speak family had also come, somewhat earlier, from Halifax.

26. *Wakefield Journal*, 22 and 29 November 1850 and see P. McCann and F.A. Young, *Samuel Wilderspin and the Infant School Movement* (London and Canberra: Croon Helm, 1982).

27. National Society School Files: Christchurch school, Christian Street, Liverpool, Trust Deed.

28. Minutes of the CCE, 1846, I, pp. 369, 370.

29. Minutes of the CCE, 1846, I, p. 369.

30. Minutes of the CCE, 1848/49, 1849/50, p. cxx and p. 135.

31. Minutes of the CCE, 1852/53, I, p. 68. Augmentation Broadsheet.

32. Minutes of the CCE, 1848/49, 1849/50, p. 146.

33. In the last year 323 had left and 249 were admitted.

34. Minutes of the CCE, 1850/51, II, p. 465.

35. Minutes of the CCE, 1853/54, p. 477.

36. Ball, *Her Majesty's Inspectorate*, p. 132.

37. Minutes of the CCE, 1852/53, p. 68. Pupil Teacher Broadsheet.

38. Minutes of the CCE, 1847/48, p. 153.

Notes to Chapter 4

1. Minutes of the Committee of Council on Education, 1853/54, I, p. 26.
2. Minutes of the CCE, 1853/54, I, pp. 457-63.
3. Minutes of the CCE, 1850/51, I, pp. xvii-xix.
4. Minutes of the CCE, 1854/55, p. 289.
5. National Society *Monthly Paper*, February 1854, pp. 37-41.
6. NS *Monthly Paper*, February 1854, pp. 37-41.
7. NS *Monthly Paper*, February 1854, p. 37.
8. Minutes of the CCE, 1853/54, II, p. 419 *et seq*.
9. Minutes of the CCE, 1850/51, II, p. 43.
10. Minutes of the CCE, 1853/54, II, pp. 438, 439.
11. Minutes of the CCE, 1845, I, p. 366.
12. Minutes of the CCE, 1850/51, II, p. 465.
13. Jones also spent two years at York; he served as drawing master at Wakefield Grammar School for a couple of years thereafter. It has not been possible to trace him further.

14. N.A.D. Scotland, 'The Centenary of Dean Close School and the Contribution of Francis Close to Education', *History of Education Society Bulletin*, 40, Autumn 1987, pp. 29-40.

S.T. Blake, *Cheltenham's Churches and Chapels AD 773–1883* (Cheltenham: Cheltenham Borough Council, 1979).

W.E. Beck, *A History of the Cheltenham Training Colleges* (Cheltenham: Cheltenham Training College, 1947).

A.F. Munden, 'The Church of England in Cheltenham 1826–56 with particular reference to Revd Francis Close' (MLitt Dissertation, Birmingham University, 1980).

15. Minutes of the CCE, 1846, I, p. 539.

16. Minutes of the CCE, 1854/55, p. 30.

17. Minutes of the CCE, 1854/55, p. 288.

18. *Wakefield Journal and Examiner*, 29 May 1852.

19. T. Adkins, *The History of St John's College, Battersea* (London: National Society, 1906), p. 123.

20. G.A. Denison, *Notes of My Life 1805–1878* (London: James Parker & Co., 1879), p. 142.

21. Revd W. Pollock, 'A reply to the letter of Mr S.F. Warren travelling agent of the National Society', Liverpool, 1853, pp. 10-18. The memorial was signed by 1051 members and 1794 non-members.

22. H.J. Burgess, *Enterprise in Education* (London: SPCK, 1958), p. 142.

23. 'Proceedings of a Public Meeting in the Royal Ampitheatre 23 June 1853', Liverpool, 1853.

24. W. Etherington, 'A History of St John's College, York 1841–1914' (MEd Dissertation, Leicester University, 1969), p.70. They noted how he read the prayers from the Communion Rails, that he did not use the metrical psalms and that he preached in a surplice.

25. *Yorkshire Gazette*, 6 September 1845.

26. Etherington, 'A History of St John's College', p. 72.

27. O. Chadwick, *The Victorian Church* (London: Adam & Charles Black, 1966), pp. 250-71.

A.O.J. Cockshut, *Anglican Attitudes* (London: Collins, 1959), pp. 39-61.

28. Chadwick, *The Victorian Church* , p. 291.

29. Revd F. Power, 'A Tract for My Parish with Reference to the Gorham Case, London, 1850, p. 1.

30. Newspaper cutting, unascribed, in Wakefield District Library c. November 1850.

31. Etherington, 'A History of St John's College', pp. 96, 97.

32. Etherington, 'A History of St John's College', p.98 and *Yorkshire Gazette*, 8 November 1853. The Principal of the Female College, Miss Cruse was accused of sympathies with a Tractarian vicar in London and of introducing a book to her students called *Steps to the Altar*.

33. York Training College. Minutes of the Governing Committee 6 September 1854 and printed pamphlet in the College archive.

34. W.R.W. Stephens, *The Life and Letters of Dean Farquhar Hook* (London: Richard Bentley & Son, 1880). In this book the college is never mentioned though it was jointly run by the two dioceses of York and Ripon and Hook was deeply involved with educational matters throughout his time in Yorkshire. See also Chapter XI 1870–1872.

35. Minutes of the CCE, 1854/55, p.278 and pp. 952-57.

NS *Monthly Paper*, February 1854, pp. 37-41.

36. Scotland, 'The Centenary of Dean Close School', Cheltenham Training College Trust Deed.

37. NS *Monthly Paper*, February 1854, p. 37. Official circular.

38. Minutes of the CCE, 1854/55 p. 307.

39. NS *Monthly Paper*, July 1856, p. 175.

Notes to Chapter 5

1. Minutes of the Committee of Council on Education, 1854/55, p. 17.

2. Minutes of the CCE, 1853, p. 28.

3. H.J. Burgess, *Enterprise in Education* (London: SPCK, 1958), Chapter 4.

4. Sir J. Kay-Shuttleworth, *Memorandum on Popular Education* (London: 1868) and Woburn Books (facsimile) 1969, p. 49.

5. National Society Annual Report, 1839.

6. York Training College, Minutes of the Governing Committee, 24 February 1842.

7. W. Etherington, 'A History of St John's College, York, 1841–1914' (MEd Dissertation, Leicester University, 1969), pp. 45, 46, 63-66.

Minutes of the CCE, 1847/48, pp. 410-412.

8. Minutes of the CCE, 1853, p. 424.

Minutes of the CCE, 1854/55, p. 278.

9. YTC, Minutes of the Governing Committee, 27 April 1854 and 15 October 1855.

10. YTC, Minutes of the Governing Committee, 29 April 1845 and Etherington, 'A History of St John's College', p. 68.

11. YTC, Minutes of the Governing Committee, 10 February 1853.

12. e.g. washing charged for at £2 a year but included after October 1855.

13. National Society *Monthly Paper*, August 1848, p. 14.

14. Minutes of the CCE, 1845, p. 14.

15. YTC, Minutes of the Governing Committee, May 1843, June 1844, November 1852, February 1855.

16. Minutes of the CCE, 1848/50, II, p. 692.

17. Royal Commission to Enquire into the State of Popular Education: Report, IV, 1861, pp. 396, 403.

18. Minutes of the CCE, 1855–56, p. 363.

19. YTC, Minutes of the Governing Committee, 15 May 1851.
20. Etherington, 'A History of St John's College', p. 85.
21. Minutes of the CCE, 1854/55, pp. 14, 15, 286, 310.
22. Minutes of the CCE, 1854/55, pp. 16, 309.
23. Minutes of the CCE, 1854/55, p. 310.
24. Minutes of the CCE, 1854/55, p. 19.
25. Minutes of the CCE, 1854/55, pp. 33-47.
26. Minutes of the CCE, 1856/57. Revd Temple quoting Moseley, 1854/55, pp. 294, 295.
27. Minutes of the CCE, 1854–55, pp. 277, 288.
28. British and Foreign School Society, *Educational Record*, III, 1857, pp. 151-55.
29. Minutes of the CCE, 1855/56, pp. 20-25.
30. Minutes of the CCE, 1853, p. 26.
31. Minutes of the CCE, 1854/55, pp. 956, 957.
32. NS *Monthly Paper*, April 1856, p. 89.
33. Royal Commission to Enquire into the State of Popular Education: Report, IV, 1861, p. 7.
34. Royal Commission, pp. 391-414.
35. Royal Commission, p. 399.
36. Minutes of the CCE, 1856/57. Letter, 22 January 1857, p. 7.
37. Royal Commission, p. 395.
38. Minutes of the CCE, 1858/59, p. 289.
39. Royal Commission, pp. 397, 398.
40. Minutes of the CCE, 1854/55, p. 49. Examination questions for religious instruction for 1854; not available for 1855.
41. Royal Commission, p. 404.

Notes to Chapter 6

1. Minutes of the Committee of Council on Education, 1854/55, p. 276.
2. Ripon Diocesan Board of Education, Annual Reports, 1854, 1855, 1856.
3. York Training College, Governors' Quarterly Meeting, 23 May 1855.
4. Minutes of the CCE, 1856/57, p. 16. Augmentation Broadsheet. In the first year of probation the government augmented the teacher's salary at a rate corresponding to the lowest class of certificate i.e. £10 or £15 a year depending on the examination results. This rate in turn determined the minimum salary the managers were obliged to offer if they wished to employ a trained teacher. The minimum was set at twice the augmentation.
5. *Post Office Directory of Cheshire*, 1857, p. 21.
6. *Liverpool Daily Post*, 11 July 1883.
7. *Osborne's Directory of Birkenhead*, 1854, p. 28.

8. National Society School Files: Holy Trinity, Birkenhead. Application for grant 13 August 1855. The population of Birkenhead was about 10,000.
9. Holy Trinity school, Birkenhead Trust Deed (C 54 PRO).
10. Holy Trinity school, Birkenhead Trust Deed, dated 27 July 1844.
11. Minutes of the CCE, 1850–51, II p. 498.
12. Minutes of the CCE, 1852–53, II p. 506.
13. Minutes of the CCE, 1852–53, II, p. 884.
14. NS School Files: Holy Trinity, Birkenhead.
15. Six square feet per pupil was regarded as the minimum space to be allowed.
Minutes of the CCE, 1845, I. Plans at end of volume.
Minutes of the CCE, 1839/40, p. 49.
16. Minutes of the CCE, 1851–52, pp. 78-91.
17. NS School Files: Holy Trinity, Birkenhead. Specifications of teacher's residence.
18. Revd J. Gratrix, *Sermons* (Halifax, 1843), p. 28.
19. Thus commented James Bury, Sub-Inspector of Factories under Robert Saunders. Select Committee on the Act for the Regulation of Mills and Factories: Second Report (Irish University Press Factories, 1840), I, pp. 64-67.
20. NS School Files: St James school, Halifax, October/November 1843.
21. NS School Files: St James school, Halifax. Letter 13 October 1845.
22. NS School Files: St James school, Halifax. Letter 15 October 1844.
23. St James Crosshills school, Halifax Trust Deed (C 54 PRO).
24. St James Crosshills school, Halifax. Sketch plan of building (West Yorkshire archives, Leeds).
25. NS School Files: St James school, Halifax. Undated letter, probably autumn 1843.
26. NS School Files: St James school, Halifax. Undated letter, probably late 1844 or early 1845.
27. Minutes of the CCE, 1848–50, I, p. 175.
28. Minutes of the CCE, 1848–50, I, p. 227, 18 October 1849.
29. Minutes of the CCE, 1847/48, I, p. cclxxxi.
30. Minutes of the CCE, 1855/56, p. 271. Watkins quotes a letter from the master Edward Stevens in which he explains exactly how the fee rise has not led to a drop in income.
31. NS *Monthly Paper*, November 1855, p. 168.
32. Minutes of the CCE, 1855/56, p. 304.
33. NS *Monthly Paper*, July 1855, p. 207. Edward Stevens read a paper at a meeting on July 21 1855.
34. Minutes of the CCE, 1855/56, p. 368.
35 Liverpool School Board First Triennial Report, 1873, p. 87.
36. Minutes of the CCE, 1855/56, p. 12.

37. Minutes of the CCE, 1856/57, pp. 16, 17. Augmentation Broadsheet.
38. Farnley Iron Work's School, Log book, 22 August 1864.
39. Minutes of the CCE, 1855/56, p. 463.
Minutes of the CCE, 1856/57, p. 415.
Minutes of the CCE, 1857/58, p. 292.

Revd Watkins noted that average salaries for certificated schoolmasters in the late 1850s ran from about £88 in Yorkshire to £98 in Lancashire: the difference he attributed to Lancashire's greater urban population.

40. Minutes of the CCE, 1857/58, pp. 292, 293.

Notes to Chapter 7

1. National Society *Monthly Paper*, April 1858, p. cxxxvii.
2. Farnley Iron Works school. Grant application 1857 (ED 7 PRO).
3. Revd G. Chappell, *Memoir of the Late Revd John Ellison MA* (privately printed, March 1913), p. 6. His MA of 1862 was a 'Lambeth degree' specially granted by the Archbishop of Canterbury for 'proficiency in theology'. A research file for this family is lodged with the Cheshire Record Office in Chester.
4 Chappell, *Memoir of the Late Revd John Ellison.*
5. Their immediate forebears were wealthy nonconformist wool merchants in Leeds.
6. Farnley Iron Works school. Grant application 1857.
7. NS School Files: Old Farnley school. Correspondence 1846–48.
8. NS School Files: Old Farnley school. Letter 3 February 1846.
9. The foundation stone was laid on 16 April 1846 in the presence of the Bishop: 'twenty clergy in surplices processed'. From handwritten notes with school log-book, possibly copied from a press report.
10. NS School Files: Old Farnley school. Trust Deed.
11. Minutes of the Committee on Council for Education, 1847/48, p. 189.
12. See Chapter IV n. 14 for the importance of Cheltenham and the evangelicalism of Revd Francis Close at this time. Both Ryder and the Morgans came from this area and two other Armitage brothers were substantial residents there before and during this period.
13. Farnley Iron Works school. Grant application 1857: sketch plan of school.
14. It is possible that John Crosfield moved elsewhere before his appointment in Cheshire in January 1862. He cannot be found in the 1861 census or in Directories in this area or for Mersyside or Cheshire.
15. Farnley Iron Works school. Grant application 1857.
16. Farnley Iron Works school, Inspectors' reports. School Board file (West Yorkshire archive, Leeds).
17. Royal Commission on the State of Popular Education. Report 1861.
Minutes of the CCE, 1863/64, pp. xxiv-lxvii.

18. *White's Directory of Leeds*, 1835, p. 301.
19. Farnley Iron Works school, log book, 31 May 1864.
20. Minutes of the CCE, 1863/64, pp. xvi, xvii.
21. Minutes of the CCE, 1863/64, p. xxxvi.
22. Farnley Iron Works school, Inspectors' reports, 31 May 1865. Inspectors' comments for most of the 1860s appear with other official documents in the School Board file (West Yorkshire archive) as well as in Barnes's log book.
23. Minutes of the CCE, 1867/68, Appendix I, p. lxxix.
24. Farnley Iron Works school, Inspectors' reports, 31 May 1865.
25. Farnley Iron Works school, log book, 8 November 1864.
26. Farnley Iron Works school, log book, 14 March 1865.
27. Sir J. Kay-Shuttleworth, *Memorandum on Popular Education* (Woburn Press, 1969 [1868]), p. 23.
28. Minutes of the CCE, 1863/64, pp. xxiv-lxvii. The Revised Code, article 52b.
29. The Revised Code, article 90.
30. Farnley Iron Works school, log book, 27 October 1862. Subsequent staff changes are all recorded here and will not be separately referenced.
31. Farnley Iron Works school, log book, 22 August 1864.
32. A Yorkshire Clergyman, 'Letter to managers of schools...on the Revised Code', London, 1861, p. 13.
33. Minutes of the CCE, 1863/64, p. 165.
34. Minutes of the CCE, 1863/64, pp. vii-xl.
35. Farnley Iron Works school, log book, 22 December 1864. William James Armitage, a son of James, managed the school at this time.
36. Farnley Iron Works school, log book, 30 November, 2 to 5 December 1867.
37. Farnley Iron Works school, log book, 11 February 1867.
38. Minutes of the CCE, 1866/67, pp. 170-73.
39. A Bill for the Regulation and Inspection of Mines, 23 and 24 Vict. c.151 1860.
40. Farnley Iron Works school, Inspectors' reports, 26 July 1868.
41. Farnley Iron Works school, log book, 2 June 1865 and 26 October 1866.
42. See later Chapter XI, 1870–72.
43. Farnley Iron Works school, log book, 2 November 1866, 31 October 1865 and 24 May 1867.
44. Farnley Iron Works school, log book, 22 March 1867.
45. Farnley Iron Works school, log book, 29 August 1864.
46. See Bishop of Carlisle's Act Books for 7 June 1868 and 19 December 1869 and the Carlisle Diocesan Year Books for this period.
47. See the Annual Reports and other records for the Casterton Clergy Daughters School held at the Record Office in Kendal.
48. Revd Joseph Preston Ward.

Notes to Chapter 8

1. *White's Directory of Cheshire*, 1860, v. 2, p. 946.
2. *Morris's Directory of Cheshire*, 1864, pp. 308, 309.
3. Her Majesty's Inspectors' Tabulated Reports: I, 1858–59, Revd Norris, 19 November 1858, p. 15; II, 1859/60, Mr Brodie, 28 October 1859, p. 76.
4. HMI Tabulated Reports: II, 1859/60, Revd Fraser, 27 October 1859, p. 75.
5. Minutes of the Committee of Council on Education, 1851/52, p. 781, 13 October 1851.
6. HMI Tabulated Reports: I, 1858–59, Revd Norris, p. 15.
7. *Morris's Directory of Cheshire*, 1864, p. 91. This school offered the usual curriculum plus mensuaration and land surveying. French, German and music were all extras.
8. Knutsford Parochial school, log book, 10 January 1866.
9. Knutsford Parochial school, application for grant 9 November 1855 (ED PRO).
10. Knutsford Parochial school, log book, 4 December 1862. Inspector's report, 21 October 1862.
11. Knutsford Parochial school, log book, 28 November 1864.
12. Minutes of the CCE, 1863/64, p. xxxviii.
13. Newspaper cutting, unascribed, undated. Crosfield's salary £113.7.9—on arrival?
14. Knutsford Parochial school, grant application.
15. Minutes of the CCE, 1863/64, p. xliii.
16. Knutsford Parochial school, log book, 11 October 1870.
17. Royal Commission on the Employment of Children, Young Persons and Women in Agriculture: Second Report (Irish University Press, Agriculture), 11, Evidence p. 65.
18. *Edinburgh Review*, 231, July 1861, pp. 5, 6.
19. *Edinburgh Review*, 231, p. 38.
20. *Edinburgh Review*, 231, p. 16.
21. Royal Commission on the State of Popular Education: Report, 1861, IV, p. 73.
22. Minutes of the CCE, 1863/64, article 88 and Apprentices Broadsheet p. xlvi .
23. Minutes of the CCE, 1847/48, p. clxxiii. Form of Indenture.
    Minutes of the CCE, 1852/53, I, p. 68, Apprentices Broadsheet.
24. Official circular in the form of a letter to William Armitage of Farnley, 12 November 1858, from the Committee of Council on Education. School Board Files (West Yorkshire archive, Leeds).
25. Minutes of the CCE, 1863/64, p. xlvi.

26. Minutes of the CCE, 1867/68, p. viii.
27. Minutes of the CCE, 1863/64, pp. xlvi, xlvii.
28. Knutsford Parochial school, log book. School and town events, staff, pupils, curriculum etc. in log book unless noted otherwise.
29. The Girls Parochial school took some small boys.
30. Minutes of the CCE, 1867/68. Code 1868 s. 466, p. lxxix.
31. Minutes of the CCE, 1867/68, p. lxiii and Royal Commission on the Employment of Children: Second Report, 1867, Appendix Part I, p. 11.
32. Royal Commission on the Employment of Children: Second Report, 1867, Appendix Part I, pp. 64, 65.
33. *Macclesfield Courier*, 22 October 1864.
34. *The Times*, 21 March 1866.
35. *Warrington and Northwich Guardian*, 7 May 1866.
J. Leach, *The History of Knutsford Royal May Day* (Knutsford, n.d.)
36. *Warrington and Northwich Guardian*, 7 May 1864.
37. *Warrington and Northwich Guardian*, 22 February 1868.
38. *Macclesfield Courier*, 23 December 1871. Meeting of Macclesfield and District Teachers Association.

Notes to Chapter 9

1. Her Majesty's Inspectors' Tabulated Reports: I, 1858/59, Revd Birley, 13 and 14 October 1859.
2. Now Queensland Street.
3. J.A. Klapas, 'Geographical Aspects of Religious Change in Victorian Liverpool 1837–1901' (MA Dissertation, Liverpool University, 1977), p. 72.
4. *Slater's Directory of Lancashire*, 1869, pp. 563-65.
5. Royal Commission on the State of Popular Education Report, 1861, V, p. 5.
6. The Charity Commissioners (Lancashire) Report 1819–37, pp. 685-88.
7. The Charity Commissioners (England and Wales) Eighth Report, 1861 PP, XX, p. 4. In 1860, revision of Trust Deeds was made simpler and cheaper by a transfer of jurisdiction from the courts to the Commissioners themselves.
8. Melling school, Trust Deed 1861 (c/o the trustees).
9. *Slater's Directory of Lancashire*, 1861, 1864, 1869.
10. C. Ratcliff, *Melling Church of England School*, booklet n.d.
11. Melling School: Education Department returns etc. 1871 (ED 2/240 PRO).
12. Census 1861.
13. Minutes of the Committee of Council on Education, 1863/64 p. xxxviii.
14. Minutes of the CCE, 1863/64, pp. xxiv-xxxviii. Revised Code.

15. Melling school, plans for extensions 1905–10 (c/o the trustees). E. Newton, *Melling with Cunscough*, booklet n.d., p. 20.
16. Minutes of the CCE, 1846, I, p. 373.
17. See Chapter VIII.
18. Melling school: Education Department returns etc., 30 October 1872.
19. Endowed Charities, Return to the House of Commons, 11 December 1908, pp. 49, 50.
20. Melling school, correspondence in school files, 6 January 1871 (ED 49 PRO). Reade and Foster were friends and colleagues, later, in Liverpool.
21. Census 1871.
22. Registrar-General, Thirty-First Annual Report 1870 for the fourth quarter 1868 PP XVI.I 1870 p. lvii.
23. *Slater's Directory of Lancashire*, 1869, p. 331.
24. S. Kelly, 'The Select Vestry of Liverpool and the Administration of the Poor Law 1821–1871' (MA Dissertation, Liverpool University, 1972), p. 76.
25. Minutes of the CCE, 1842/43, bound at end of volume.
26. J.A. Picton, *Memorials of Liverpool* (Liverpool: Longmans Green & Co., 1875), II, p. 140.
27. *The Builder*, 10 October 1868, pp. 746, 747.
28. *The Porcupine*, 9 January 1869, p. 397.
29. *The Porcupine*, 7 November 1868, p. 309.
30. Liverpool School Board First Triennial Report, 1870–1873, p. 76. *The Schoolmaster*, 13 January 1872, p. 13.
31. The Poor Law Board became the Local Government Board in 1871.
32. Liverpool Select Vestry Minutes of the Industrial Schools Committee, 19 October 1868.
33. Liverpool Select Vestry Minutes, 15 September 1868.
34. Kirkdale Industrial School, records of the Poor Law Board, 1869 (MH 12 PRO). Mary Eliza Flockton had left the household by 1871. She was married in Yorkshire in 1873.
35. Liverpool Select Vestry Minutes, 2 March 1869.
36. Liverpool Select Vestry Minutes, 5 April 1870.
37. *Slater's Directory of Lancashire*, 1861, I p. 190.
38. Picton, *Memorials of Liverpool*, II, p. 425, 426.
39. Liverpool Select Vestry Minutes, 5 January 1869.
40. Liverpool Borough Council Proceedings, 1866/67, pp. 244-51.
41. Kirkdale Industrial School, classification register (column heads).
42. *The Porcupine*, 8 May 1869, p. 48.
43. Liverpool School Board First Triennial Report, p. 31.
44. Kirkdale Industrial School, records of the Poor Law Board, 1869.
45. Liverpool School Board First Triennial Report, p. 81.
46. Kirkdale Industrial School, records of the Poor Law Board, 22 June 1869, 18 September 1868.

47. D.R. Fearon, HMI Return to the House of Commons (on schools in Liverpool and Manchester) 18 March 1869, p. 169.

48. Kirkdale Industrial School, records of the Poor Law Board, 11 and 12 May 1869.

49. Kirkdale School, records of the Poor Law Board, 1 December 1870.

50. Poor Law Board, Sixteenth Annual Report, 1863–64 PP XXV.I 1864 p. 19. Transfer of responsibility from the Committee of Council for Education to the Poor Law Board.

51. Kirkdale School, records of the Poor Law Board, May 1869.

52. Kirkdale School, records of the Poor Law Board, May 1869. Pupil-teachers could sit for Queen's Scholarships and proceed to training college; their pay was laid by for them by the Industrial School.

53. Kirkdale School, records of the Poor Law Board, 15 December 1870.

54. Liverpool Select Vestry Minutes, 1 June 1869.

55. Kirkdale School, records of the Poor Law Board. Letters from H.J. Hagger to Poor Law Board, 30 December and 10 January.

56. Letter from H.J. Hagger to Poor Law Board, 5 August 1870.

57. Letter from H.J. Hagger to Poor Law Board, 11 February 1871.

58. Liverpool Select Vestry Minutes, 15 August 1871. Kirkdale School, records to the Poor Law Board. Letter from H.J. Hagger to Poor Law Board, 21 August 1871.

59. *Liverpool Mercury*, 16 August 1871.

Notes to Chapter 10

1. M. Arnold, *The Twice Revised Code* (Harmondsworth: Penguin Education, 1973), pp. 43, 44, 51.

2. See *A Verbatim Report...of the Debate in Parliament during the Progress of the Elementary Education Bill 1870* (Manchester and London: National Education Union, n.d.).

3. J.G. Fitch and D.R. Fearon, 'Return...of all Schools for the Poorer Classes of Children (Birmingham, Leeds, Liverpool and Manchester)' for the House of Commons, 2 March 1870.

4. Elementary Education Act 1870, Vict. c.75 clause 70.

5. For example Birkenhead, whose School Board was set up in 1890, and Preston where no School Board was ever formed.

6 Elementary Education Act 1876 (Sandon Act) 39 and 40 Vict. c.79.

7. Elementary Education Act 1870, clause 14 (2).

8. Elementary Education Act 1870, clause 7 (2).

9. General Regulations for the First Election of School Boards in Boroughs (in the Verbatim Report), pp. 615-19 n. 2.

10. Elementary Education Act 1870, second schedule.

11. *Liverpool Daily Post*, 15 November 1870.

12. *Liverpool Mercury*, 12 November 1870.
Liverpool Daily Post, 12 November 1870. Mr Williams of St Mary's, Edgehill withdrew his nomination.
13. *Liverpool Mercury*, 27 April 1858.
14. *Liverpool Daily Post*, 15 November 1870.
15 *Liverpool Mercury*, 16 November 1870.
16. *Liverpool Mercury*, 12 November 1870.
Liverpool School Board First Triennial Report, 1873 Appendix, pp. 2-13.
17. Liverpool School Board First Triennial Report, 1873, pp. 73, 97.
18. Liverpool School Board First Triennial Report, 1873, pp. 76, 81.
19. Liverpool and Birkenhead Official Red Book 1901, p. 190.
20. Liverpool Select Vestry Minutes of Industrial Schools Committee, 15 August 1871.
21. Liverpool School Board Minutes of General Purposes Committee, 15 January 1872.
22. Liverpool School Board First Triennial Report, 1873, p.102.
23. Liverpool School Board Minutes of District Education Committee, 8 July 1872.
24. Liverpool School Board First Triennial Report, 1873, p. 18.
25. Liverpool School Board Proceedings, 8 March 1875.
26. Liverpool School Board Proceedings, 10 April 1876.
27. Liverpool School Board Minutes of Education and Management Committee 10 March 1873.
28. Liverpool School Board Proceedings, 12 January 1874.
29. *Liverpool Mercury*, 16 January 1872.
30. R.M. Jennings, 'The Role of Managers under the Liverpool School Board 1870–1903' (MEd Dissertation, Liverpool University, 1986), Chapter VI.
31. *The Schoolmaster*, 24 May 1873, p. 307.
32. *School Board Chronicle*, 24 May 1873, p. 347.
33. Jennings, 'The Role of Managers', pp. 212-15.
34. Jennings, 'The Role of Managers', p. 87. List of Board schools with date of opening and appointment of managers.
35. Liverpool School Board Proceedings, 12 February 1872.
36. Liverpool School Board Minutes, 23 March 1874.
37. Liverpool School Board Minutes, 16 February 1874.
38. Liverpool School Board Minutes, 9 November 1874.
39. Liverpool School Board Minutes, 31 August 1874.
40. Liverpool School Board Minutes, 9 September 1874.
41. Liverpool School Board Proceedings, 13 March 1876. M.E. Bailey, *Hints on Introducing the Kindergarten System into English Infant Schools* (London: George Philip & Son, 1876).

References to Froebel Society Minute Book etc. c/o archivist, Roehampton Institute.

42. Liverpool School Board Proceedings, 6 December 1875.

43. J. Collins, 'The Training of Elementary Schoolteachers in England and Wales 1840–90' (DPhil Dissertation, Bulmershe College, 1985) p. 68.

Miss Yelf went on to Edge Hill College, Liverpool in 1884; see F.A. Montgomery, *Edge Hill College: A History 1885–1985* (Ormskirk: Edge Hill College, 1985).

44. Liverpool School Board Minutes, 15 October 1876.

45. Liverpool School Board Minutes, 22 September 1879. *Suggestions to Managers of Public Elementary Schools* (Liverpool: School Board, 1879, 1880).

46. D.R. Fearon, *Inspection of Schools* (London: Macmillan, 1876).

47. Liverpool School Board Minutes, 29 September and 27 October 1879.

48. As in *Suggestions to Managers*, pp. 76, 77.

49. Liverpool School Board General Rules, 1888.

50. *Liverpool Mercury*, 7 July 1871.

51. Liverpool School Board Proceedings, 9 June 1873 and Pleasant Street log book, 7 May 1873.

52. Liverpool School Board Minutes, 23 April 1875.

53. Liverpool School Board Minutes, 1 and 15 November 1875.

54. Liverpool School Board Minutes, 16 October 1876.

55. Liverpool School Board Minutes, 10 October 1884.

56. R.E.L. *Reminiscences of St Philip's Church, Hardman Street 1867–82* (Liverpool, 1882).

57. Liverpool School Board Minutes, 31 October and 12 December 1884.

58. Liverpool School Board Proceedings, 7 February 1884.

59. Liverpool School Board Proceedings, 12 January 1874.

60. She replaced Kate Saunders who was born to a single woman in Hertfordshire and who trained later at Norwich.

61. Liverpool School Board Minutes, 3 April 1884.

62. Liverpool School Board Minutes, 5 April 1888.

63. Liverpool Geological Society Minutes, 10 October 1876 and 8 October 1889.

64 A.L. Reade, *The Mellards and Their Descendants* (London, 1915), pp. 147, 156.

65. Liverpool School Board Minutes, 5 June 1890.

66. St Mark's College, Chelsea Archive, c/o The College of St John Foundation, Plymouth.

St Bede's College, Durham Archive, c/o College of St Hild and St Bede, Durham.

L. Grove, *The Model School, Bede College 1881–1933* (Durham: The College of St Hild and Bede, n.d.), pp. 8, 9.

67. For a full account of this episode see Jennings, 'The Role of Managers', Chapter IV.

68. *Liverpool Mercury*, 14 July 1893.

69. *Liverpool Mercury*, 6 September 1893.

Notes to Chapter 11, Section 1870–1872

1. Revd R.V. Taylor, *The Biographia Leodiensis* or *Leeds Worthies* (London: Simkin, Marshall & Co, 1865), pp. 364-66, 411.

2. See J. Burgess (ed.), *Bishop of the Lake Counties: Letters of Samuel Waldegrave* (Carlisle, 1987) for correspondence between the Bishop and Revd Francis Armitage on the subject of Barnes's ordination, in particular his academic background, 1868–69.

3. W.R.W. Stephens, *The Life and Letters of Walter Farquhar Hook* (London: Richard Bentley & Son, 1880), p. 377.

4. Stephens, *The Life and Letters*, Chapters V–X.

5. Stephens, *The Life and Letters*, p. 376.

6. Stephens, *The Life and Letters*, pp. 384, 381.

7. See W.G. Rimmer, *Marshall's of Leeds: Flax Spinners 1788–1886* (Cambridge: Cambridge University Press, 1960), p. 109.

8. J. Mayhall, *The Annals and History of Leeds* (Leeds: Joseph Johnson, 1860), pp. 551, 552. The first vicar, Revd J.H.F. Kendall, left in 1855 for the church of St Matthew's Holbeck and was replaced at St John's by Barnes's predecessor, Revd J.P. Ward.

9. *Kelly's Directory of Yorkshire*, 1888, p. xxxiii.

10. Clergy List, 1862 and *Crockford's Clerical Directory*, 1872.

11. W.J. Conybeare, 'Church Parties', *Edinburgh Review*, October 1853, XCVIII, pp. 273 *et seq*.

D.G. Wigmore-Beddoes, 'The Affinity Between Unitarianism and Broad Church Anglicanism in the Nineteenth Century' (MA Dissertation, Birmingham University, 1963/64), p. 1.

12. *Dictionary of National Biography*, XX, p. 1371.

13. Revd F. Myers, *Catholic Thoughts on the Bible and Theology* (Isbister: Daldy, 1879), pp. ix-xviii.

14. Myers, *Catholic Thoughts*, p. 365.

15. *The Times*, 22 September 1869. In his ordination sermon Revd Close said it was 'the direct tendency of knowledge and science' to be 'the perversion and destruction of God's truth'.

16. Myers, *Catholic Thoughts*, p. vi.

17. Wigmore-Beddoes, 'The Affinity Between Unitarianism', p. 147.

18. O. Chadwick, *The Victorian Church* (London: Adam & Charles Black, 1966) p. 475.

19. N. Yates, *Leeds and the Oxford Movement* (Leeds: Thoresby Society Publications, 1975), LV, no. 121, p. 11.

20. Revd F.J. Wood, *Four Notable Vicars* (Leeds: Richard Jackson, 1912–13).

21. Yates, *Leeds and the Oxford Movement*, p. 16.

N. Yates, *The Oxford Movement and Parish Life: St Saviour's Leeds 1839–1929* (York: Borthwick Papers, 1975), no. 48, pp. 35, 59.

22. C.G. Lang, *Church and Town for Fifty Years* (Leeds: Richard Jackson, 1891), p. 25.

23. *Yorkshire Post*, 21 October 1870.

24. Lang, *Church and Town for Fifty Years*, p. 29.

25. *Yorkshire Post*, 27 October 1870. Meetings of the Leeds Church Union. Yates, *Leeds and the Oxford Movement*, p. 35.

26. 'Public Testimonial to Revd Samuel Flood DD'. Includes extract from the *Leeds Mercury*, September 30 1880.

27. L. and K. Sykes (eds.), *Sketches of the Life of Edward Jackson* (London: Christian Knowledge Society, 1913).

28. *Leeds Mercury*, 4 December 1884.

29. Marshall's school, Holbeck, log book, 1870.

30. Rimmer, *Marshall's of Leeds*, p. 109.

31. Little Holbeck Board school 1871 (ED 7 PRO).

32. Marshall's school, Holbeck, log book, 1870.

33. J.G. Fitch and D.R. Fearon, 'Return...of all Schools for the Poorer Classes of Children: Birmingham, Leeds, Liverpool and Manchester' for the House of Commons, 2 March 1870.

34. Fitch, 'Return...of all Schools: Leeds', p. 120.

35. *A Verbatim report...of the debate in Parliament during the progress of the Elementary Education Bill in 1870* (Manchester and London: National Education Union, n.d.), pp. 255-57.

36. For example the Halifax Lancastrian school mentioned in Chapter II.

37. *Yorkshire Post*, 21 October.

38. *Yorkshire Post*, for example, 17 November gives 42 candidates; 22 November gives 59 candidates and the final list of 38 candidates, with votes cast, appears on 29 November.

39. *Yorkshire Post*, 9 and 14 November 1870.

40. *Yorkshire Post*, 26 November 1870.

41. *Yorkshire Post*, 29 November 1870.

42. Thoresby Society Publications Miscellany 14, 1968 p. 55. This school was rented by the School Board for several years; see later for John Crosfield's first post in Leeds.

43. *Yorkshire Post*, 10 February 1879. Revd Kendall died in 1879.

44. *School Board Chronicle*, 23 December 1871, p. 168.

45. *School Board Chronicle*, 30 December 1871, p. 201.

46. Leeds School Board Memorandum 28 December 1871 (ED 16 PRO).

47. National Society school files: St Matthew's Holbeck. Undated letter, probably written in the early 1880s.

48. *School Board Chronicle*, 20 January 1872, p. 296.

49. Leeds School Board Education Committee Minutes, 27 November to 16 December 1871.

50. Sheepscar Board school (School Board files, Leeds District Archive) Letter, Goodall to Jowitt, 29 November 1871.

51. Sheepscar Board school, Forms and Inspectors' Reports, 20 November 1872 to 20 November 1875.

52. Leeds School Board Minutes, 8 January 1874 to 19 February 1874.

Notes to Chapter 11, section 1872–79

1. R.B. McDowell and D.A. Webb, *Trinity College Dublin 1592–1892* (Cambridge: Cambridge University Press, 1982).

2. Harpham received only £80 per annum and was allowed to live at his parents home two miles away.

3. Trinity College Dublin, Calendar and Year Books.

4. Leeds School Board Letter from W. Lee (the Clerk) to the Education Department, 13 February 1873 (ED 7 PRO).

5. Sheepscar Board school, Form, 21 December 1875 (ED 7 PRO).

6. Sheepscar Board school, Form, 1 August 1872.

7. *The Builder,* 22 February 1873, p. 141.

8. *School Board Chronicle,* 27 May 1876, p. 524.

9. Sheepscar Board school, School Board files (Leeds District Archive), 24 November 1876.

10. Sheepscar Board school, Girls log book, 5 September 1878. It is clear that Crosfield had some overall responsibility for the teaching in the school for he sometimes 'examined' pupils in the other departments.

11. Sheepscar Board school, Girls log book, 2 and 23 June 1876.

12. Minutes of the Committee on Council for Education, 1874/75, pp. clx, clxi. *The Schoolmaster,* 9 February 1878, pp. 162, 163.

13. Minutes of the CCE, 1876/77, p. 318.

14. Minutes of the CCE, 1877/78, p. 306.

15. Minutes of the CCE, 1874/75, p. cxlix.

16. G. Sutherland, *Policy-making in Elementary Education 1870–1895* (Oxford: Oxford University Press, 1973), pp. 191-99.

17. Minutes of the CCE, 1874/75, p. cxlix.

18. Leeds School Board Minutes, 10 February 1876.

19. Leeds School Board Minutes, 13 January 1876.

20. Sheepscar Board school, Girls log book, 29 November 1876. A 'main room' used for one or more teaching groups (the rest in classrooms) evolved into the modern 'school hall' used only for assemblies.

21. C. Treen, 'Building and Estate Development in the Northern Out-Townships of Leeds 1781–1914' (PhD Dissertation, Leeds University, 1977), pp. 277-79.

22. The street was in a poor state in 1872 as a resident complained in a letter to the *Leeds Mercury* on 2 January that year.

23. Leeds School Board, Triennial Report 1879–1882, p. 25.

24. P. Pritchard, 'The Churches and the Liverpool School Board 1870–1903' (PhD Dissertation, Liverpool University, 1981).

R.M. Jennings, 'The Role of Managers under the Liverpool School Board 1870–1903' (MEd Dissertation, Liverpool University, 1986).

25. Revd Samuel Flood and Revd Edward Jackson.

26. *Leeds Mercury*, 12 November 1879.

27. Poll book Leeds Parliamentary Elections, 1865 Barnes appears as a Conservative voter along with William James Armitage, Revd Kendall, Revd Flood and the vicar of Leeds, Revd J. Atlay.

28. *Leeds Mercury*, 12 November 1879.

29. *Leeds Mercury*, 21 November 1879.

30. *Leeds Mercury*, 19 November 1879.

31. *Yorkshire Post*, 24 November 1879.

32. *Yorkshire Post*, 25 November 1879.

Notes to Chapter 11, section 1879–82

1. Leeds School Board Minutes, 5 December 1879.

2. Leeds School Board Minutes, 8 January 1880.

School Board Chronicle, 24 January 1880, p. 83.

3. Leeds School Board Minutes, 21 October 1880 and 22 April 1881.

4. Leeds School Board Minutes, 3 April 1873 and 12 November 1874.

5. *Yorkshire Post*, 26 November 1870.

6. Leeds School Board Minutes, 13 April 1872.

7. Leeds School Board Minutes, 13 May 1880 and 10 February 1881. It was still ineffective as late as 1970.

8. Leeds School Board Minutes, 9 June 1881. See the references to Miss Bailey in Chapter X.

9. Leeds School Board Minutes, 10 November 1881.

10. 30 September 1880. Marshall's school was transferred to the School Board in April 1880.

11. Yorkshire College Annual Reports, 1881–82, p. 18.

12. *School Board Chronicle*, 29 May 1880, p. 513.

13. G. Sutherland, *Policy-making in Elementary Education 1870–1895* (Oxford: Oxford University Press, 1973), p. 199.

14. Leeds School Board Minutes, 16 April and 3 August 1874; 5 August 1875.

15. Leeds School Board Minutes, 28 September 1882.

School Board Chronicle, 14 October 1882, p. 383.

16. Leeds School Board Minutes, 24 November 1871.

17. Leeds School Board Minutes, 14 March 1872.

18. Leeds School Board Minutes, 4 April 1872.

19. Leeds School Board Minutes, 14 October, 11 November and 2 December 1875.

20. *School Board Chronicle*, 18 August 1877; for School Board meeting, 2 August 1877

21. Leeds School Board Minutes, 7 August 1879.

22. Leeds School Board Minutes, 15 April 1880.

School Board Chronicle, 1 May 1880, p. 419.

23. *School Board Chronicle*, 29 May 1880, pp. 513-15.

24. See *A Verbatim Report of the Debate in Parliament during the progress of the Elementary Education Bill 1870* (London and Manchester: National Education Union, n.d.).

25. The Scripture extracts were compiled by a respected Quaker, Thomas Harvey, an earlier Board member welcomed back unanimously in 1880 to fill a vacancy on the Board. See Thoresby Society Publications Miscellany 14, Leeds, 1968, p. 47 *et seq.*

Leeds School Board Minutes, 20 January 1881.

Notes to Chapter 11, section 1882–89

1. *Leeds Mercury*, 21 November 1882.

2. Leeds School Board, Triennial Report 1879–82.

School Board Chronicle, 27 January 1883, p. 96.

Minutes of the Committee of Council on Education, 1881/82, pp. 132, 133.

3. Minutes of the CCE, 1883/84 p. 324.

4. Leeds School Board, Triennial Report 1879–82, p. 25. *Leeds Mercury*, 17 November 1882.

5. *Leeds Mercury*, 17 and 18 November 1882; letters, reports of meetings. *Leeds Mercury*, 20 November 1882, leading article.

6. *Leeds Mercury*, 13, 16 and 18 November 1882.

7. *Leeds Mercury*, 16 and 17 November 1882. Gott was proved correct when 'higher' education in Board schools was declared illegal in the Cockerton judgment against the London School Board in 1900. This was one factor which led to the demise of the School Board system in 1902.

8. *Leeds Mercury*, 21 November 1882.

9. *Yorkshire Post*, 21 November 1882.

10. Leeds School Board, Minutes, 7 December 1882.

11. Leeds School Board, Minutes, 11 January 1883.

12. Leeds School Board, Minutes, 10 May 1883. *School Board Chronicle*, 26 May 1883, p. 515.

13. Leeds School Board, Minutes, 14 June 1883. *School Board Chronicle*, 7 July 1883, p. 11.

14. Leeds School Board, Minutes, 17 January 1884.

15. They chose the Governess of Derby Training College.

16. Leeds School Board, Minutes, 11 December 1884.

17. *Leeds Mercury*, 4 December 1884.

18. *Leeds Mercury*, 8 December 1884.

19. Sheepscar Board school, Inspectors Reports, 1879–86 (Leeds District Archives).

20. Sheepscar Board school, Inspectors Reports, 24 November 1882.

21. Leeds School Board, Minutes, 2 November 1883.

22. Leeds School Board, Minutes, 4 December 1883.

23. R.M. Jennings, 'The Role of Managers under the Liverpool School Board, 1870–1903, (MEd Dissertation, Liverpool University, 1986), pp. 54-56.

24. Sheepscar Board school, Inspectors Reports, 1888.

25. *Yorkshire Post*, 2 August 1889.

Notes to Chapter 12

1. Mrs Beeton, *Household Management* (London: S.O. Beeton, 1861), p. 8.

2. A sizar worked his way through university by performing menial tasks such as serving at table. Though earlier regarded as socially inferior and excluded from membership of college societies, by Arthur Foster's time the sizars seem to have been fully integrated into college life.

3. A colleague of Crosfield's published a series of arithmetic questions; two of these, significantly, started 'A man earns 25s a week...' and 'A gentleman with an income of £200...'—the latter a typical schoolmaster's salary. A. Gardner, *Home Lessons* (London and Manchester: 1883 and 1884).

4. T. Thomas, 'Four Centuries of Leeds Grammar School', *University of Leeds Review*, III, no. 1, (1952–53), pp. 54-61.

'The Register of Leeds Grammar School 1820–96', Leeds, 1897.

E. Wilson (ed.) *Leeds Grammar School Admission Books 1820–1900* (Leeds: Thoresby Society Publications, 1906), XIV.

5. W. Hewitt, *The Liverpool Council of Education 1874–1904* (Liverpool: Northern Publishing Company, 1928).

6. H.J. Tiffen, *History of the Liverpool Institute*, (Liverpool: Institute of Old Boys, 1935). Also registers, prospectuses and annual reports in Liverpool Local History Library.

7. J.R.de S. Honey, *Tom Brown's Universe* (London: Millington, 1977), p. 245.

8. R. Symonds, 'Oxford and India', in Madden and Fieldhouse (eds.) *Oxford and the Idea of Commonwealth* (London: Croon Helm, 1982), pp. 57-59.

E. Abbott and L. Campbell (eds.), *The Letters of Benjamin Jowett* (London: J. Murray, 1897), I, p. 185; II, pp. 65, 66, 135-40, 348, 349.

J.M. Compton, 'Open Competition and the Indian Civil Service', *English Historical Review*, 83, (1968), pp. 272-79.

Sir M. O'Dwyer, *India As I Knew It* (London: Constable, 1926), p. 20.

9. India List 1882–96.

10. St John's College, Cambridge, *Eagle*, XIV, (1887), pp. 402, 403.

11. British and Foreign Schools Society Annual Report 1876, p. 46 and 1877, p. 59.

O.M. Stanton, *Our Present Opportunities* (Darlington, 1966).

12. Royal Commission to Enquire into the working of the Elementary Education Acts: First Report (Dublin: Irish University Press Education, 1886), 34, pp. 496-99, 504; and Second Report (1887), p. 984.

13. Information supplied by Dr H.M. Jewell.

14. Yorkshire Ladies Council of Education Fifth Annual Report, 1876, p. 7.

H.M. Jewell, *A School of Unusual Excellence: Leeds Girls High School 1876–1976* (Leeds: Leeds Girls High School, 1976).

15. Royal Commission on Secondary Education Report, 1895, VII, p. 154.

16. Dr J.D. Heaton, 'Journals', c/o Thoresby Society, Leeds.

17. A.B. White (ed.), *Register of Newnham College Cambridge 1871–1950* (Cambridge: Newnham College, 1963), I, pp. ii, iii.

M.A. Hamilton, *Newnham: An Informal Biography* (London: Faber and Faber, 1936).

D. Bennett, *Emily Davies and the Liberation of Women 1830–1921* (London: Andre Deutsch, 1990).

18. Worcester High School, 'White and Blue', no. 1, (June 1890), p. 6.

M.J. Williamson Jones and A. Garrood, *The Alice Ottley School: The Record of a Century 1883–1893* (Worcester, 1983).

19. Asylum Press Almanac, Madras, 1896, p. lxviii.

20. J. Garnett, 'Diary' 11 October 1895 (c/o Manchester Public Library).

21. Merseyside County Museums, Department of Maritime History, Letter from V. Burton to author, 17 March 1986.

O. Ashmore (ed.), *The Diary of James Garnett of Low Moor, Clitheroe, 1858–1865* (Liverpool: Transactions of the Historic Society of Lancashire and Cheshire, 1969), 121.

Notes to Conclusion

1. Minutes of the Committee of Council on Education, 1853/54, p. 421.
2. Minutes of the CCE, 1858/59, p. 273.
3. Minutes of the CCE, 1865/66, p. lx.
4. Minutes of the CCE, 1886/87, p. 226.
5. Revd H. J. Ellison, 'The Church Schoolmaster in Relation to the Church', (London and Derby, 1854). Speaking to a group of masters and mistresses in Lichfield he concluded with a promise to one who gave faithful service: 'as they gathered to pay him the last tributes of respect...good men's tears would fall into his grave'.
6. Minutes of the CCE, 1857/58, p. 293.

7. No longer bound to serve in church schools after training.
8. (Now) College of Ripon and York St John , 'White Rose', 1894.
9. see Chapter XI, 1870–1872, n. 2
10. E.L. Edmonds, *The School Inspector* (London: Routledge & Kegan Paul, 1962), pp. 83, 84, 144, 145.

Index